ROBOTECH

BYE-BYE MARS

TITAN COMICS

Harmony GOLD

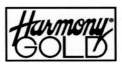

BYE-BYE MARS

PLOT
BRIAN WOOD & SIMON FURMAN

SCRIPT
SIMON FURMAN

ART
MARCO TURINI

COLORS
MARCO LESKO

LETTERING
JIM CAMPBELL

THANK YOU TO: The amazing Tommy Yune and all of the incredible people at Harmony Gold. Also, Chris Schell.
And finally, thank you to Carl Macek for creating such an incredible series.

For rights information contact: jenny.boyce@titanemail.com

Published by Titan Comics. A division of Titan Publishing Group Ltd., 144 Southwark St. London SE1 0UP.
Titan Comics is a registered trademark of Titan Publishing Group Ltd.

First edition: June 2018

ISBN: 9781785859144

10 9 8 7 6 5 4 3 2 1

Printed in China.

www.titan-comics.com

Follow us on Twitter @ComicsTitan

Visit us at facebook.com/comicstitan

ROBOTECH GRAPHIC NOVELS FROM TITAN

AVAILABLE NOW
ROBOTECH: COUNTDOWN,
GRAPHIC NOVEL ONE

ROBOTECH: BYE-BYE MARS,
GRAPHIC NOVEL TWO

ROBOTECH ARCHIVES – THE MACROSS SAGA
VOLUME ONE

COMING SOON
ROBOTECH ARCHIVES – THE MACROSS SAGA
VOLUME TWO (On sale August 2018)

ROBOTECH GRAPHIC NOVEL THREE (Oct 2018)

ROBOTECH ARCHIVES – THE MACROSS SAGA
VOLUME THREE (November 2018)

ROBOTECH ARCHIVES – THE SENTINELS
VOLUME ONE (February 2019)

ROBOTECH ARCHIVES – THE SENTINELS
VOLUME TWO (May 2019)

ROBOTECH ARCHIVES – THE SENTINELS
VOLUME THREE (August 2019)

ROBOTECH ARCHIVES – THE SENTINELS
VOLUME FOUR (November 2019)

...and more to come!

TITAN COMICS

SENIOR EDITOR Martin Eden
DESIGNER Donna Askem
MANAGING/LAUNCH EDITOR Andrew James
PRODUCTION CONTROLLER Peter James
PRODUCTION SUPERVISOR Maria Pearson
SENIOR PRODUCTION CONTROLLER Jackie Flook
ART DIRECTOR Oz Browne
SALES & CIRCULATION MANAGER Santosh Maharaj
PRESS OFFICER Will O'Mullane
COMICS BRAND MANAGER Chris Thompson
DIRECT SALES & MARKETING MANAGER Ricky Claydon
COMMERCIAL MANAGER Michelle Fairlamb
HEAD OF RIGHTS Jenny Boyce
PUBLISHING MANAGER Darryl Tothill
PUBLISHING DIRECTOR Chris Teather
OPERATIONS DIRECTOR Leigh Baulch
EXECUTIVE DIRECTOR Vivian Cheung
PUBLISHER Nick Landau

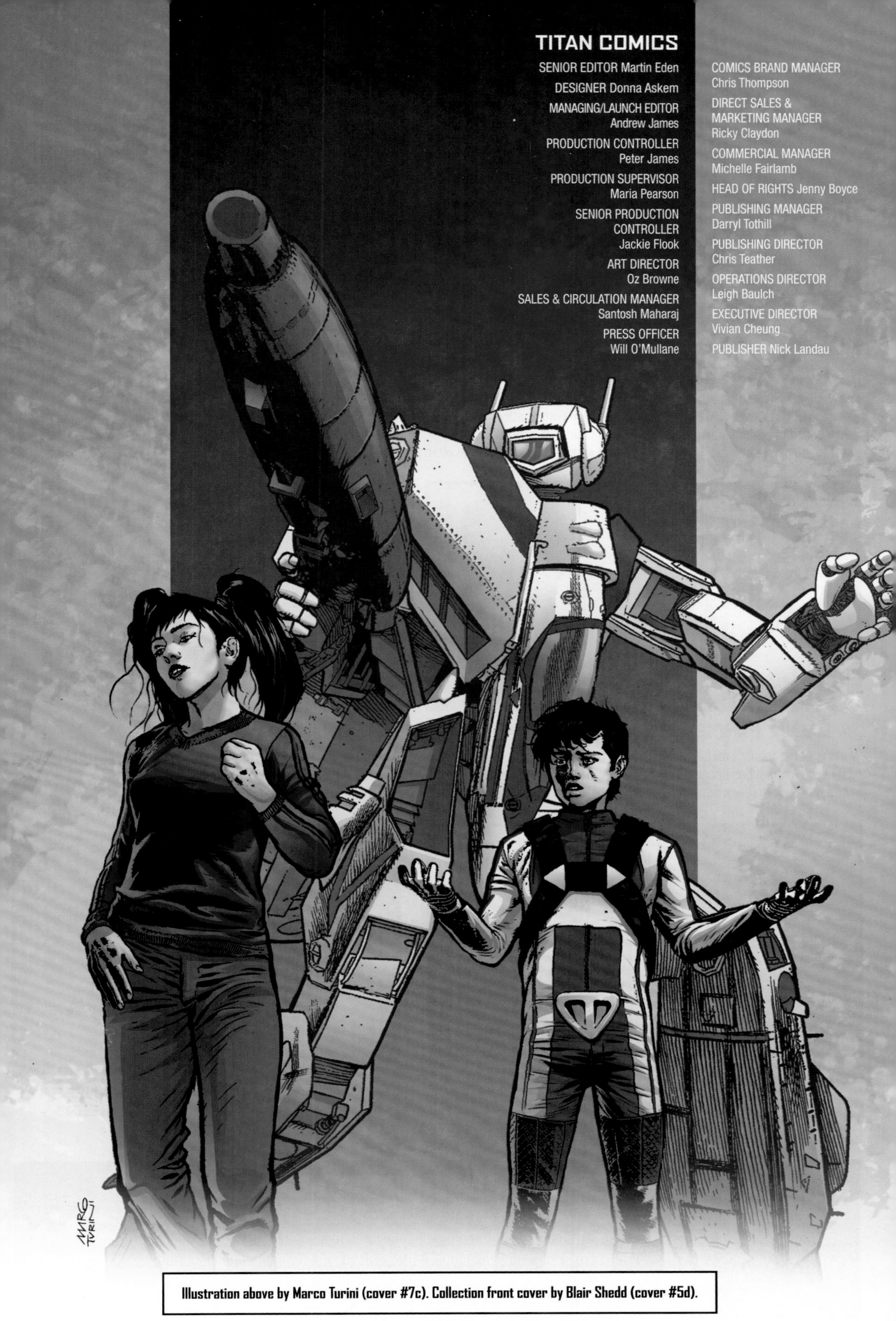

Illustration above by Marco Turini (cover #7c). Collection front cover by Blair Shedd (cover #5d).

CAST OF CHARACTERS

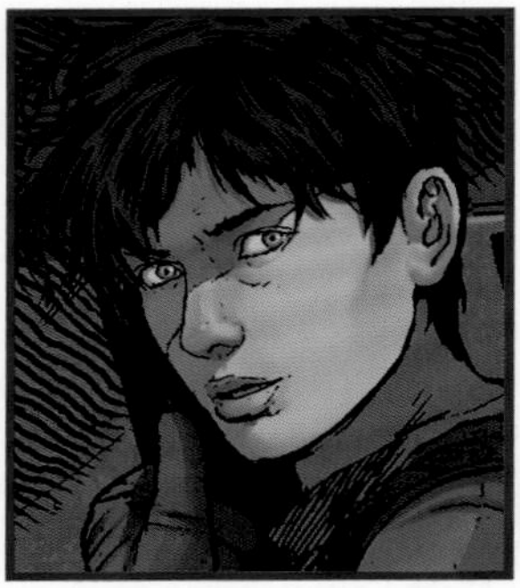

RICK HUNTER

Following in his 'big brother' Roy's footsteps, Rick is a talented but cocky pilot and has become an asset to the defense force.

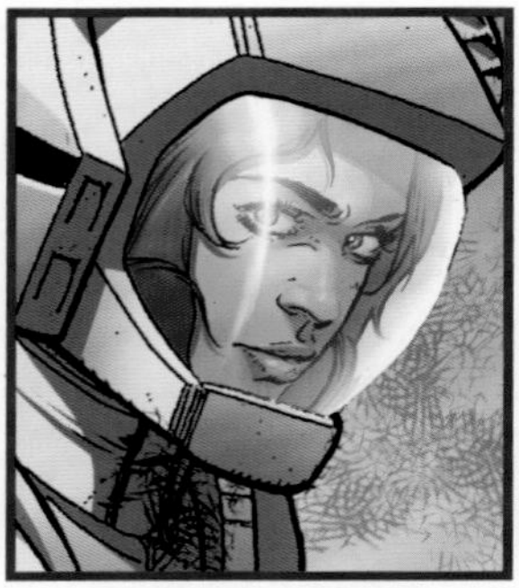

LISA HAYES

The First Officer of the Super Dimension Fortress One (the SDF-1). The daughter of a military officer, Lisa's serious side can emerge often.

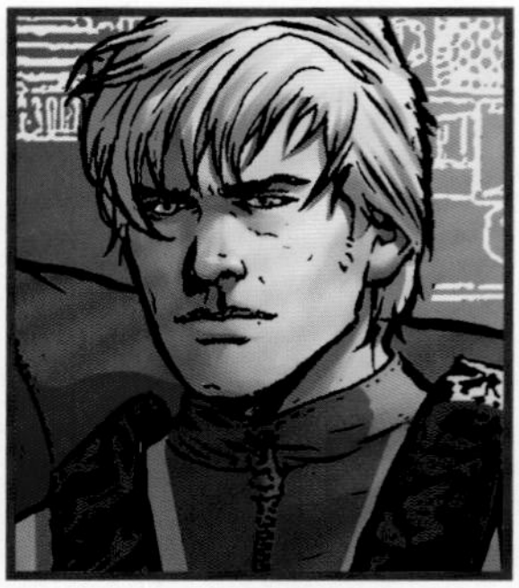

ROY FOKKER

A highly skilled and brave pilot, Roy becomes the leader of the legendary Skull Squadron in the Robotech Defence Force.

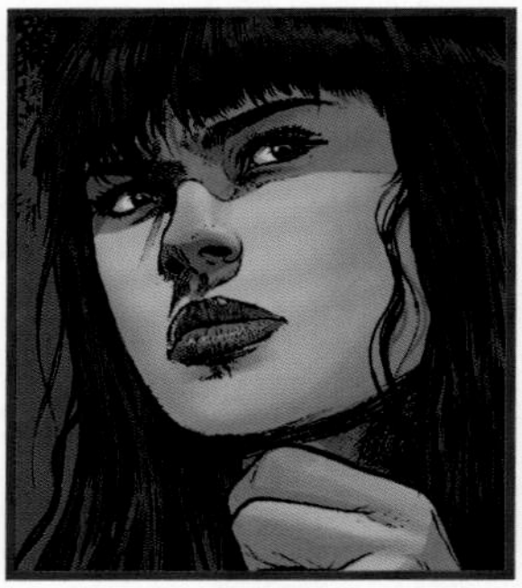

LYNN MINMEI

Working at her family's restaurant, feisty Lynn Minmei has become involved in Rick Hunter's adventures...

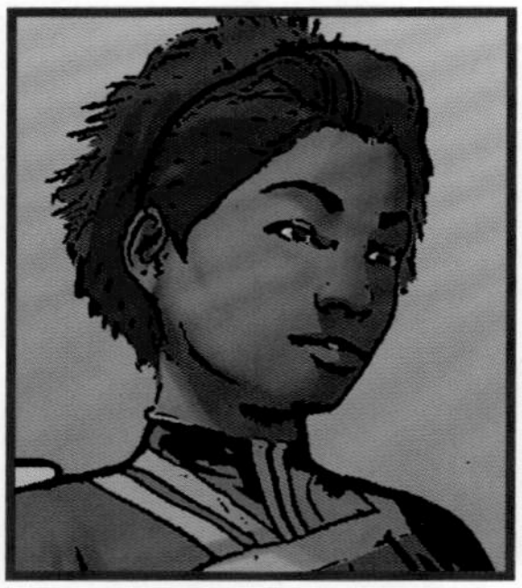

CLAUDIA GRANT

The confident Chief Communications officer of the SDF-1. In a relationship with Roy.

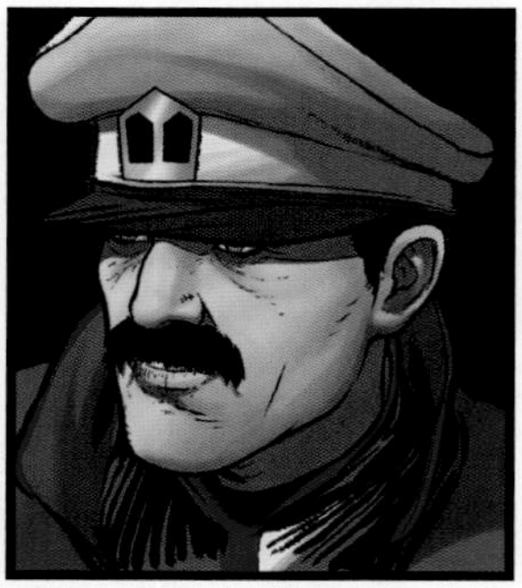

HENRY GLOVAL

A born leader, Gloval rose through the ranks of the Robotech Defense Force to become captain of the SDF-1.

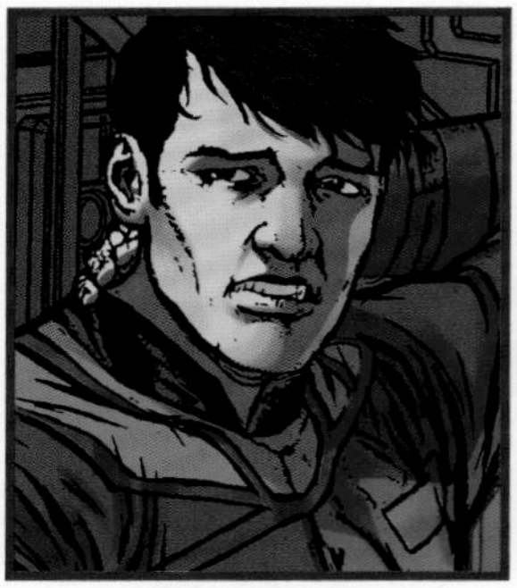

DR LANG

A brilliant scientist and engineer on board the SDF-1. One of Earth's foremost Robotechnology experts.

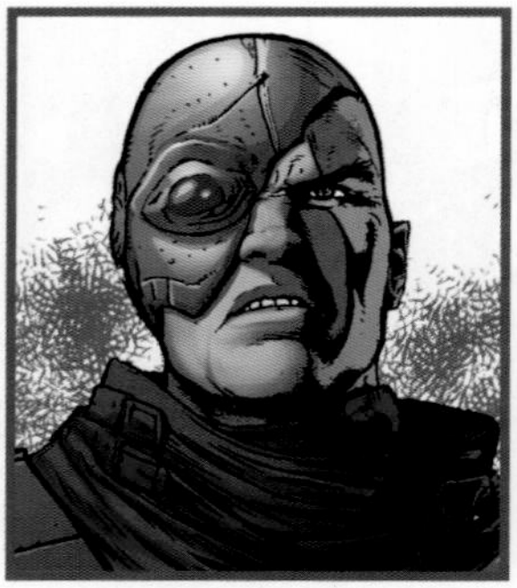

BREETAI

The commander of a mysterious alien race's armada. The alien race consists of giant humanoids.

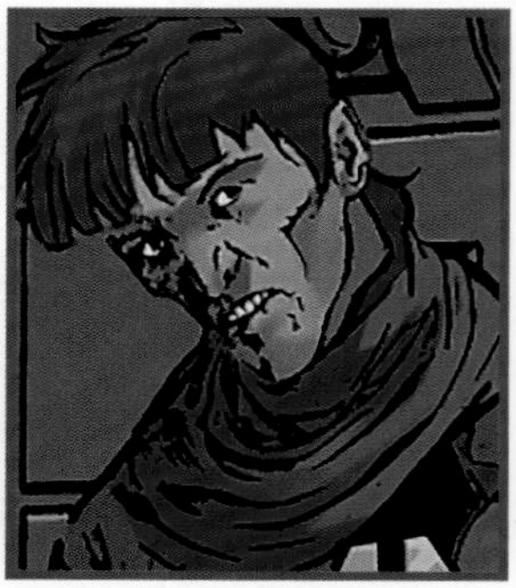

EXODORE

Breetai's loyal second-in-command…

MEMBERS OF THE SDF-1'S BRIDGE CREW

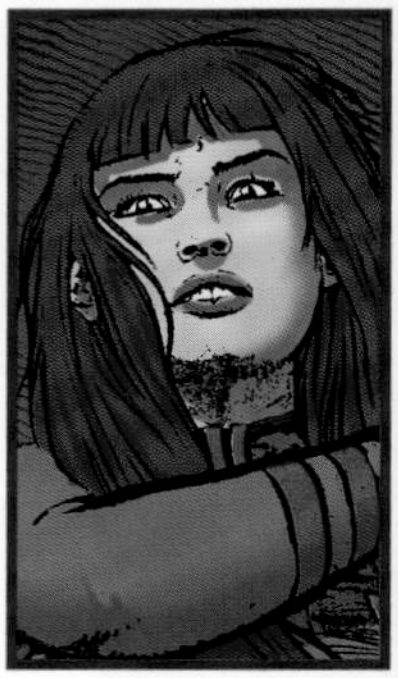

SAMMIE PORTER

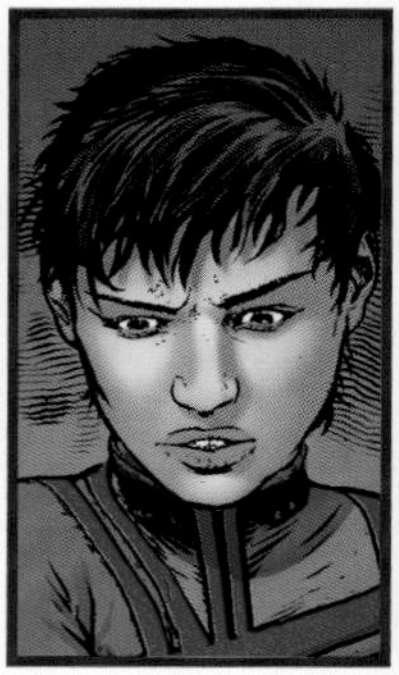

KIM YOUNG

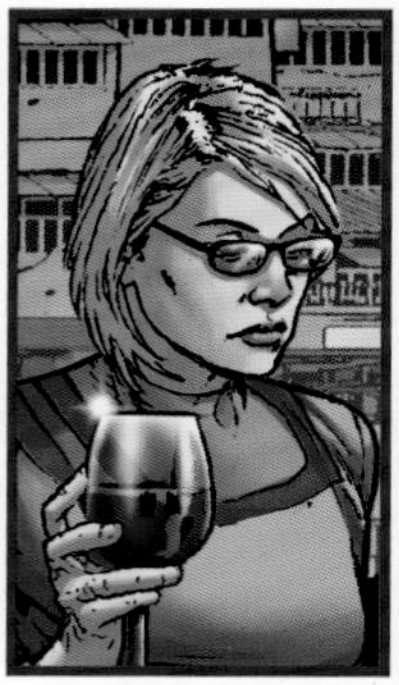

VANESSA LEEDS

THE ROBOTECH ANIMATED SERIES

Robotech producer Carl Macek was recruited by Harmony Gold to adapt Macross for the US market. To meet television syndication requirements of the time, Carl deftly edited three Japanese anime series (*Super Dimension Fortress Macross, Super Dimension Cavalry Southern Cross* and *Genesis Climber MOSPEADA*) and created the concept of Robotechnology to tie them together into one epic 85-episode saga. *Robotech* introduced a whole new generation of Western fans to anime, and audiences grew to love Rick, Lisa, Minmei, Roy, Claudia, Gloval, and many more.

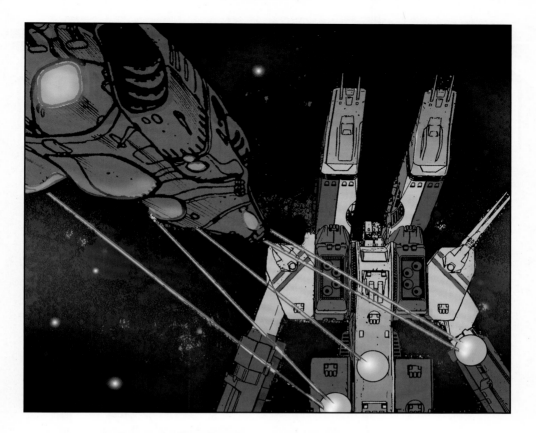

THE STORY SO FAR...

Ten years ago, a mysterious ship crashed on Macross Island in the South Pacific. In the intervening years, the people of Earth have used the 'Robotechnology' from the ship to significantly advance their own technology.

On the launch day of Earth's Super-Dimension Fortress (the SDF-1), Earth is attacked by mysterious aliens. The SDF-1 is eventually forced to space-fold into space – but takes a chunk of Macross City with them (the city and its citizens are now inside the massive SDF-1). The SDF-1 is now in the midst of a long journey back to Earth.

During a fierce space battle, the SDF-1 was forced to execute a modular transformation – causing considerable damage to the city within it. The humans won – but Captain Gloval's body was found buried under the SDF-1's internal wreckage...

And while all this is happening, it's becoming evident that some of the crew know more about the origins of the SDF-1 crash than they are letting on...

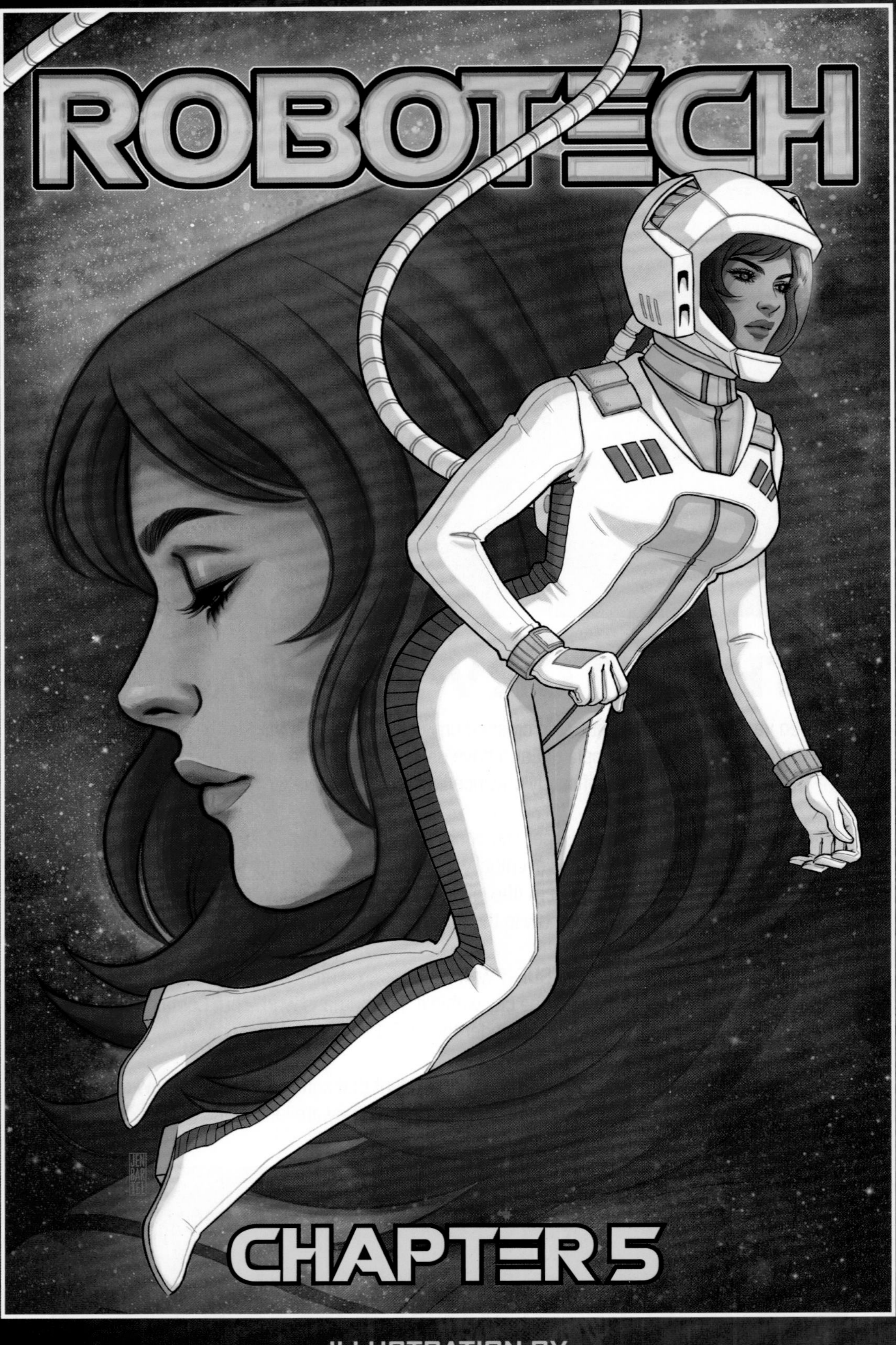
ROBOTECH
JEN BARTEL
CHAPTER 5

ILLUSTRATION BY
JEN BARTEL

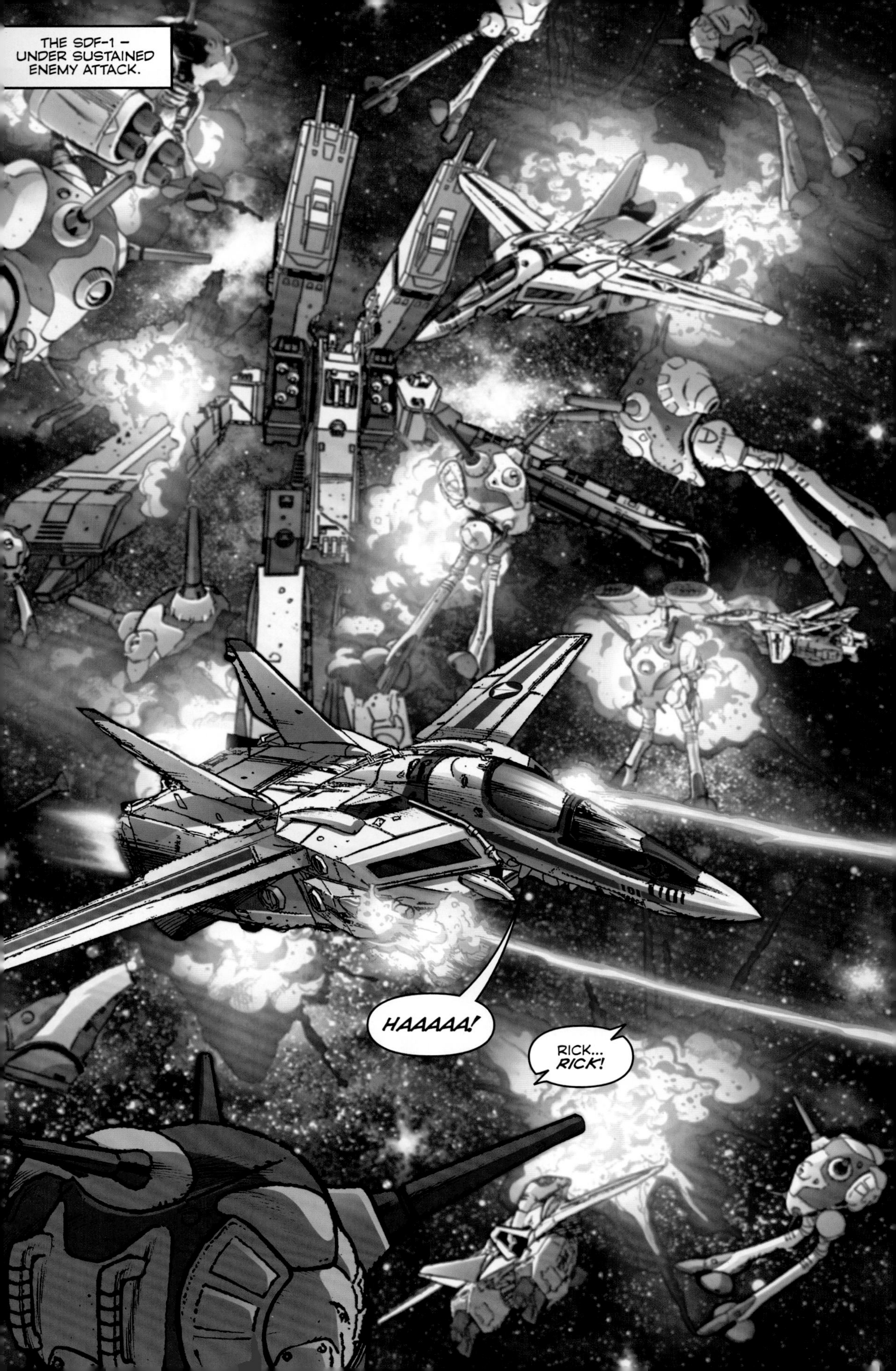
THE SDF-1 — UNDER SUSTAINED ENEMY ATTACK.
HAAAAA!
RICK... RICK!

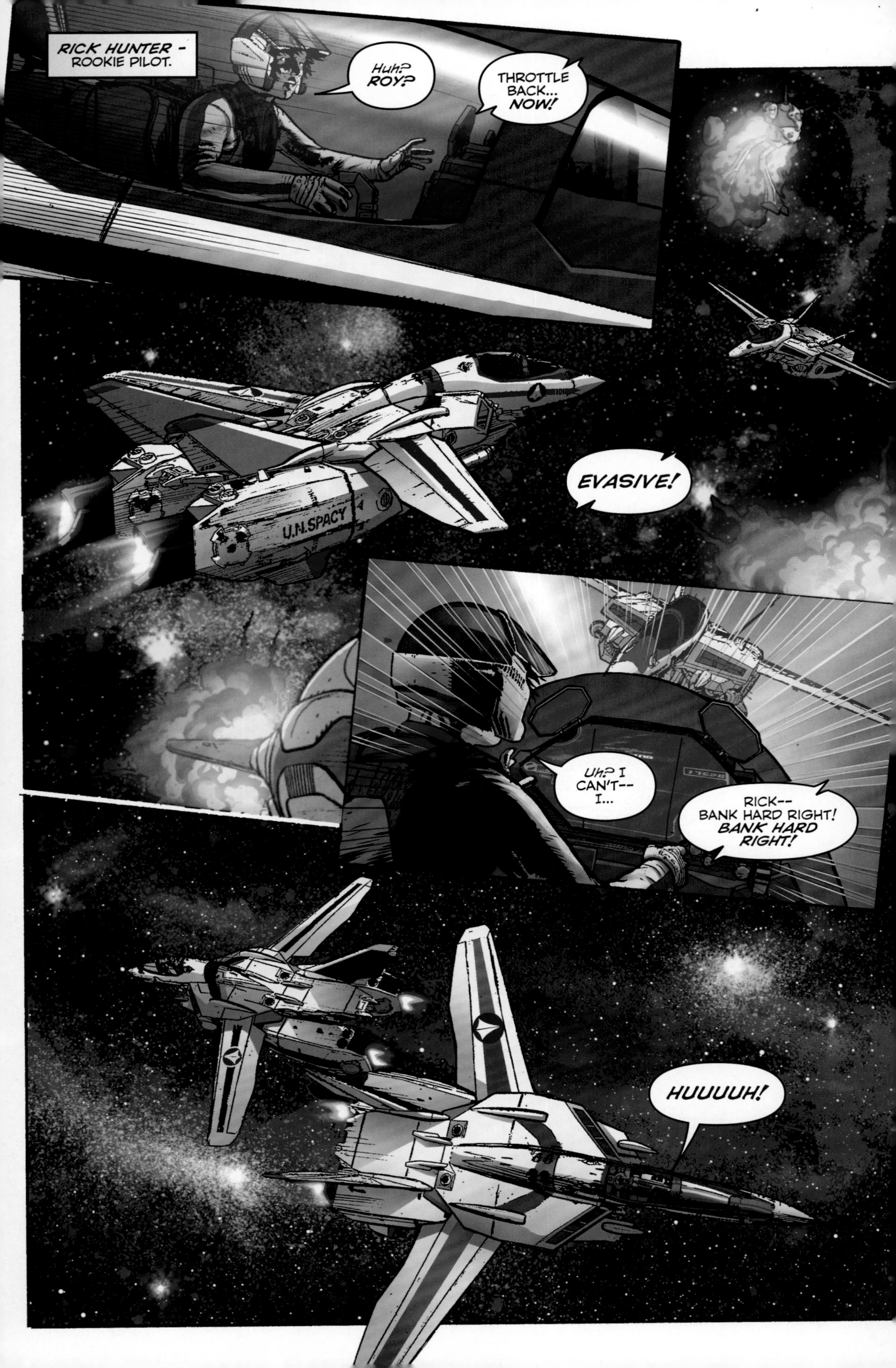
RICK HUNTER - ROOKIE PILOT.
Huh? ROY?
THROTTLE BACK... NOW!
U.N.SPACY
EVASIVE!
Uh? I CAN'T-- I...
RICK-- BANK HARD RIGHT! BANK HARD RIGHT!
HUUUUH!

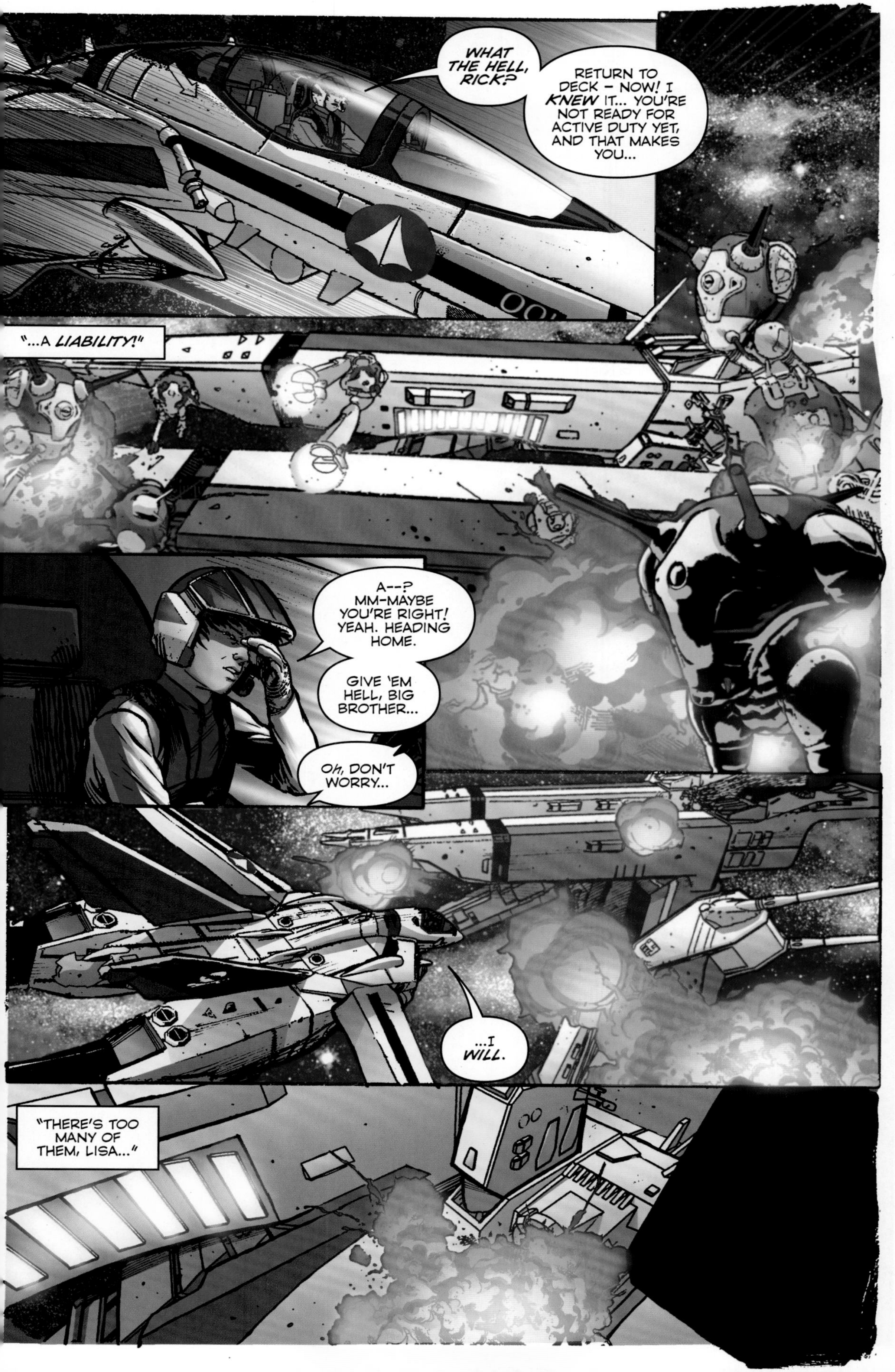
WHAT THE HELL, RICK?
RETURN TO DECK – NOW! I KNEW IT... YOU'RE NOT READY FOR ACTIVE DUTY YET, AND THAT MAKES YOU...
"...A LIABILITY!"
A--? MM-MAYBE YOU'RE RIGHT! YEAH. HEADING HOME.
GIVE 'EM HELL, BIG BROTHER...
OH, DON'T WORRY...
...I WILL.
"THERE'S TOO MANY OF THEM, LISA..."

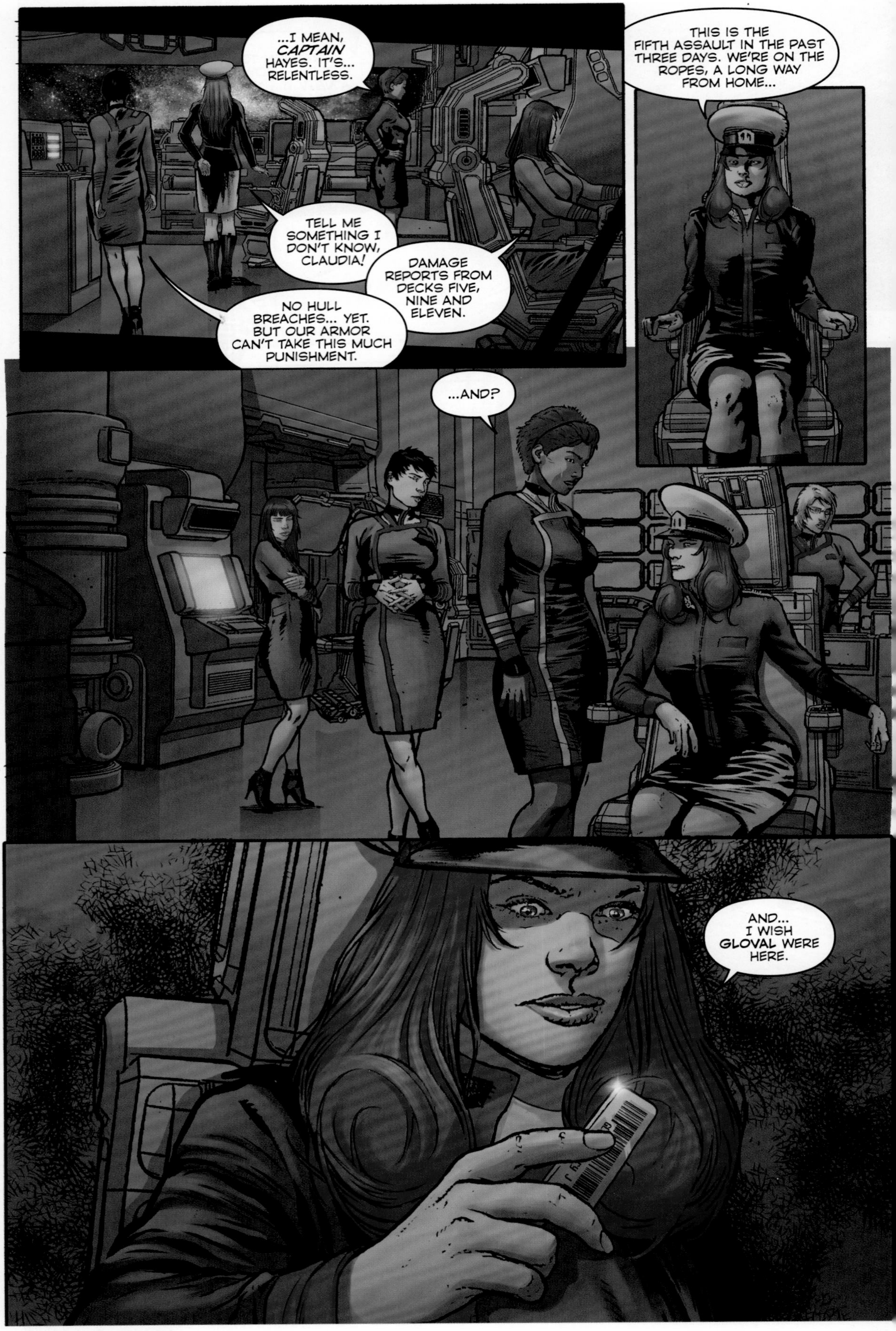

...I MEAN, *CAPTAIN* HAYES. IT'S... RELENTLESS.
THIS IS THE FIFTH ASSAULT IN THE PAST THREE DAYS. WE'RE ON THE ROPES, A LONG WAY FROM HOME...
TELL ME SOMETHING I DON'T KNOW, CLAUDIA!
DAMAGE REPORTS FROM DECKS FIVE, NINE AND ELEVEN.
NO HULL BREACHES... YET. BUT OUR ARMOR CAN'T TAKE THIS MUCH PUNISHMENT.
...AND?
AND... I WISH GLOVAL WERE HERE.

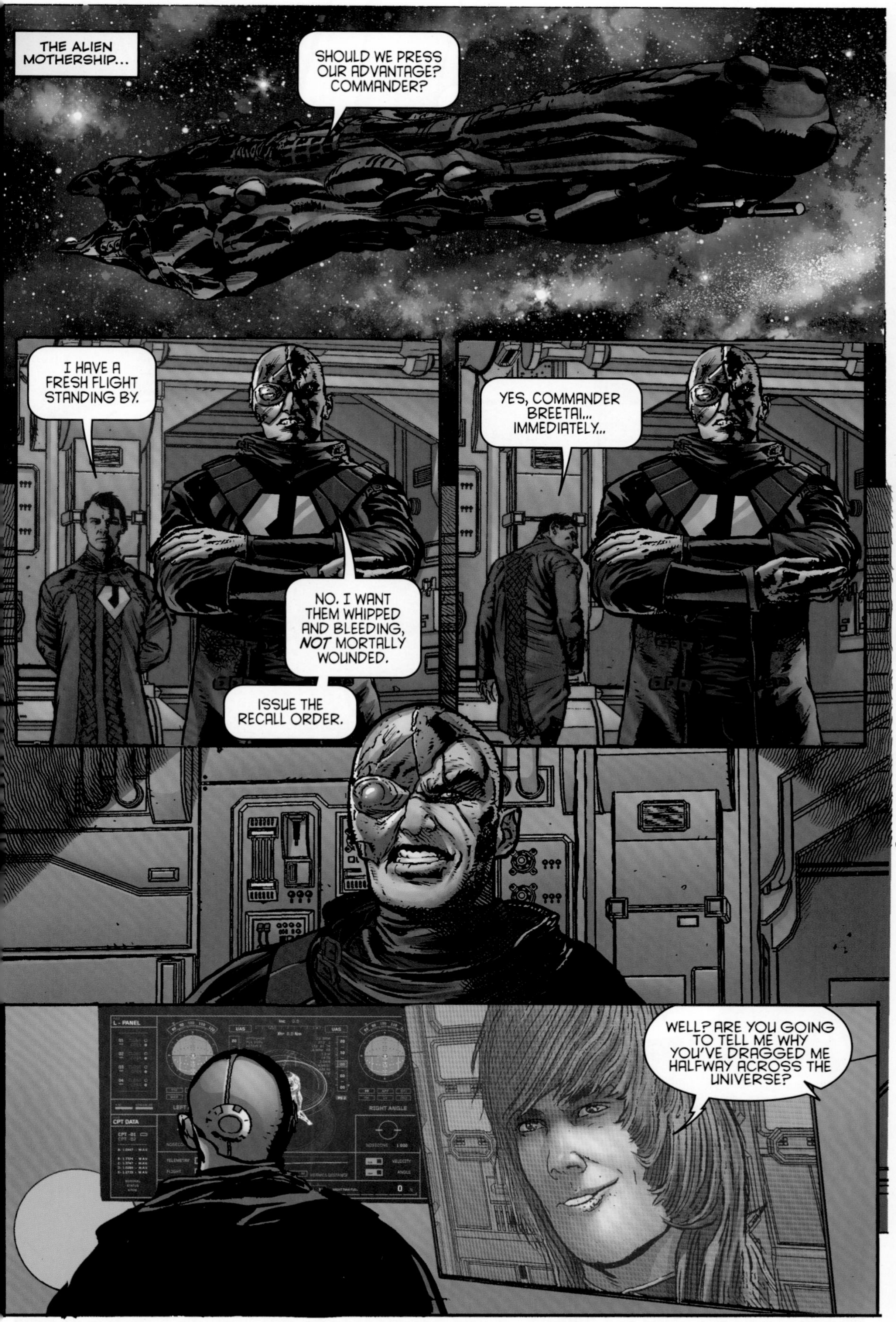
THE ALIEN MOTHERSHIP...
SHOULD WE PRESS OUR ADVANTAGE? COMMANDER?
I HAVE A FRESH FLIGHT STANDING BY.
NO. I WANT THEM WHIPPED AND BLEEDING, *NOT* MORTALLY WOUNDED.
ISSUE THE RECALL ORDER.
YES, COMMANDER BREETAI... IMMEDIATELY...
WELL? ARE YOU GOING TO TELL ME WHY YOU'VE DRAGGED ME HALFWAY ACROSS THE UNIVERSE?

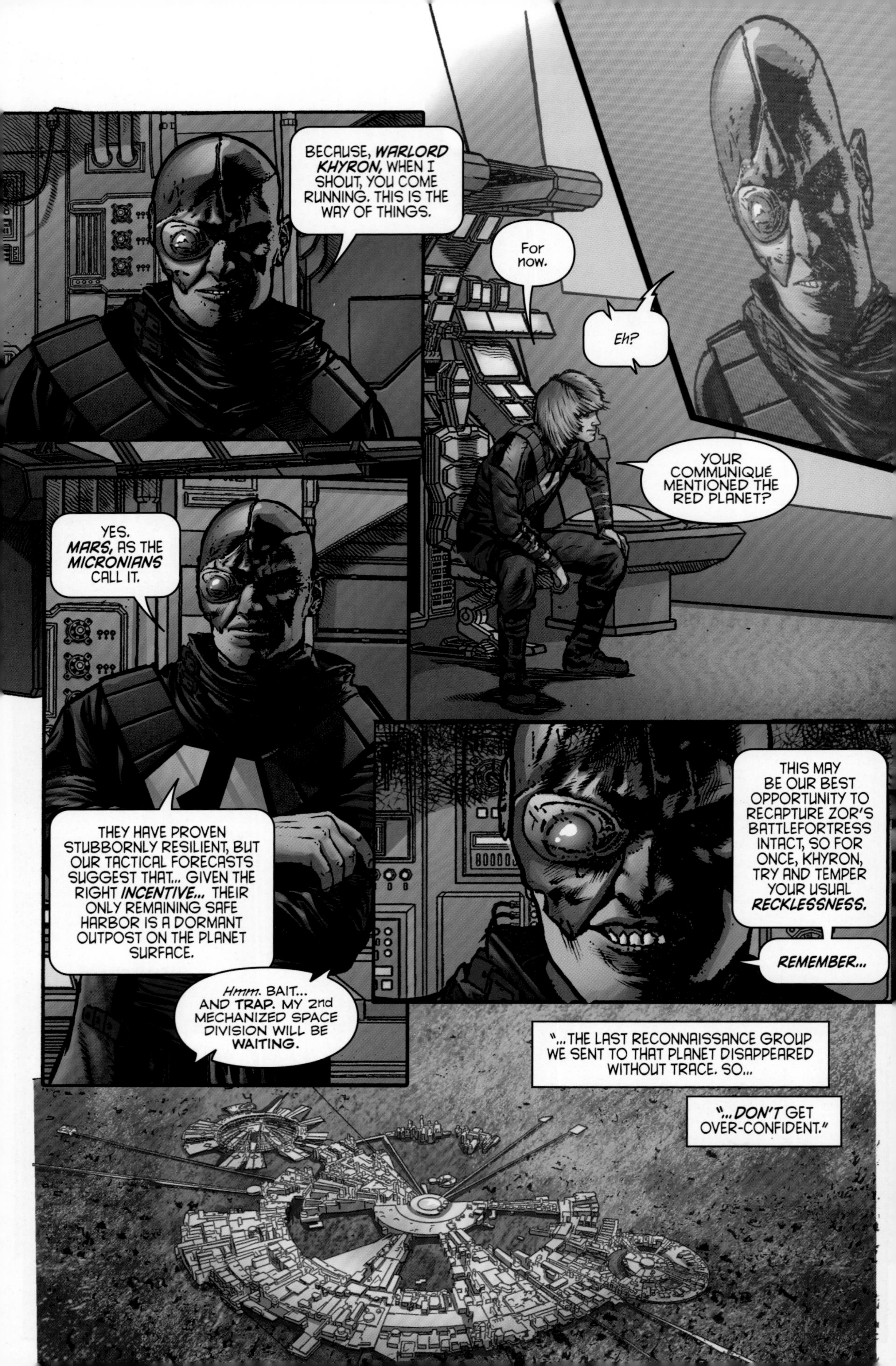

BECAUSE, WARLORD KHYRON, WHEN I SHOUT, YOU COME RUNNING. THIS IS THE WAY OF THINGS.
For now.
Eh?
YOUR COMMUNIQUÉ MENTIONED THE RED PLANET?
YES. MARS, AS THE MICRONIANS CALL IT.
THEY HAVE PROVEN STUBBORNLY RESILIENT, BUT OUR TACTICAL FORECASTS SUGGEST THAT... GIVEN THE RIGHT INCENTIVE... THEIR ONLY REMAINING SAFE HARBOR IS A DORMANT OUTPOST ON THE PLANET SURFACE.
Hmm. BAIT... AND TRAP. MY 2nd MECHANIZED SPACE DIVISION WILL BE WAITING.
THIS MAY BE OUR BEST OPPORTUNITY TO RECAPTURE ZOR'S BATTLEFORTRESS INTACT, SO FOR ONCE, KHYRON, TRY AND TEMPER YOUR USUAL RECKLESSNESS.
REMEMBER...
"...THE LAST RECONNAISSANCE GROUP WE SENT TO THAT PLANET DISAPPEARED WITHOUT TRACE. SO...
"...DON'T GET OVER-CONFIDENT."

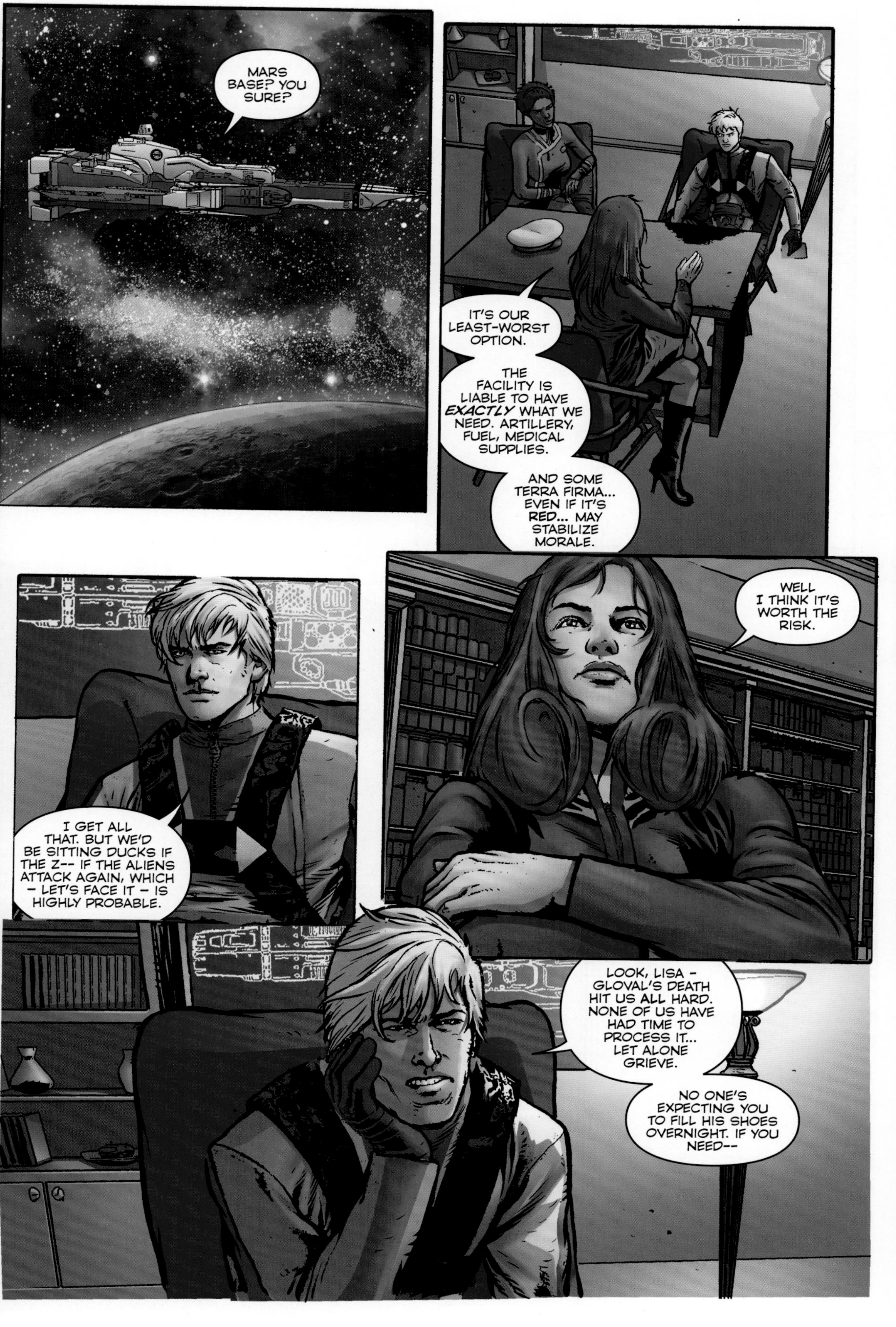
MARS BASE? YOU SURE?
IT'S OUR LEAST-WORST OPTION.
THE FACILITY IS LIABLE TO HAVE *EXACTLY* WHAT WE NEED. ARTILLERY, FUEL, MEDICAL SUPPLIES.
AND SOME TERRA FIRMA... EVEN IF IT'S **RED...** MAY STABILIZE MORALE.
I GET ALL THAT. BUT WE'D BE SITTING DUCKS IF THE Z-- IF THE ALIENS ATTACK AGAIN, WHICH – LET'S FACE IT – IS HIGHLY PROBABLE.
WELL I THINK IT'S WORTH THE RISK.
LOOK, LISA - GLOVAL'S DEATH HIT US **ALL** HARD. NONE OF US HAVE HAD TIME TO PROCESS IT... LET ALONE GRIEVE.
NO ONE'S EXPECTING YOU TO FILL HIS SHOES OVERNIGHT. IF YOU NEED--

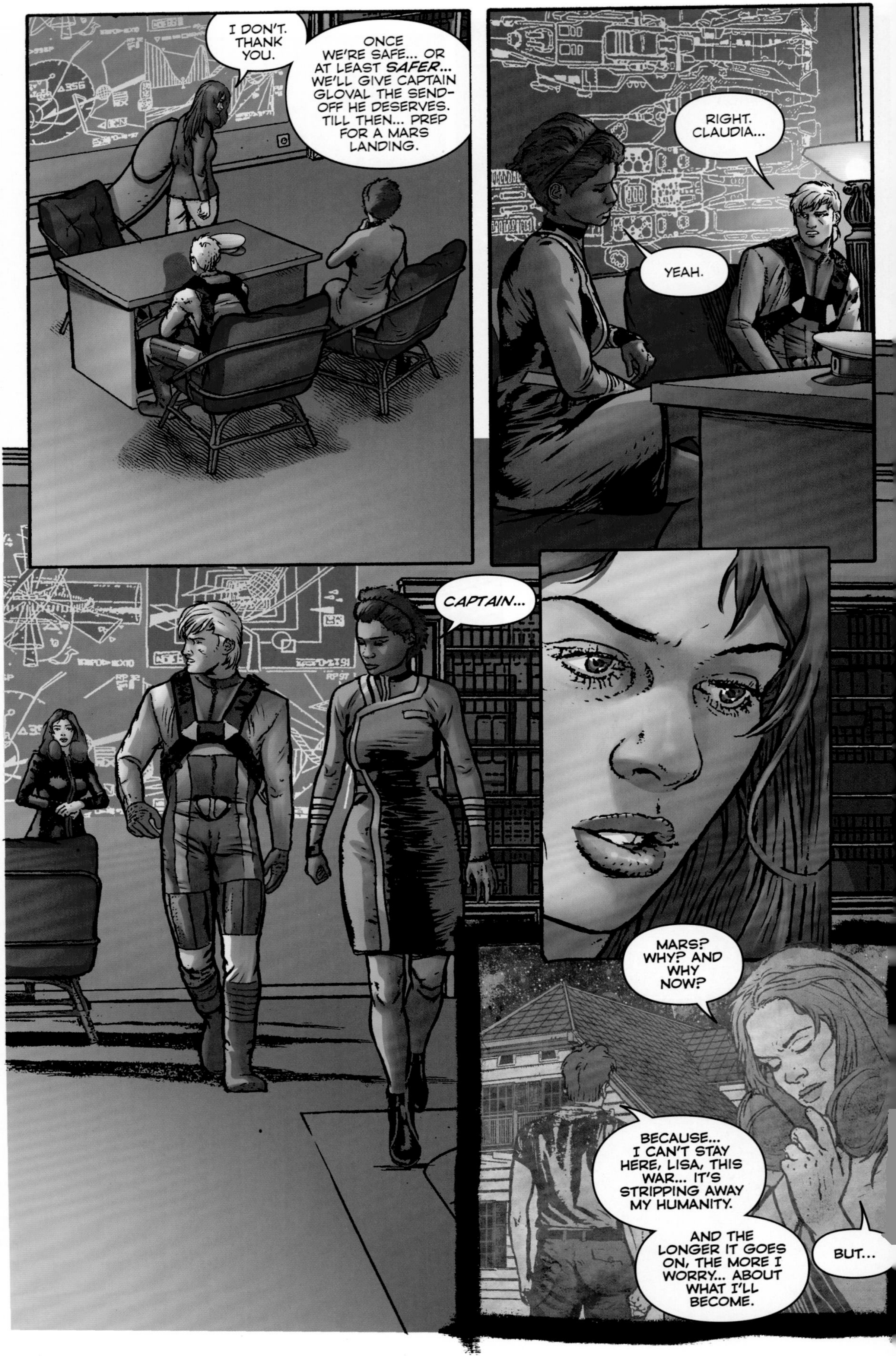
I DON'T. THANK YOU.
ONCE WE'RE SAFE... OR AT LEAST *SAFER*... WE'LL GIVE CAPTAIN GLOVAL THE SEND-OFF HE DESERVES. TILL THEN... PREP FOR A MARS LANDING.
RIGHT. CLAUDIA...
YEAH.
CAPTAIN...
MARS? WHY? AND WHY NOW?
BECAUSE... I CAN'T STAY HERE, LISA, THIS WAR... IT'S STRIPPING AWAY MY HUMANITY.
AND THE LONGER IT GOES ON, THE MORE I WORRY... ABOUT WHAT I'LL BECOME.
BUT...

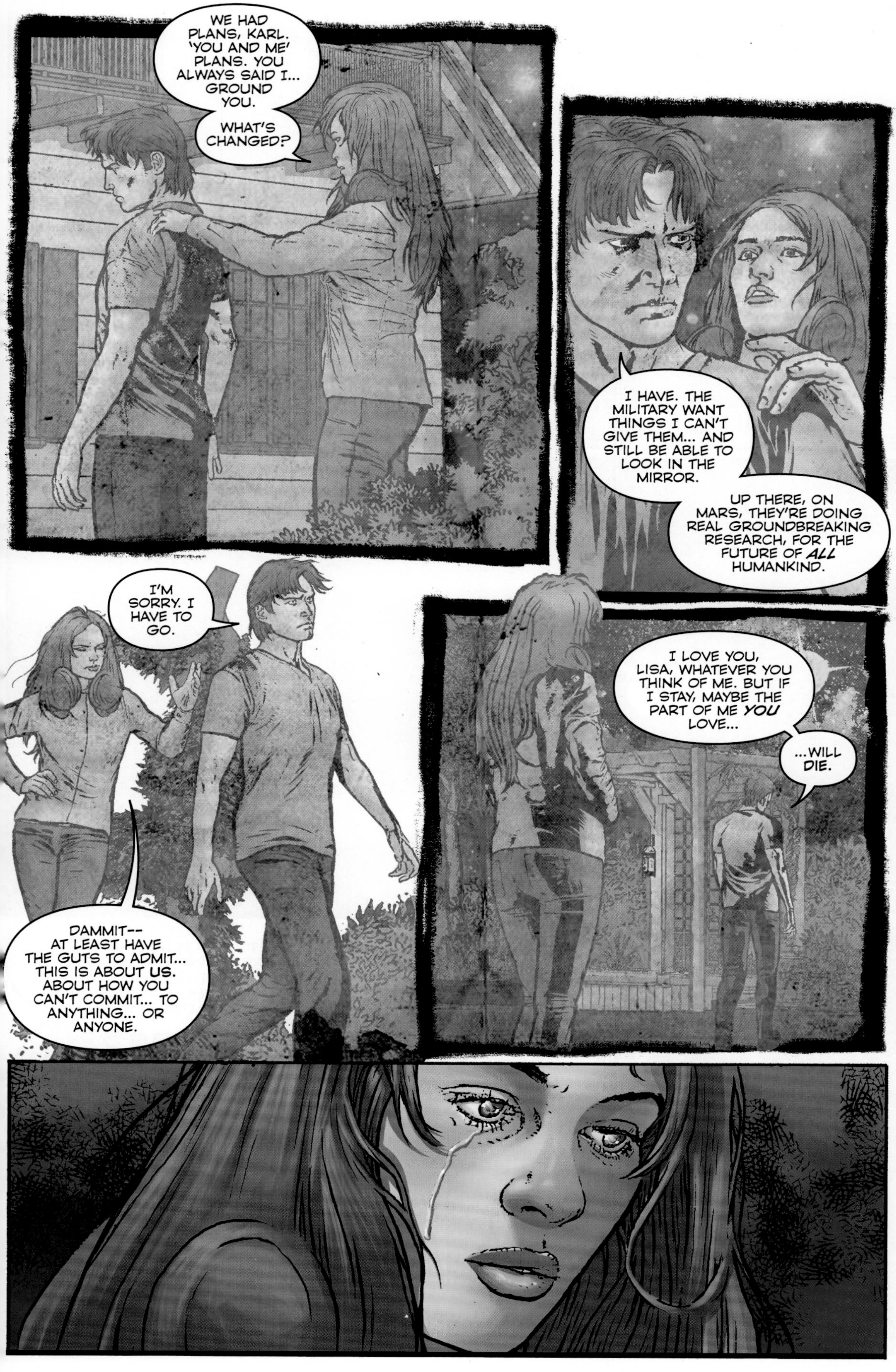
WE HAD PLANS, KARL. 'YOU AND ME' PLANS. YOU ALWAYS SAID I... GROUND YOU.
WHAT'S CHANGED?
I HAVE. THE MILITARY WANT THINGS I CAN'T GIVE THEM... AND STILL BE ABLE TO LOOK IN THE MIRROR.
UP THERE, ON MARS, THEY'RE DOING REAL GROUNDBREAKING RESEARCH, FOR THE FUTURE OF *ALL* HUMANKIND.
I'M SORRY. I HAVE TO GO.
DAMMIT-- AT LEAST HAVE THE GUTS TO ADMIT... THIS IS ABOUT **US**. ABOUT HOW YOU CAN'T COMMIT... TO ANYTHING... OR ANYONE.
I LOVE YOU, LISA, WHATEVER YOU THINK OF ME. BUT IF I STAY, MAYBE THE PART OF ME *YOU* LOVE...
...WILL **DIE**.

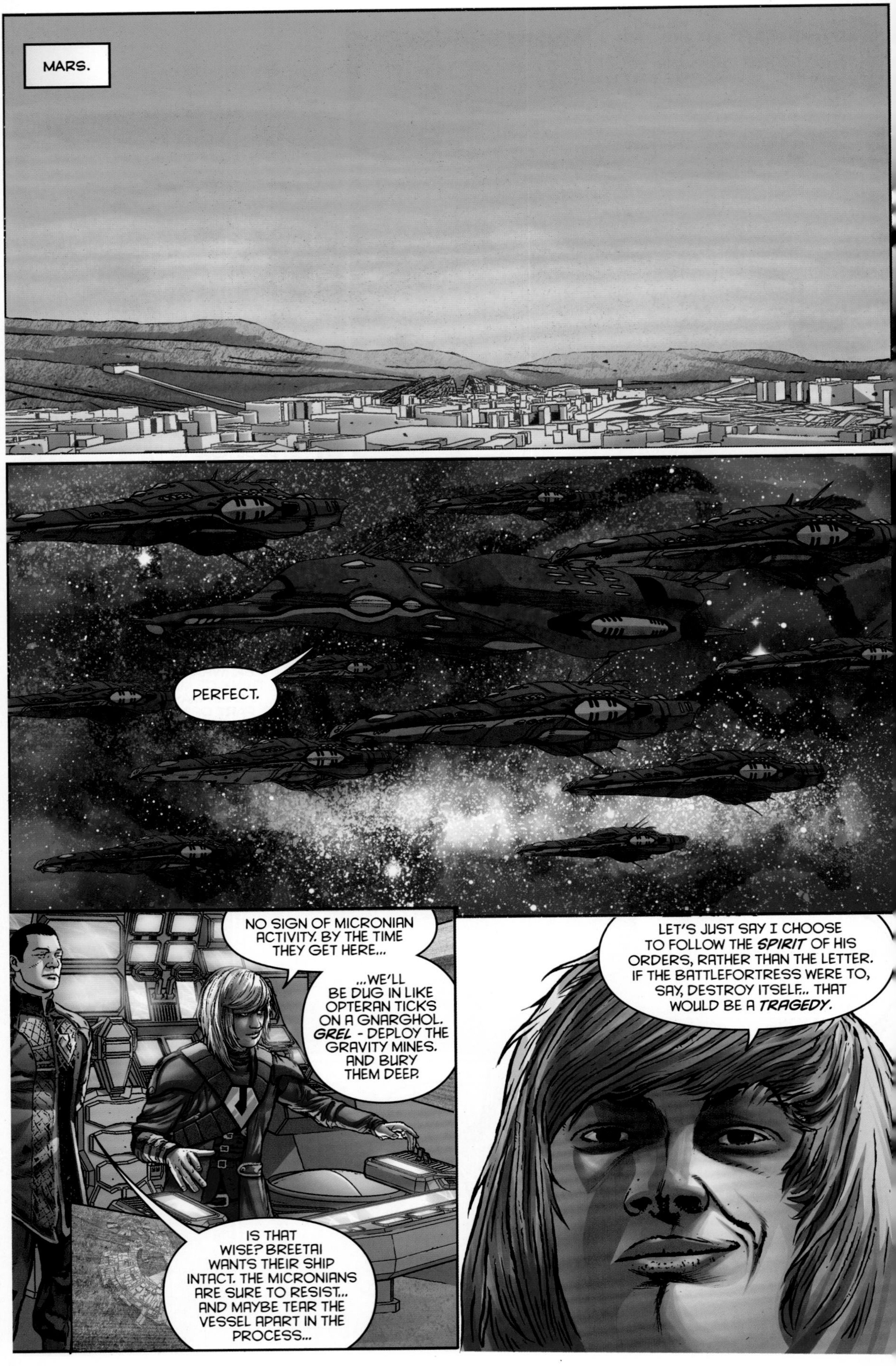

MARS.
PERFECT.
NO SIGN OF MICRONIAN ACTIVITY. BY THE TIME THEY GET HERE...
...WE'LL BE DUG IN LIKE OPTERAN TICKS ON A GNARGHOL. GREL - DEPLOY THE GRAVITY MINES. AND BURY THEM DEEP.
IS THAT WISE? BREETAI WANTS THEIR SHIP INTACT. THE MICRONIANS ARE SURE TO RESIST... AND MAYBE TEAR THE VESSEL APART IN THE PROCESS...
LET'S JUST SAY I CHOOSE TO FOLLOW THE SPIRIT OF HIS ORDERS, RATHER THAN THE LETTER. IF THE BATTLEFORTRESS WERE TO, SAY, DESTROY ITSELF... THAT WOULD BE A TRAGEDY.

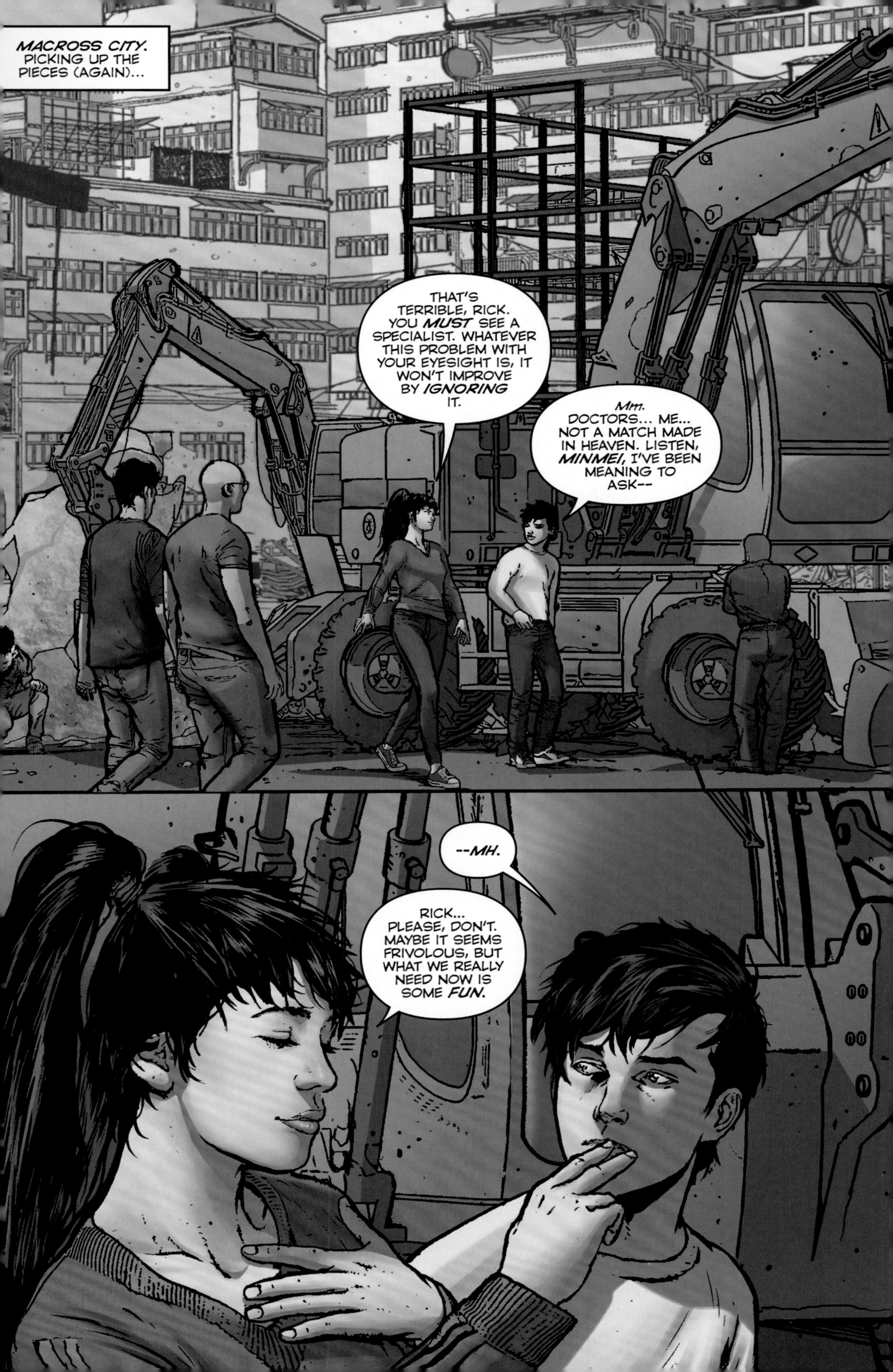
MACROSS CITY. PICKING UP THE PIECES (AGAIN)...
THAT'S TERRIBLE, RICK. YOU MUST SEE A SPECIALIST. WHATEVER THIS PROBLEM WITH YOUR EYESIGHT IS, IT WON'T IMPROVE BY IGNORING IT.
Mm. DOCTORS... ME... NOT A MATCH MADE IN HEAVEN. LISTEN, MINMEI, I'VE BEEN MEANING TO ASK--
--MH.
RICK... PLEASE, DON'T. MAYBE IT SEEMS FRIVOLOUS, BUT WHAT WE REALLY NEED NOW IS SOME FUN.

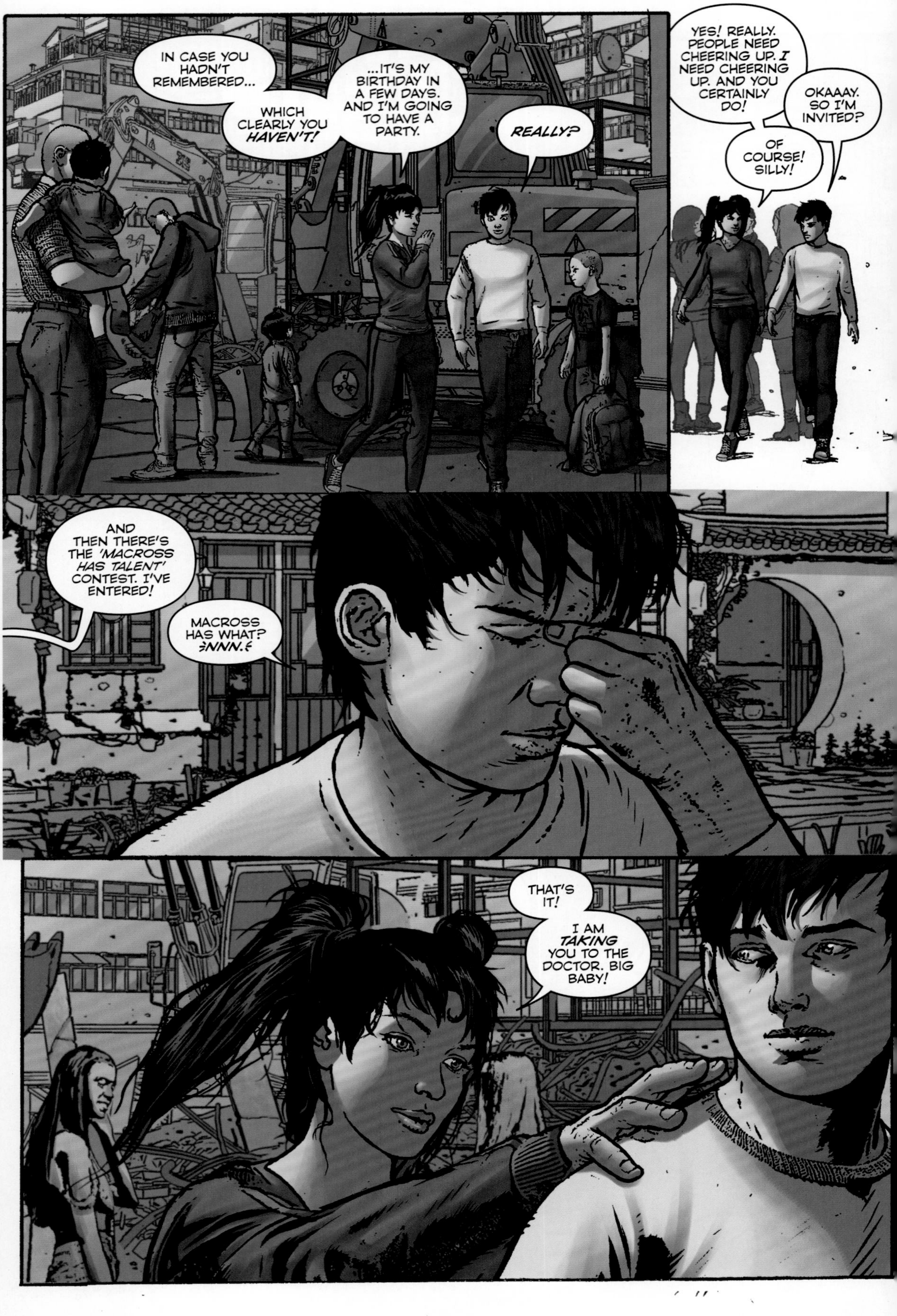
IN CASE YOU HADN'T REMEMBERED...
WHICH CLEARLY YOU HAVEN'T!
...IT'S MY BIRTHDAY IN A FEW DAYS. AND I'M GOING TO HAVE A PARTY.
REALLY?
YES! REALLY. PEOPLE NEED CHEERING UP. I NEED CHEERING UP. AND YOU CERTAINLY DO!
OKAAAY. SO I'M INVITED?
OF COURSE! SILLY!
AND THEN THERE'S THE 'MACROSS HAS TALENT' CONTEST. I'VE ENTERED!
MACROSS HAS WHAT? NNN.
THAT'S IT!
I AM TAKING YOU TO THE DOCTOR. BIG BABY!

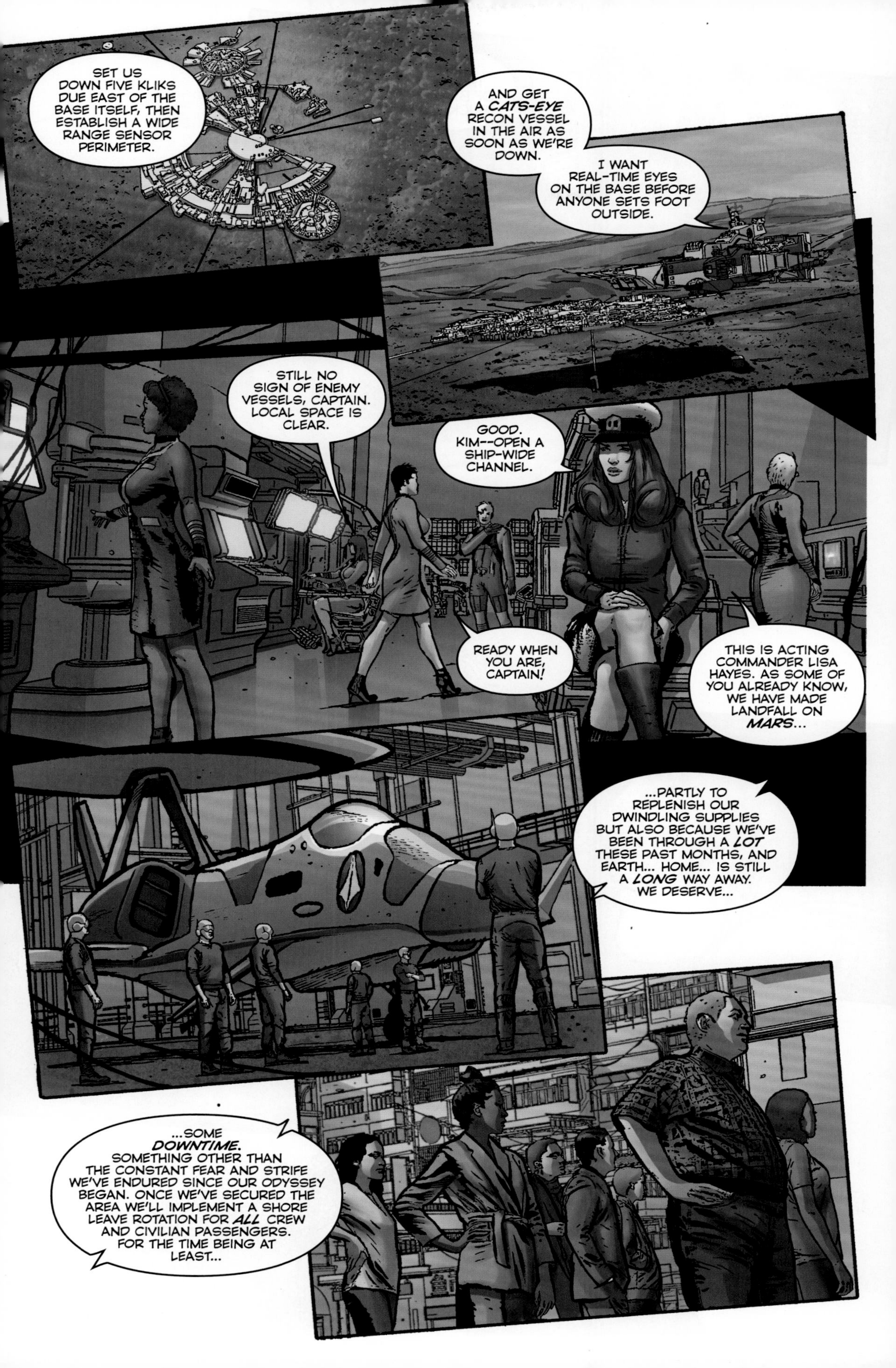
SET US DOWN FIVE KLIKS DUE EAST OF THE BASE ITSELF, THEN ESTABLISH A WIDE RANGE SENSOR PERIMETER.
AND GET A CATS-EYE RECON VESSEL IN THE AIR AS SOON AS WE'RE DOWN.
I WANT REAL-TIME EYES ON THE BASE BEFORE ANYONE SETS FOOT OUTSIDE.
STILL NO SIGN OF ENEMY VESSELS, CAPTAIN. LOCAL SPACE IS CLEAR.
GOOD. KIM--OPEN A SHIP-WIDE CHANNEL.
READY WHEN YOU ARE, CAPTAIN!
THIS IS ACTING COMMANDER LISA HAYES. AS SOME OF YOU ALREADY KNOW, WE HAVE MADE LANDFALL ON MARS...
...PARTLY TO REPLENISH OUR DWINDLING SUPPLIES BUT ALSO BECAUSE WE'VE BEEN THROUGH A LOT THESE PAST MONTHS, AND EARTH... HOME... IS STILL A LONG WAY AWAY. WE DESERVE...
...SOME DOWNTIME. SOMETHING OTHER THAN THE CONSTANT FEAR AND STRIFE WE'VE ENDURED SINCE OUR ODYSSEY BEGAN. ONCE WE'VE SECURED THE AREA WE'LL IMPLEMENT A SHORE LEAVE ROTATION FOR ALL CREW AND CIVILIAN PASSENGERS. FOR THE TIME BEING AT LEAST...

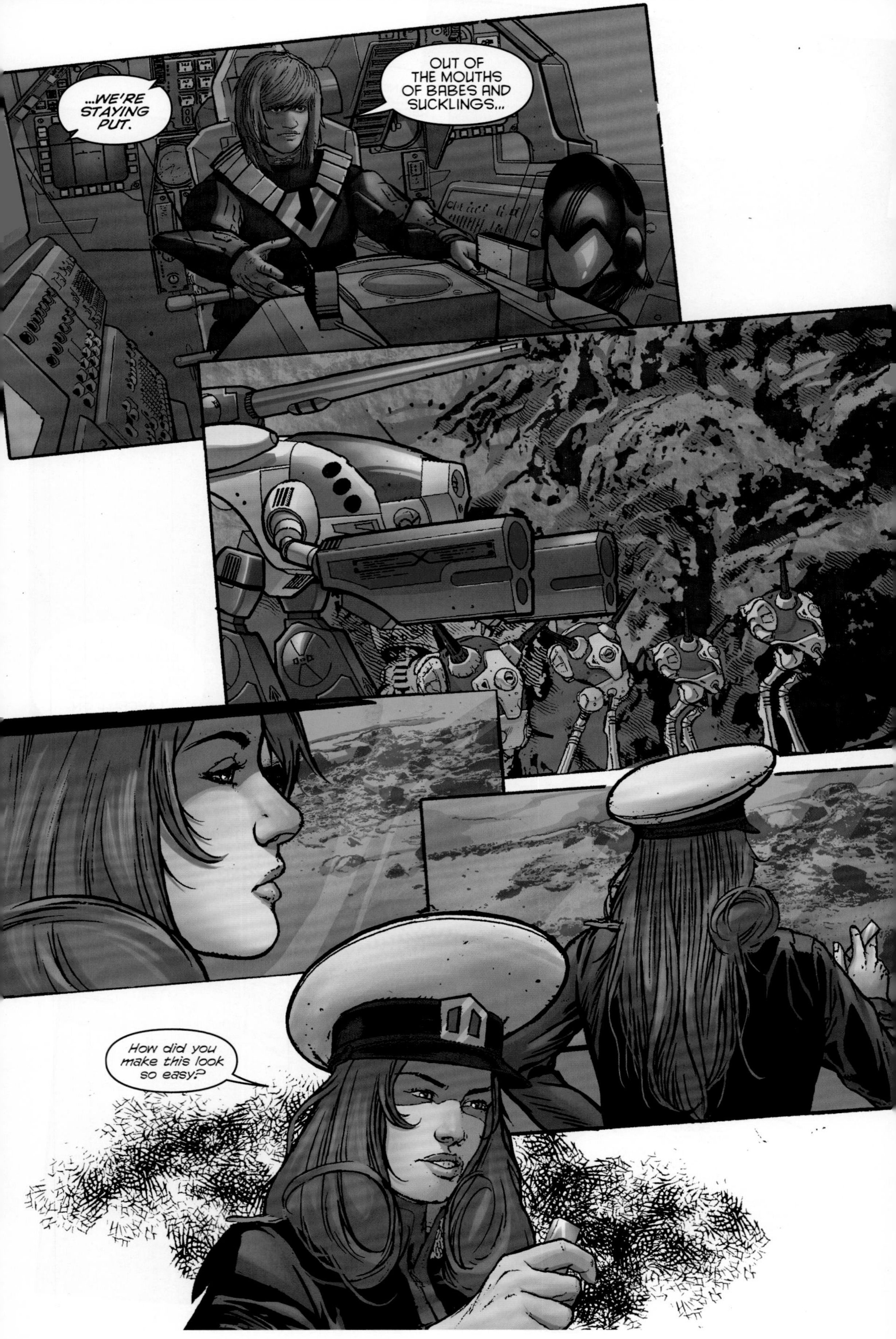
...WE'RE STAYING PUT.
OUT OF THE MOUTHS OF BABES AND SUCKLINGS...
How did you make this look so easy?

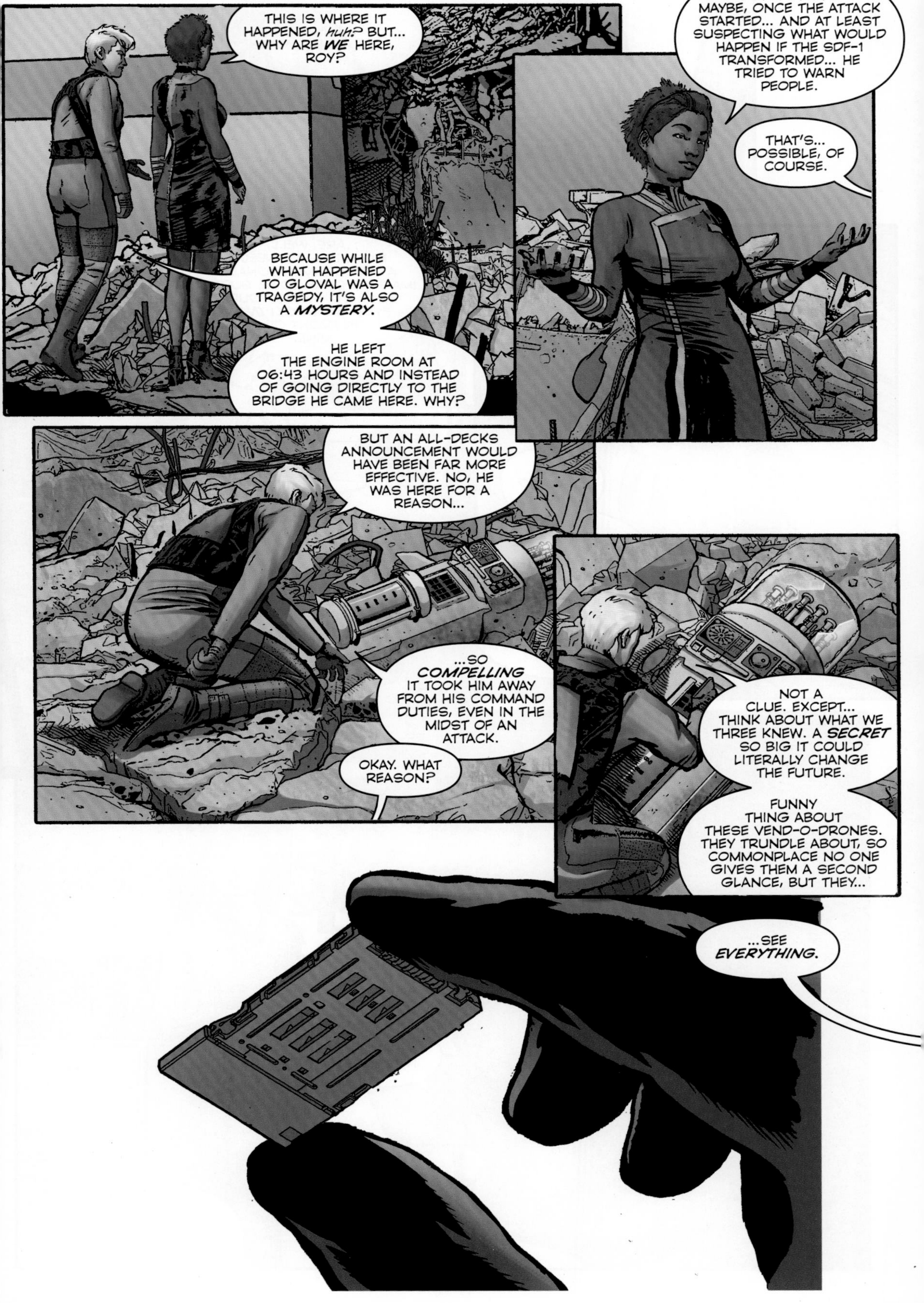
THIS IS WHERE IT HAPPENED, *huh?* BUT... WHY ARE ***WE*** HERE, ROY?
BECAUSE WHILE WHAT HAPPENED TO GLOVAL WAS A TRAGEDY, IT'S ALSO A ***MYSTERY.***
HE LEFT THE ENGINE ROOM AT 06:43 HOURS AND INSTEAD OF GOING DIRECTLY TO THE BRIDGE HE CAME HERE. WHY?
DON'T KNOW. MAYBE, ONCE THE ATTACK STARTED... AND AT LEAST SUSPECTING WHAT WOULD HAPPEN IF THE SDF-1 TRANSFORMED... HE TRIED TO WARN PEOPLE.
THAT'S... POSSIBLE, OF COURSE.
BUT AN ALL-DECKS ANNOUNCEMENT WOULD HAVE BEEN FAR MORE EFFECTIVE. NO, HE WAS HERE FOR A REASON...
...SO ***COMPELLING*** IT TOOK HIM AWAY FROM HIS COMMAND DUTIES, EVEN IN THE MIDST OF AN ATTACK.
OKAY. WHAT REASON?
NOT A CLUE. EXCEPT... THINK ABOUT WHAT WE THREE KNEW. A ***SECRET*** SO BIG IT COULD LITERALLY CHANGE THE FUTURE.
FUNNY THING ABOUT THESE VEND-O-DRONES. THEY TRUNDLE ABOUT, SO COMMONPLACE NO ONE GIVES THEM A SECOND GLANCE, BUT THEY...
...SEE ***EVERYTHING.***

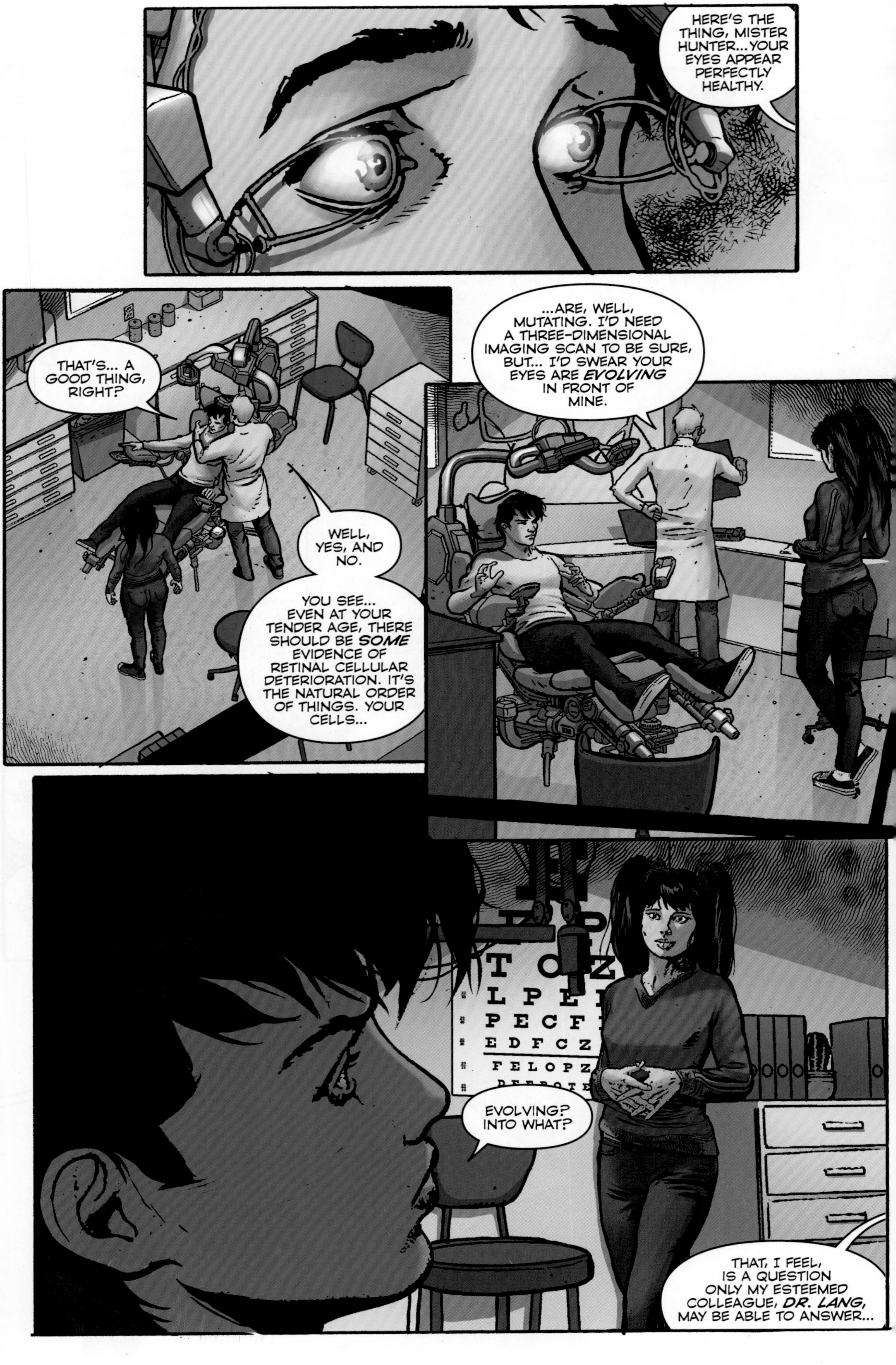
HERE'S THE THING, MISTER HUNTER...YOUR EYES APPEAR PERFECTLY HEALTHY.
THAT'S... A GOOD THING, RIGHT?
WELL, YES, AND NO.
YOU SEE... EVEN AT YOUR TENDER AGE, THERE SHOULD BE *SOME* EVIDENCE OF RETINAL CELLULAR DETERIORATION. IT'S THE NATURAL ORDER OF THINGS. YOUR CELLS...
...ARE, WELL, MUTATING. I'D NEED A THREE-DIMENSIONAL IMAGING SCAN TO BE SURE, BUT... I'D SWEAR YOUR EYES ARE *EVOLVING* IN FRONT OF MINE.
EVOLVING? INTO WHAT?
THAT, I FEEL, IS A QUESTION ONLY MY ESTEEMED COLLEAGUE, *DR. LANG,* MAY BE ABLE TO ANSWER...

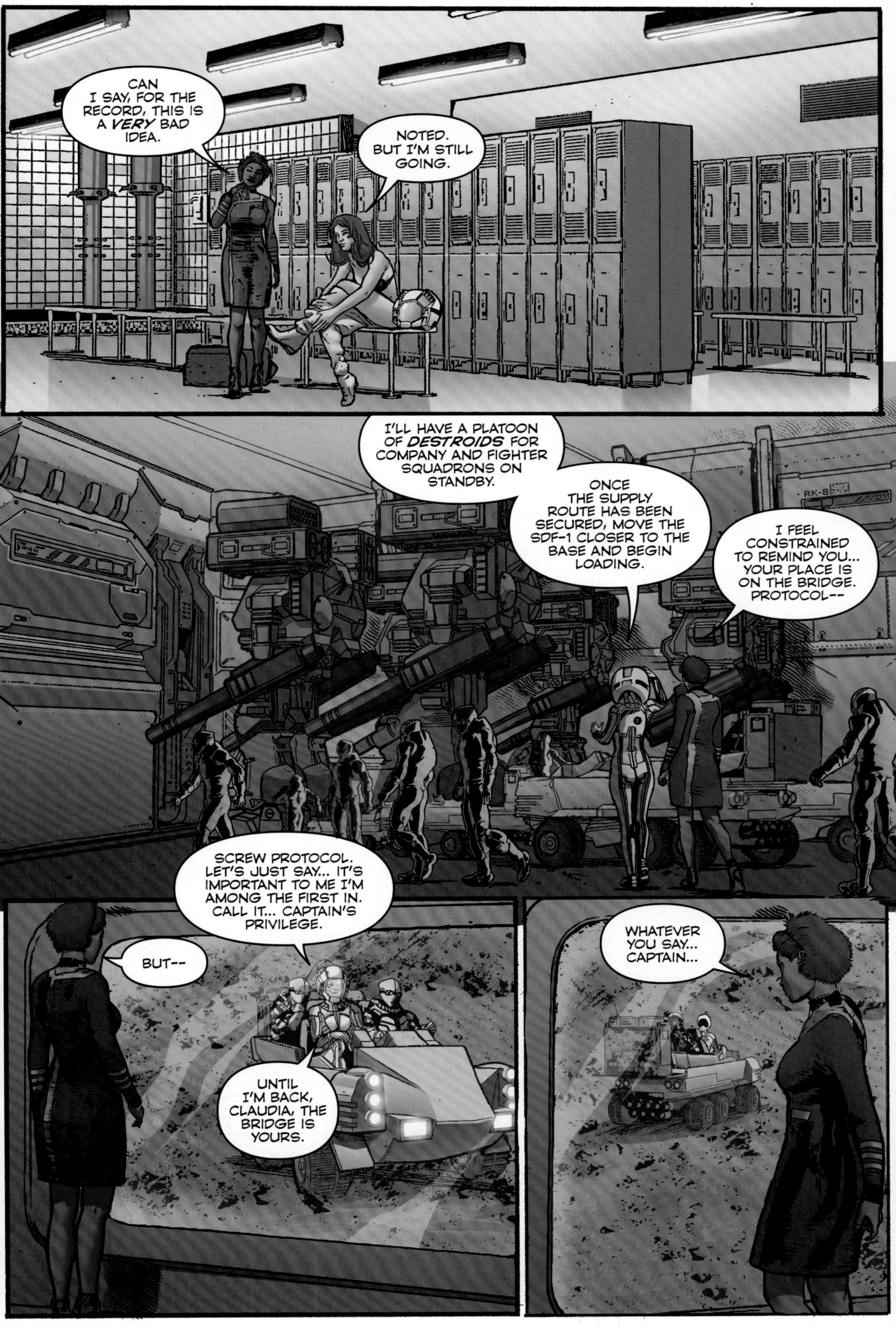
CAN I SAY, FOR THE RECORD, THIS IS A *VERY* BAD IDEA.
NOTED. BUT I'M STILL GOING.
I'LL HAVE A PLATOON OF *DESTROIDS* FOR COMPANY AND FIGHTER SQUADRONS ON STANDBY.
ONCE THE SUPPLY ROUTE HAS BEEN SECURED, MOVE THE SDF-1 CLOSER TO THE BASE AND BEGIN LOADING.
I FEEL CONSTRAINED TO REMIND YOU... YOUR PLACE IS ON THE BRIDGE. PROTOCOL--
SCREW PROTOCOL. LET'S JUST SAY... IT'S IMPORTANT TO ME I'M AMONG THE FIRST IN. CALL IT... CAPTAIN'S PRIVILEGE.
BUT--
UNTIL I'M BACK, CLAUDIA, THE BRIDGE IS YOURS.
WHATEVER YOU SAY... CAPTAIN...

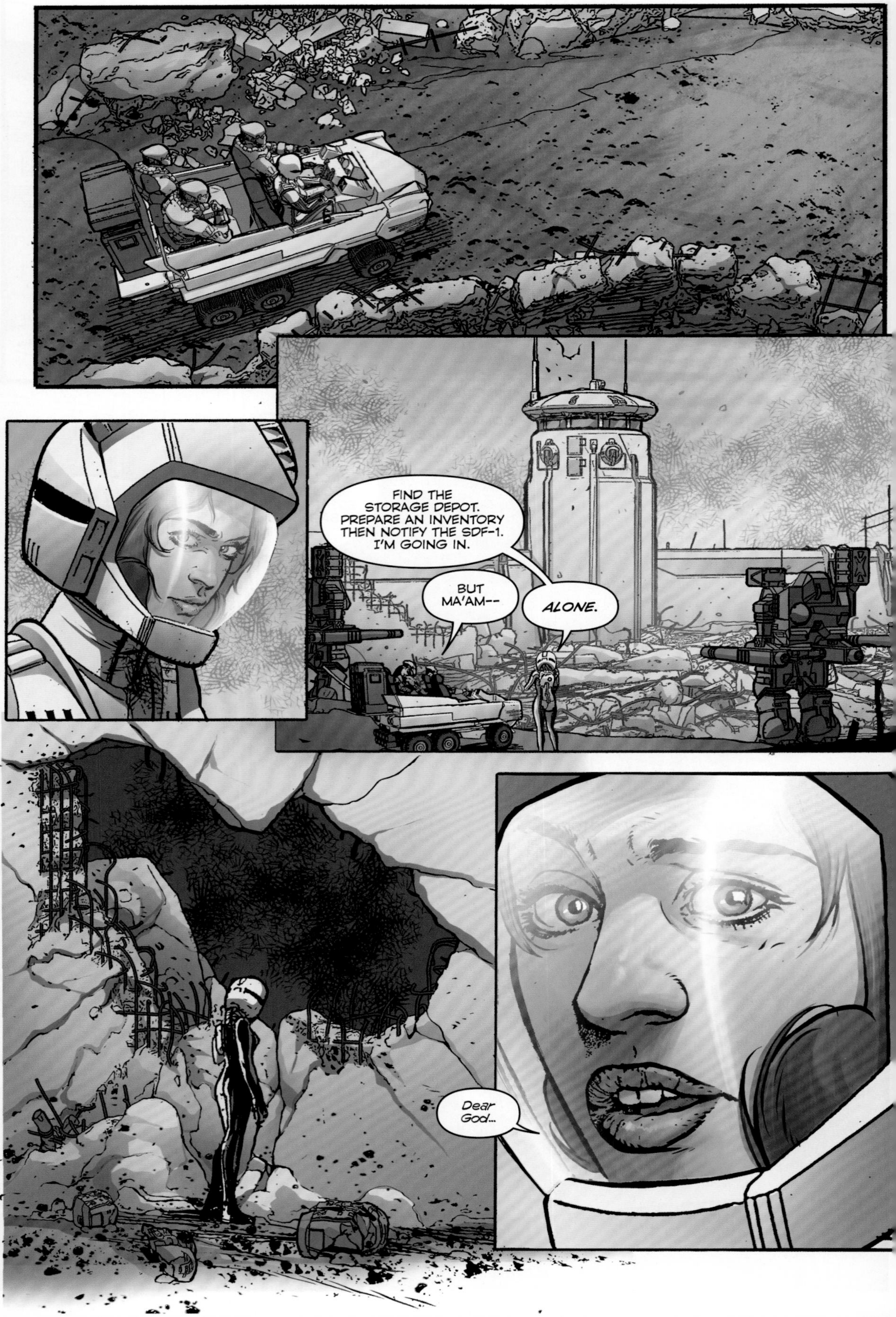
FIND THE STORAGE DEPOT. PREPARE AN INVENTORY THEN NOTIFY THE SDF-1. I'M GOING IN.
BUT MA'AM--
ALONE.
Dear God...

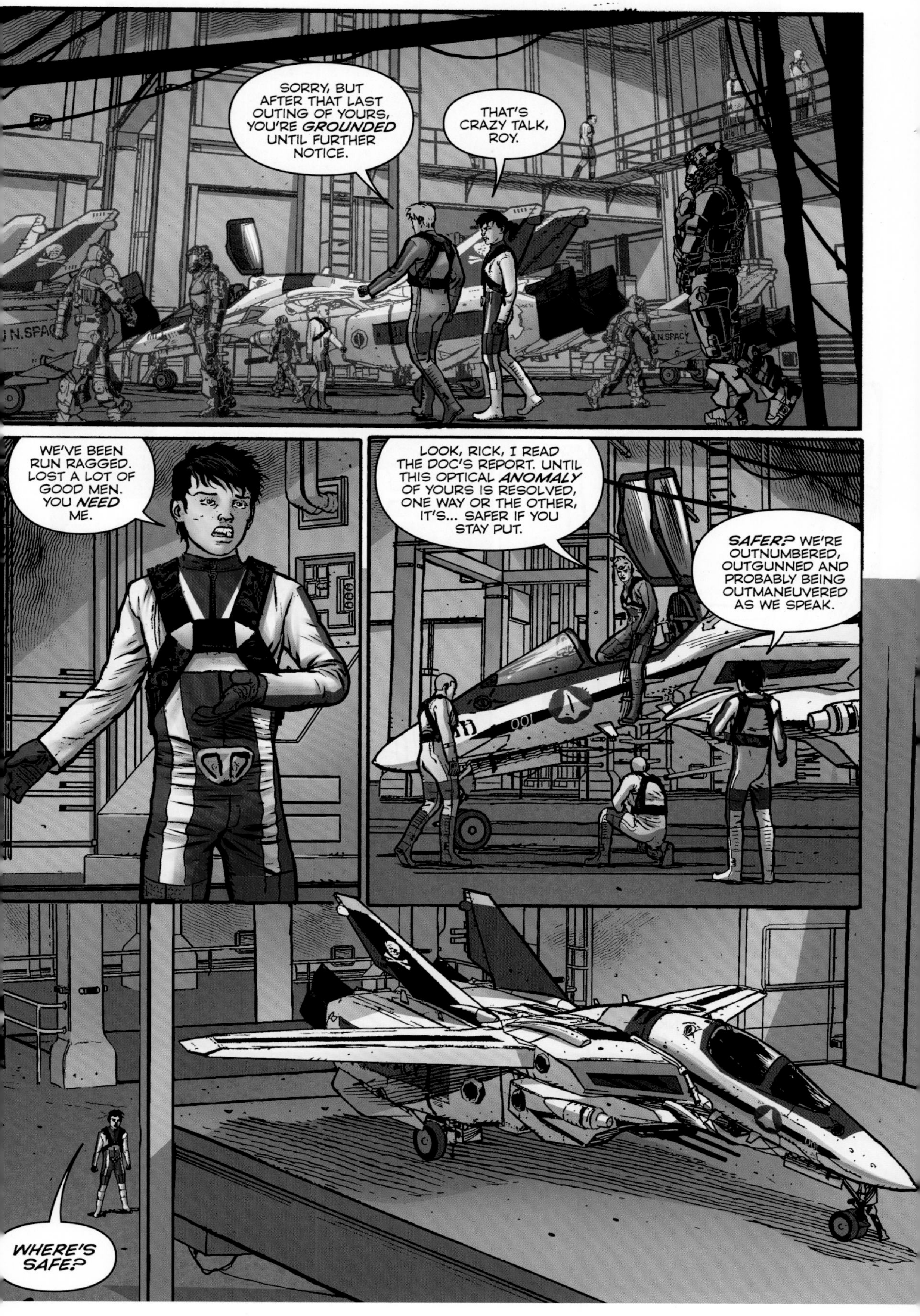
SORRY, BUT AFTER THAT LAST OUTING OF YOURS, YOU'RE GROUNDED UNTIL FURTHER NOTICE.
THAT'S CRAZY TALK, ROY.
U.N.SPACY
U.N.SPACY
WE'VE BEEN RUN RAGGED. LOST A LOT OF GOOD MEN. YOU NEED ME.
LOOK, RICK, I READ THE DOC'S REPORT. UNTIL THIS OPTICAL ANOMALY OF YOURS IS RESOLVED, ONE WAY OR THE OTHER, IT'S... SAFER IF YOU STAY PUT.
SAFER? WE'RE OUTNUMBERED, OUTGUNNED AND PROBABLY BEING OUTMANEUVERED AS WE SPEAK.
001
WHERE'S SAFE?

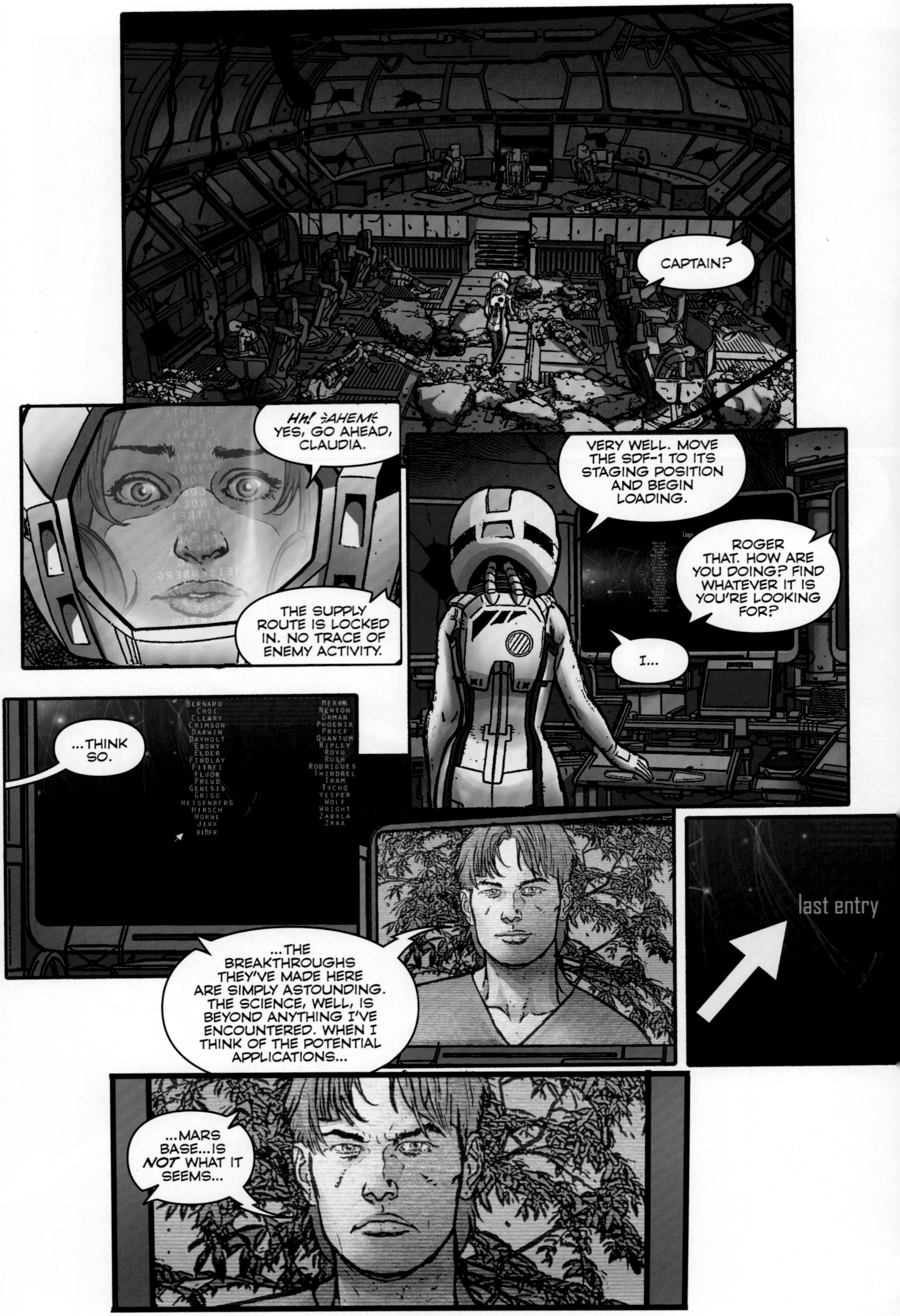
CAPTAIN?
HH! AHEM!
YES, GO AHEAD, CLAUDIA.
THE SUPPLY ROUTE IS LOCKED IN. NO TRACE OF ENEMY ACTIVITY.
VERY WELL. MOVE THE SDF-1 TO ITS STAGING POSITION AND BEGIN LOADING.
ROGER THAT. HOW ARE YOU DOING? FIND WHATEVER IT IS YOU'RE LOOKING FOR?
I...
...THINK SO.
BERNARD
CHOI
CLEARY
CRIMSON
DARWIN
DAYHOLT
EBONY
ELDER
FINDLAY
FITREI
FLUOR
FREUD
GENESIS
GRIGG
HEISENBERG
HIRSCH
HORNE
JINX
RIBER
MERKA
NEWTON
ORMAN
PHOENIX
PRICE
QUANTUM
RIPLEY
ROYU
RUSH
RODRIGUES
THINDREL
TRAM
TYCHO
VESPER
WOLF
WRIGHT
ZABALA
ZRAA
last entry
...THE BREAKTHROUGHS THEY'VE MADE HERE ARE SIMPLY ASTOUNDING. THE SCIENCE, WELL, IS BEYOND ANYTHING I'VE ENCOUNTERED. WHEN I THINK OF THE POTENTIAL APPLICATIONS...
...MARS BASE...IS NOT WHAT IT SEEMS...

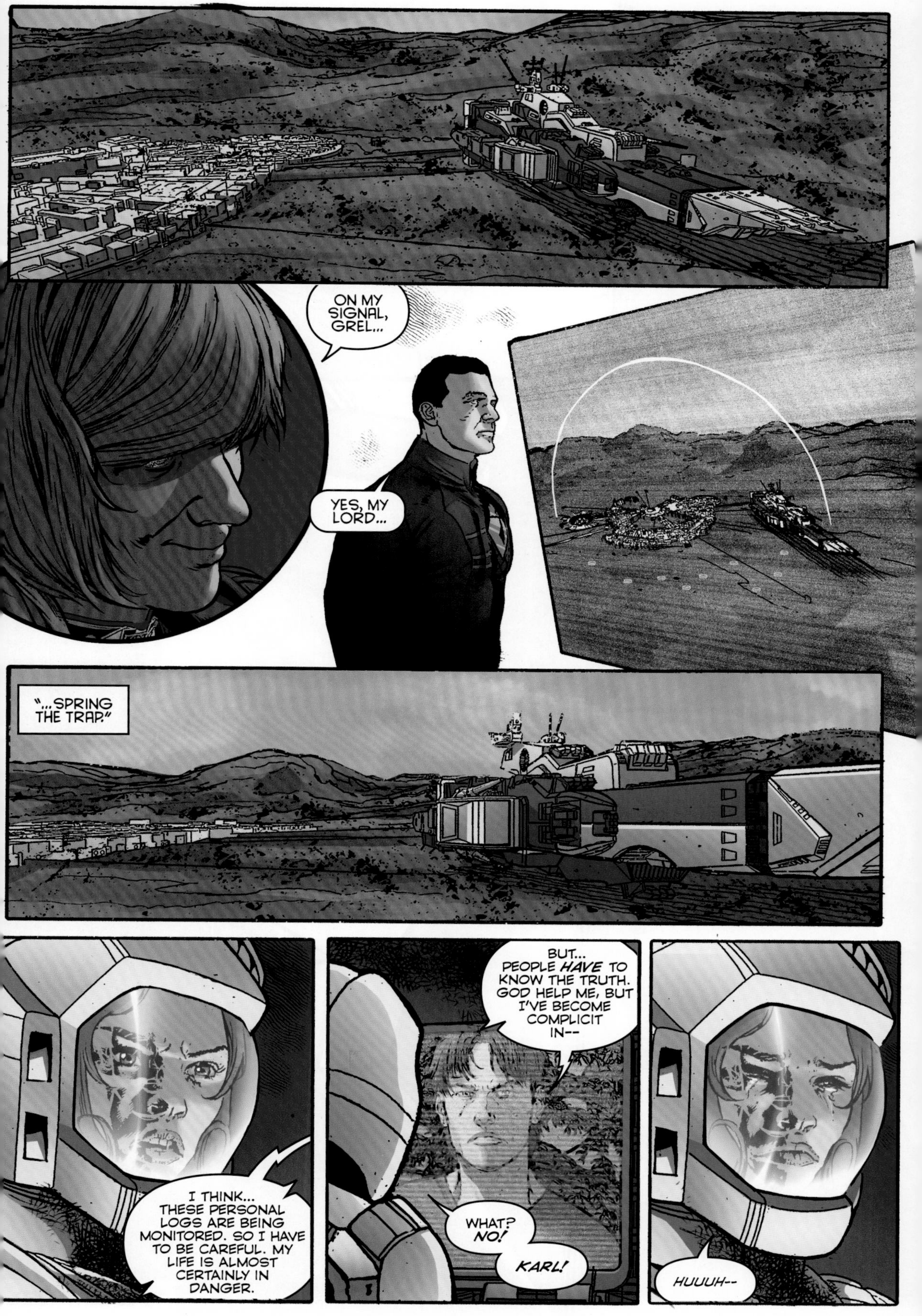
ON MY SIGNAL, GREL...
YES, MY LORD...
"...SPRING THE TRAP."
I THINK... THESE PERSONAL LOGS ARE BEING MONITORED. SO I HAVE TO BE CAREFUL. MY LIFE IS ALMOST CERTAINLY IN DANGER.
BUT... PEOPLE *HAVE* TO KNOW THE TRUTH. GOD HELP ME, BUT I'VE BECOME COMPLICIT IN--
WHAT? *NO!*
KARL!
HUUUH--

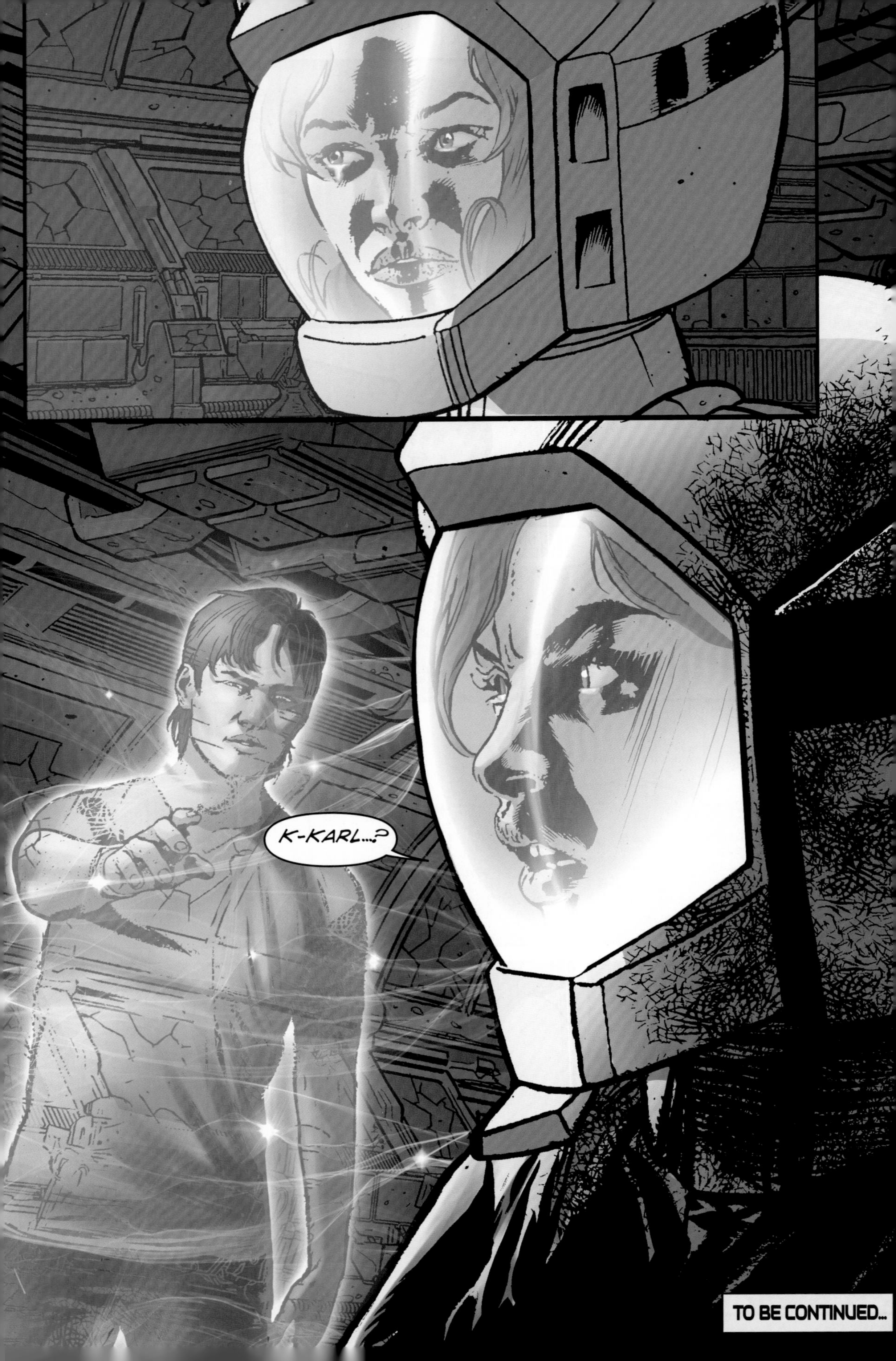
K-KARL...?
TO BE CONTINUED...

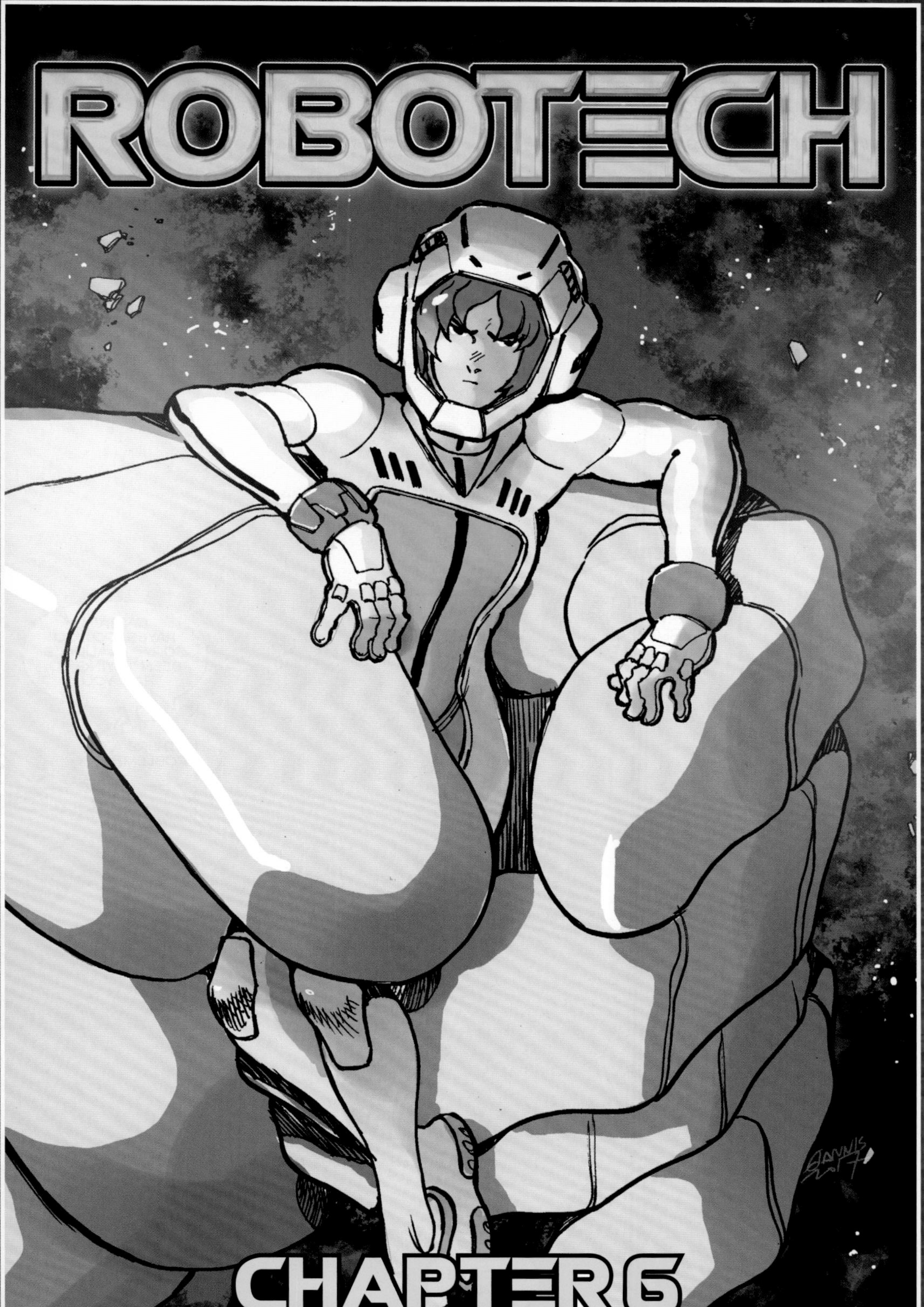
ROBOTECH
CHAPTER 6

ILLUSTRATION BY
GIANNIS MILONOGIANNIS

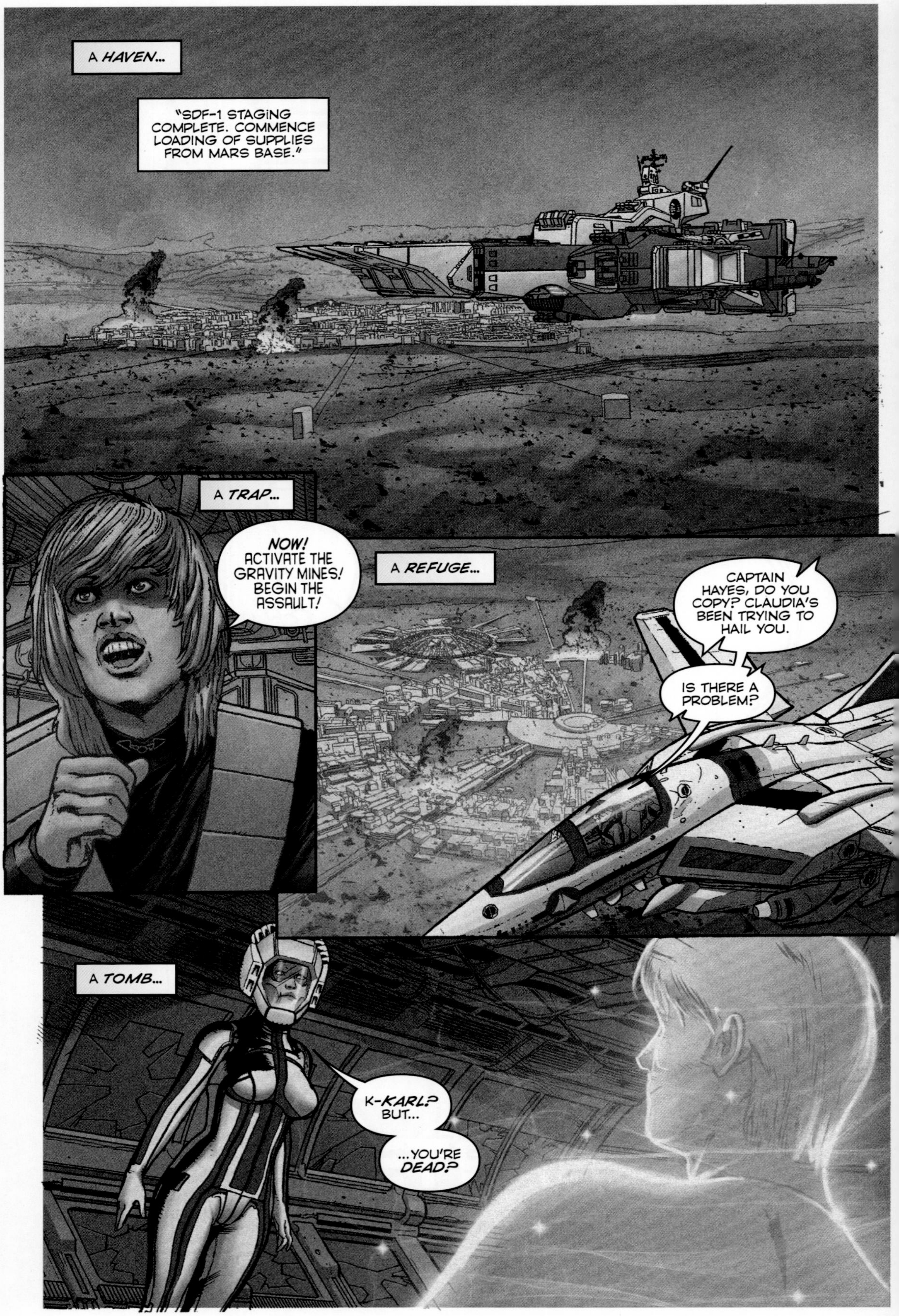
A HAVEN...
"SDF-1 STAGING COMPLETE. COMMENCE LOADING OF SUPPLIES FROM MARS BASE."
A TRAP...
NOW! ACTIVATE THE GRAVITY MINES! BEGIN THE ASSAULT!
A REFUGE...
CAPTAIN HAYES, DO YOU COPY? CLAUDIA'S BEEN TRYING TO HAIL YOU.
IS THERE A PROBLEM?
A TOMB...
K-KARL? BUT...
...YOU'RE DEAD?

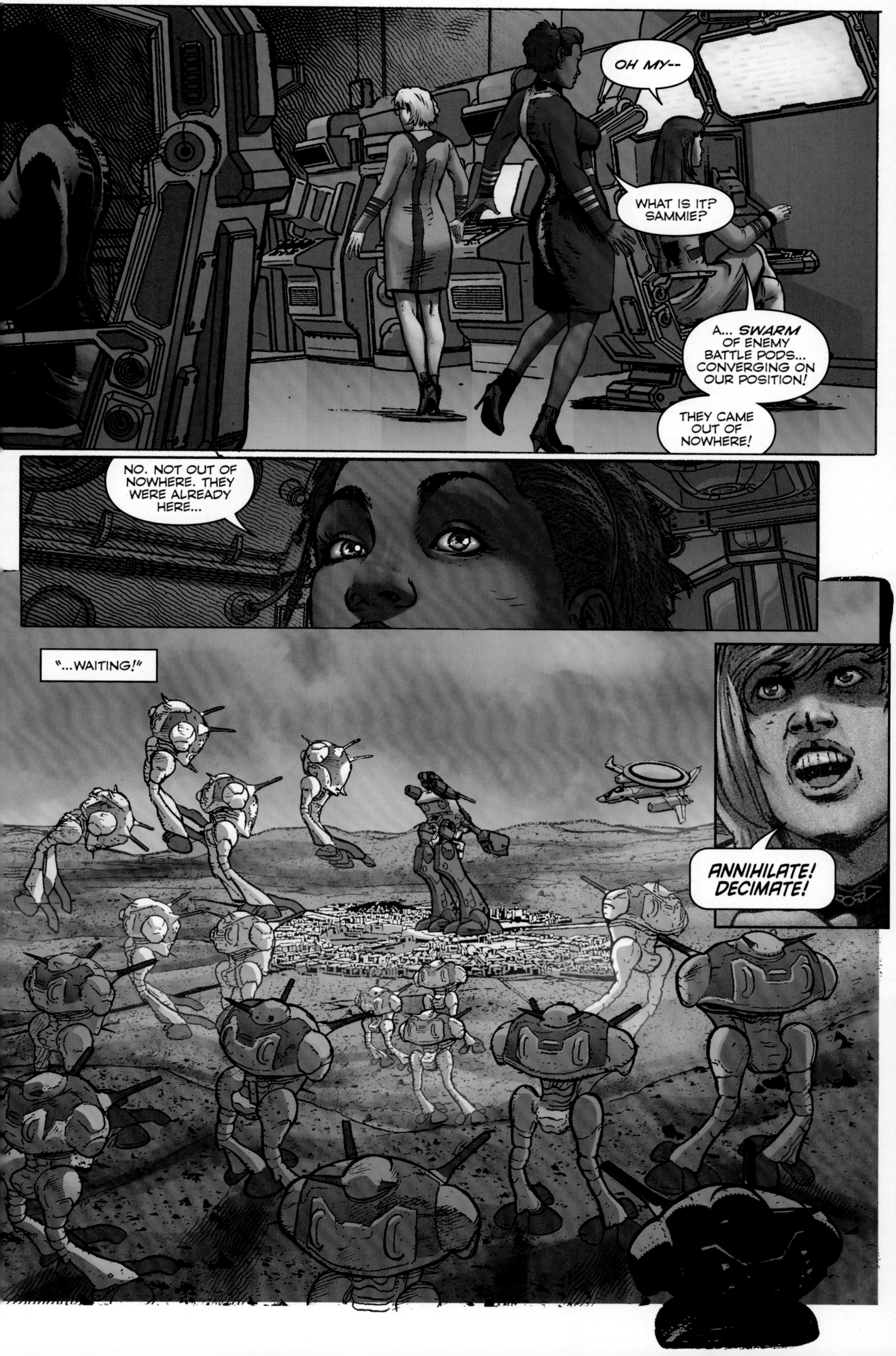
OH MY--
WHAT IS IT? SAMMIE?
A... SWARM OF ENEMY BATTLE PODS... CONVERGING ON OUR POSITION!
THEY CAME OUT OF NOWHERE!
NO. NOT OUT OF NOWHERE. THEY WERE ALREADY HERE...
"...WAITING!"
ANNIHILATE! DECIMATE!

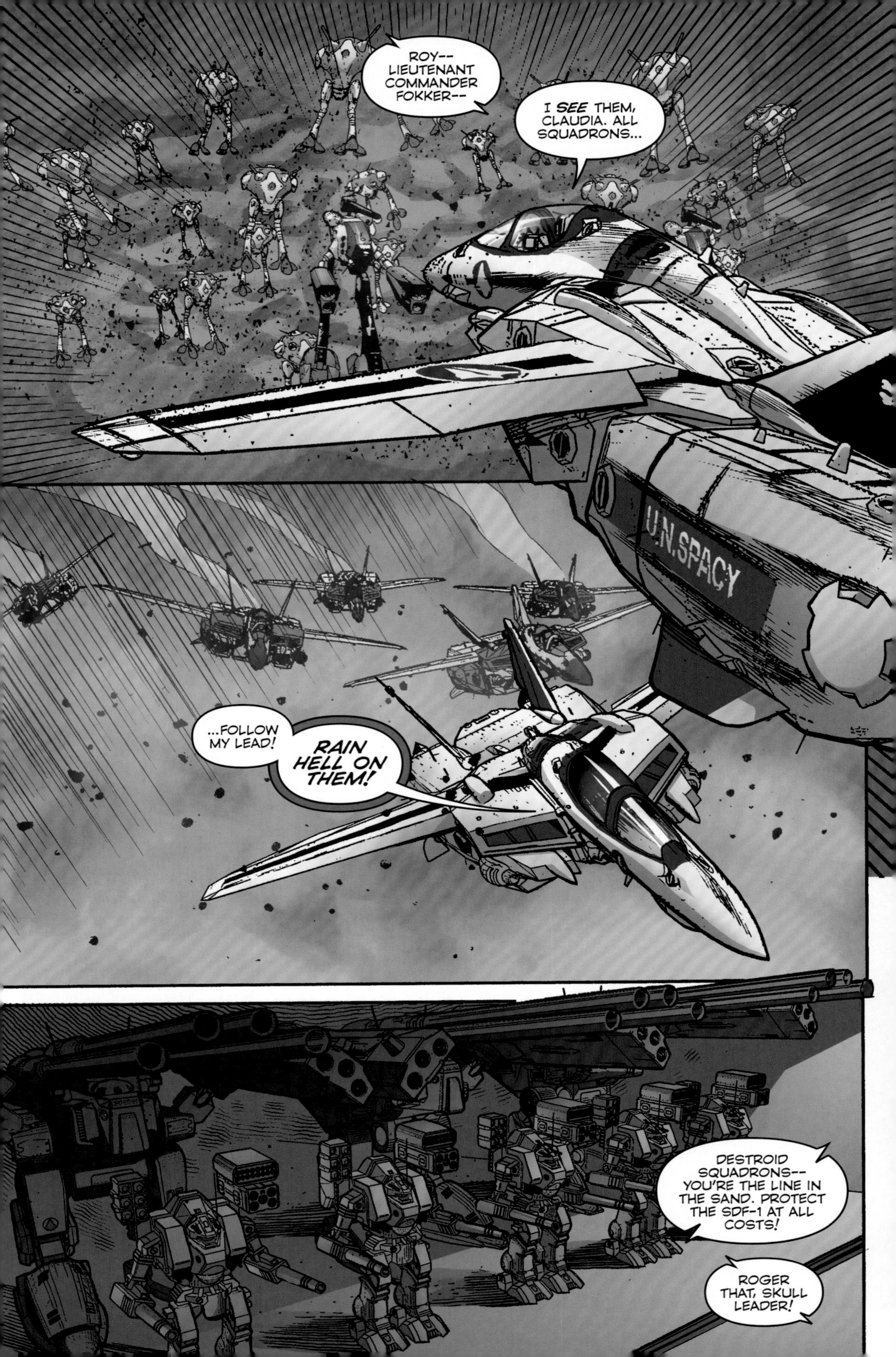

ROY-- LIEUTENANT COMMANDER FOKKER--
I SEE THEM, CLAUDIA. ALL SQUADRONS...
U.N.SPACY
...FOLLOW MY LEAD!
RAIN HELL ON THEM!
DESTROID SQUADRONS-- YOU'RE THE LINE IN THE SAND. PROTECT THE SDF-1 AT ALL COSTS!
ROGER THAT, SKULL LEADER!

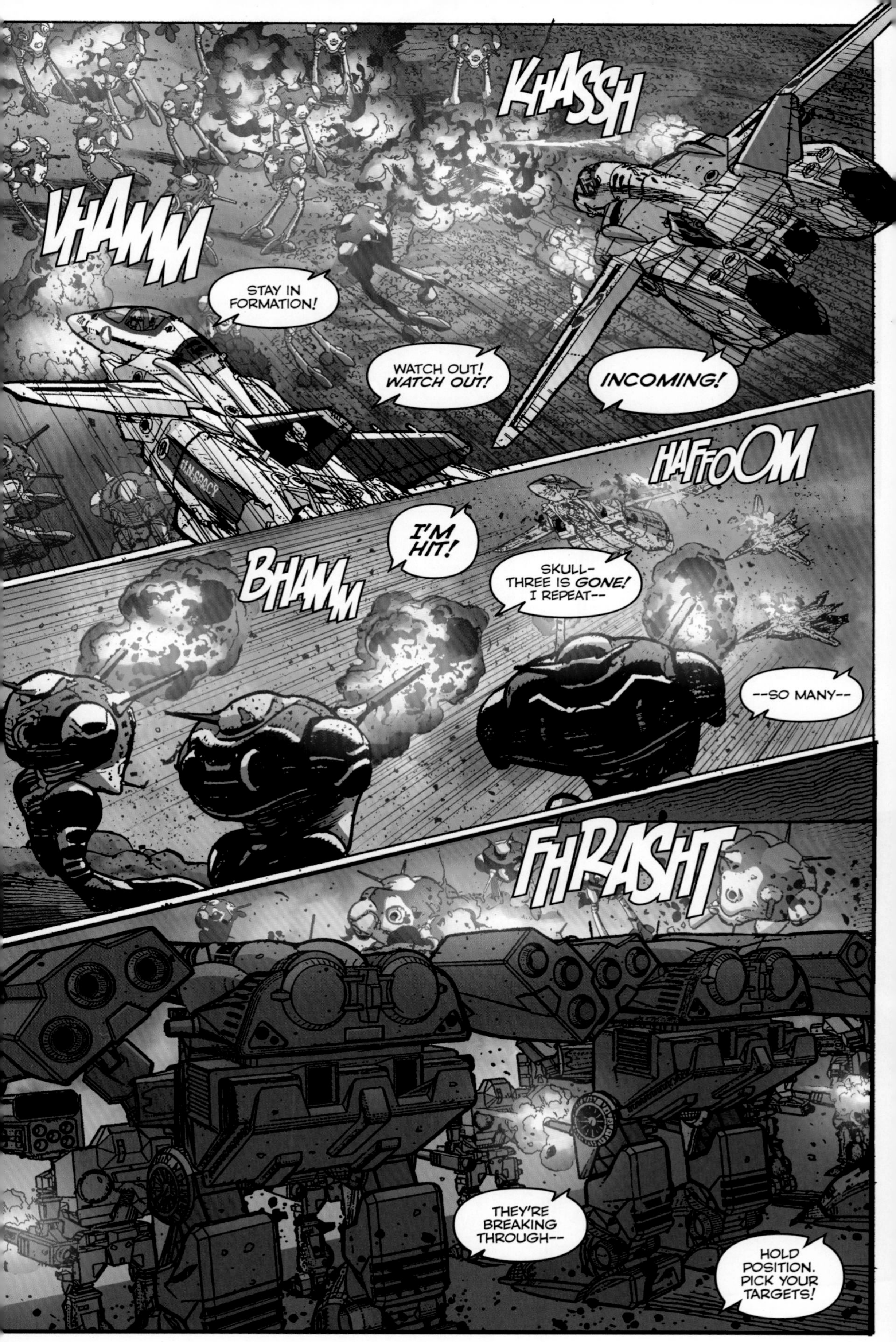
KHASSH
VHAMM
STAY IN FORMATION!
WATCH OUT! WATCH OUT!
INCOMING!
HAFFOOM
I'M HIT!
BHAMM
SKULL-THREE IS GONE! I REPEAT--
--SO MANY--
FHRASHT
THEY'RE BREAKING THROUGH--
HOLD POSITION. PICK YOUR TARGETS!

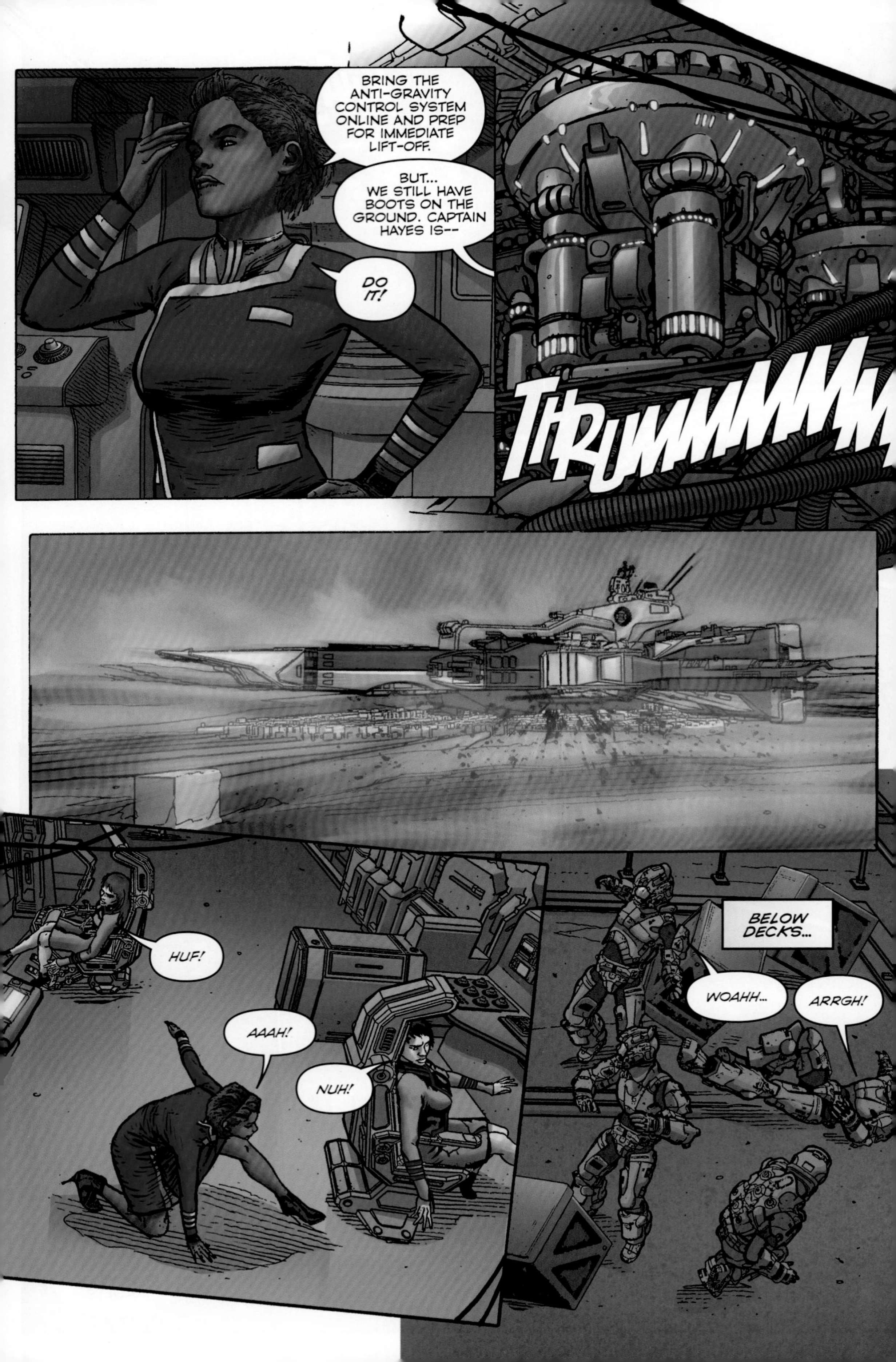
BRING THE ANTI-GRAVITY CONTROL SYSTEM ONLINE AND PREP FOR IMMEDIATE LIFT-OFF.
BUT... WE STILL HAVE BOOTS ON THE GROUND. CAPTAIN HAYES IS--
DO IT!
THRUMMMMMM
HUF!
AAAH!
NUH!
BELOW DECKS...
WOAHH...
ARRGH!

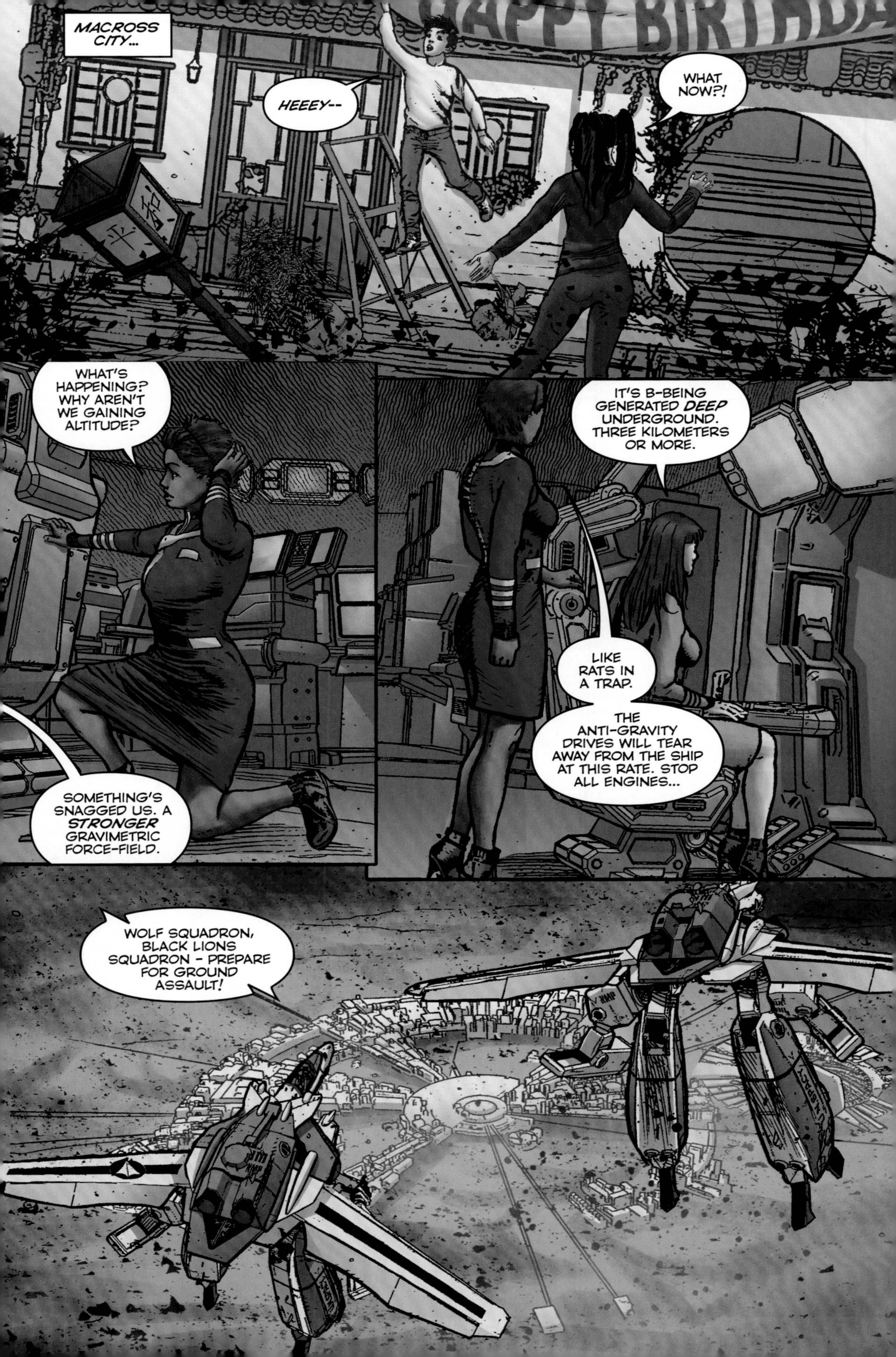
HAPPY BIRTHDA
MACROSS CITY...
HEEEY--
WHAT NOW?!
WHAT'S HAPPENING? WHY AREN'T WE GAINING ALTITUDE?
SOMETHING'S SNAGGED US. A STRONGER GRAVIMETRIC FORCE-FIELD.
IT'S B-BEING GENERATED DEEP UNDERGROUND. THREE KILOMETERS OR MORE.
LIKE RATS IN A TRAP.
THE ANTI-GRAVITY DRIVES WILL TEAR AWAY FROM THE SHIP AT THIS RATE. STOP ALL ENGINES...
WOLF SQUADRON, BLACK LIONS SQUADRON - PREPARE FOR GROUND ASSAULT!

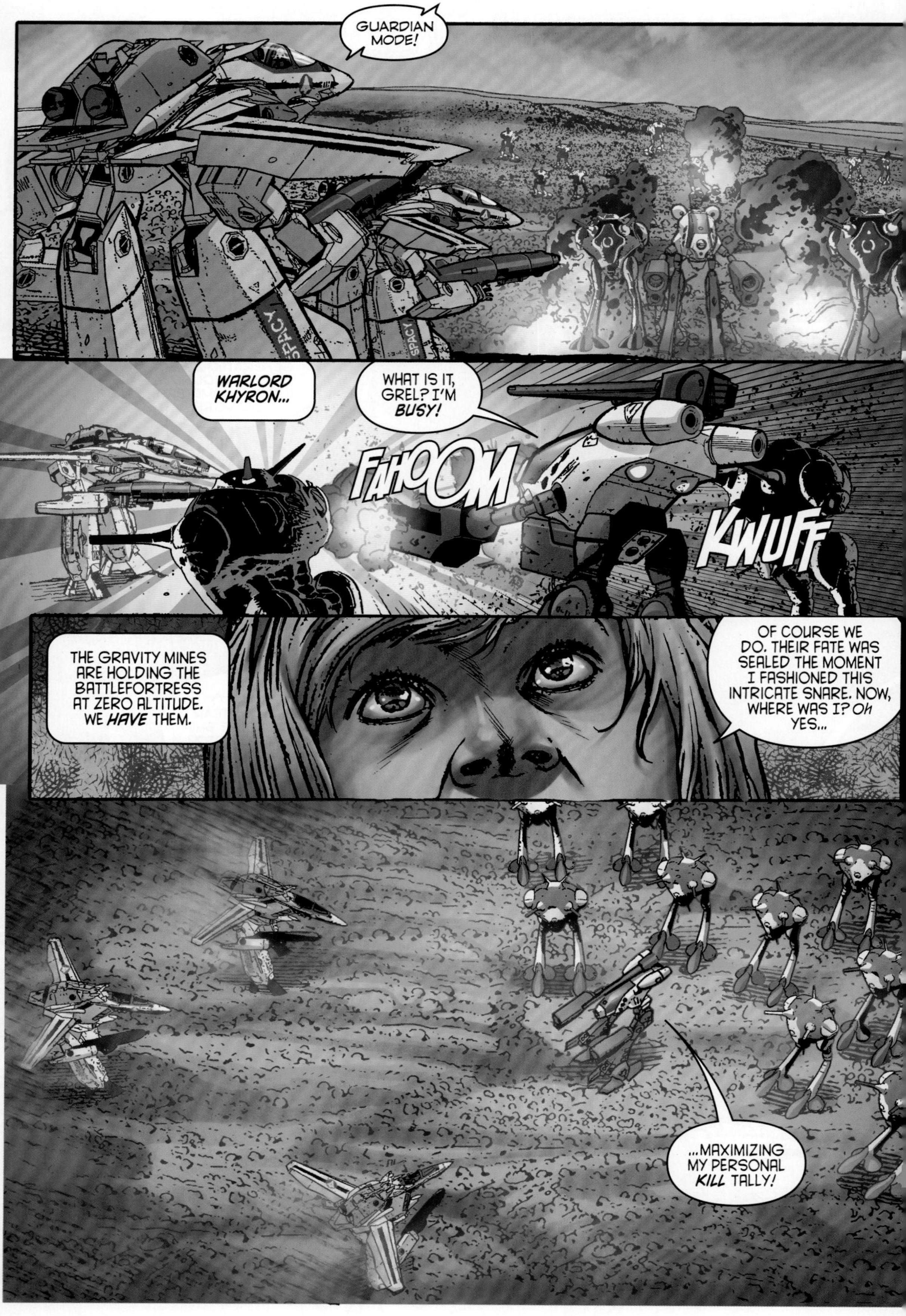
GUARDIAN MODE!
WARLORD KHYRON...
WHAT IS IT, GREL? I'M BUSY!
FAHOOM
KWUFF
THE GRAVITY MINES ARE HOLDING THE BATTLEFORTRESS AT ZERO ALTITUDE. WE HAVE THEM.
OF COURSE WE DO. THEIR FATE WAS SEALED THE MOMENT I FASHIONED THIS INTRICATE SNARE. NOW, WHERE WAS I? OH YES...
...MAXIMIZING MY PERSONAL KILL TALLY!

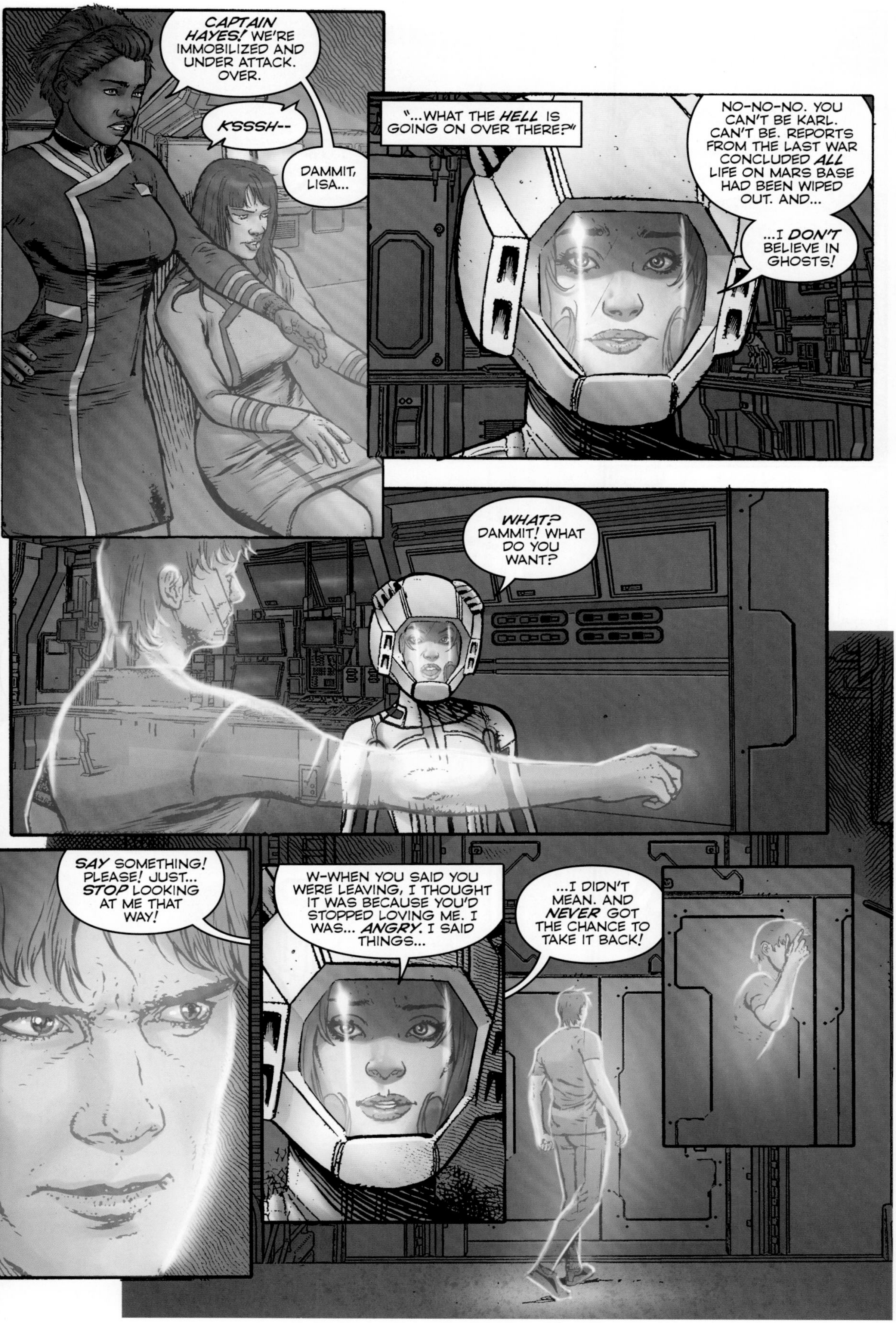
CAPTAIN HAYES! WE'RE IMMOBILIZED AND UNDER ATTACK. OVER.
KSSSH--
DAMMIT, LISA...
"...WHAT THE HELL IS GOING ON OVER THERE?"
NO-NO-NO. YOU CAN'T BE KARL. CAN'T BE. REPORTS FROM THE LAST WAR CONCLUDED ALL LIFE ON MARS BASE HAD BEEN WIPED OUT. AND...
...I DON'T BELIEVE IN GHOSTS!
WHAT? DAMMIT! WHAT DO YOU WANT?
SAY SOMETHING! PLEASE! JUST... STOP LOOKING AT ME THAT WAY!
W-WHEN YOU SAID YOU WERE LEAVING, I THOUGHT IT WAS BECAUSE YOU'D STOPPED LOVING ME. I WAS... ANGRY. I SAID THINGS...
...I DIDN'T MEAN. AND NEVER GOT THE CHANCE TO TAKE IT BACK!

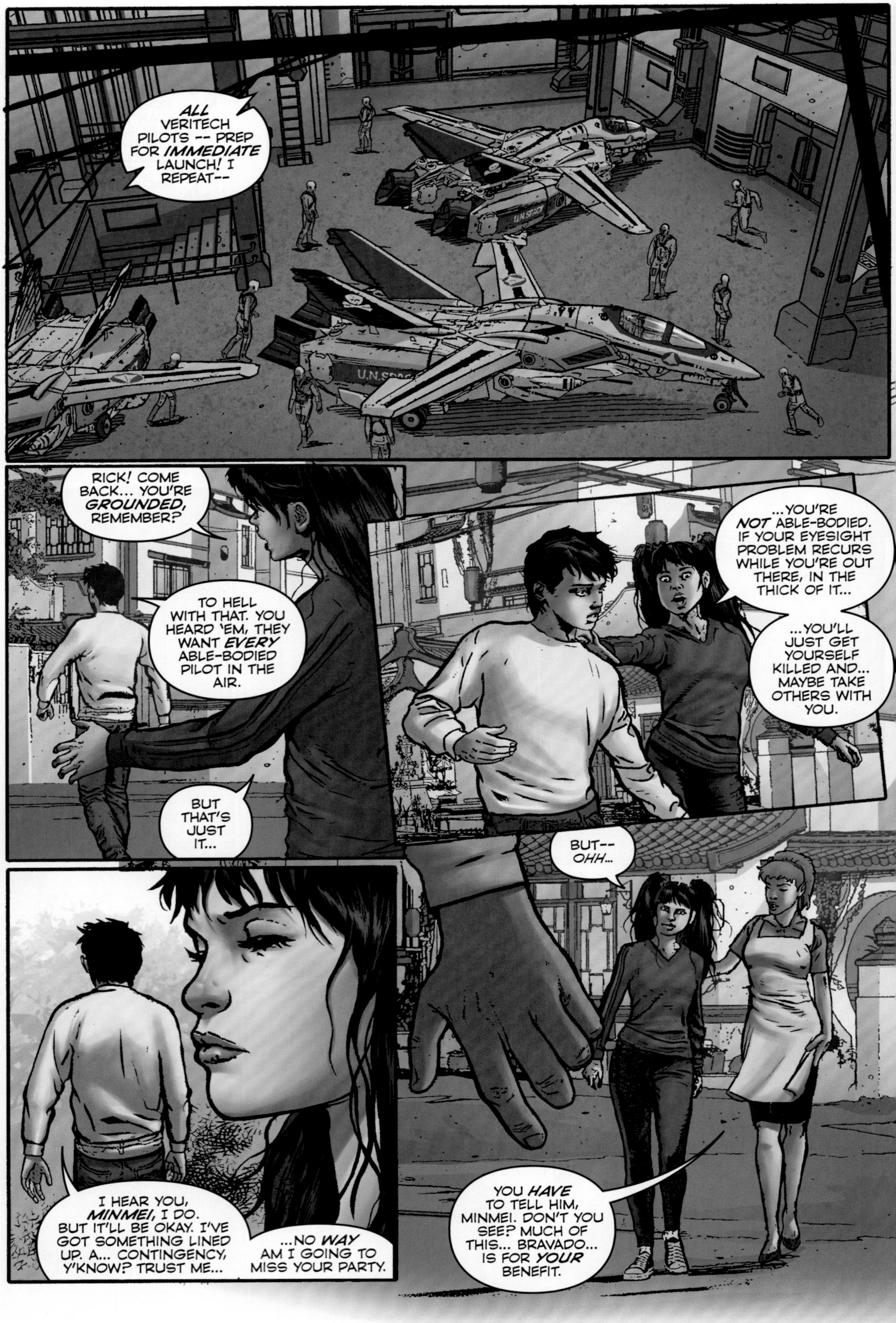
ALL VERITECH PILOTS -- PREP FOR IMMEDIATE LAUNCH! I REPEAT--
U.N.SPACY
RICK! COME BACK... YOU'RE GROUNDED, REMEMBER?
TO HELL WITH THAT. YOU HEARD 'EM, THEY WANT EVERY ABLE-BODIED PILOT IN THE AIR.
BUT THAT'S JUST IT...
...YOU'RE NOT ABLE-BODIED. IF YOUR EYESIGHT PROBLEM RECURS WHILE YOU'RE OUT THERE, IN THE THICK OF IT...
...YOU'LL JUST GET YOURSELF KILLED AND... MAYBE TAKE OTHERS WITH YOU.
I HEAR YOU, MINMEI, I DO. BUT IT'LL BE OKAY. I'VE GOT SOMETHING LINED UP. A... CONTINGENCY, Y'KNOW? TRUST ME...
...NO WAY AM I GOING TO MISS YOUR PARTY.
BUT-- OHH...
YOU HAVE TO TELL HIM, MINMEI. DON'T YOU SEE? MUCH OF THIS... BRAVADO... IS FOR YOUR BENEFIT.

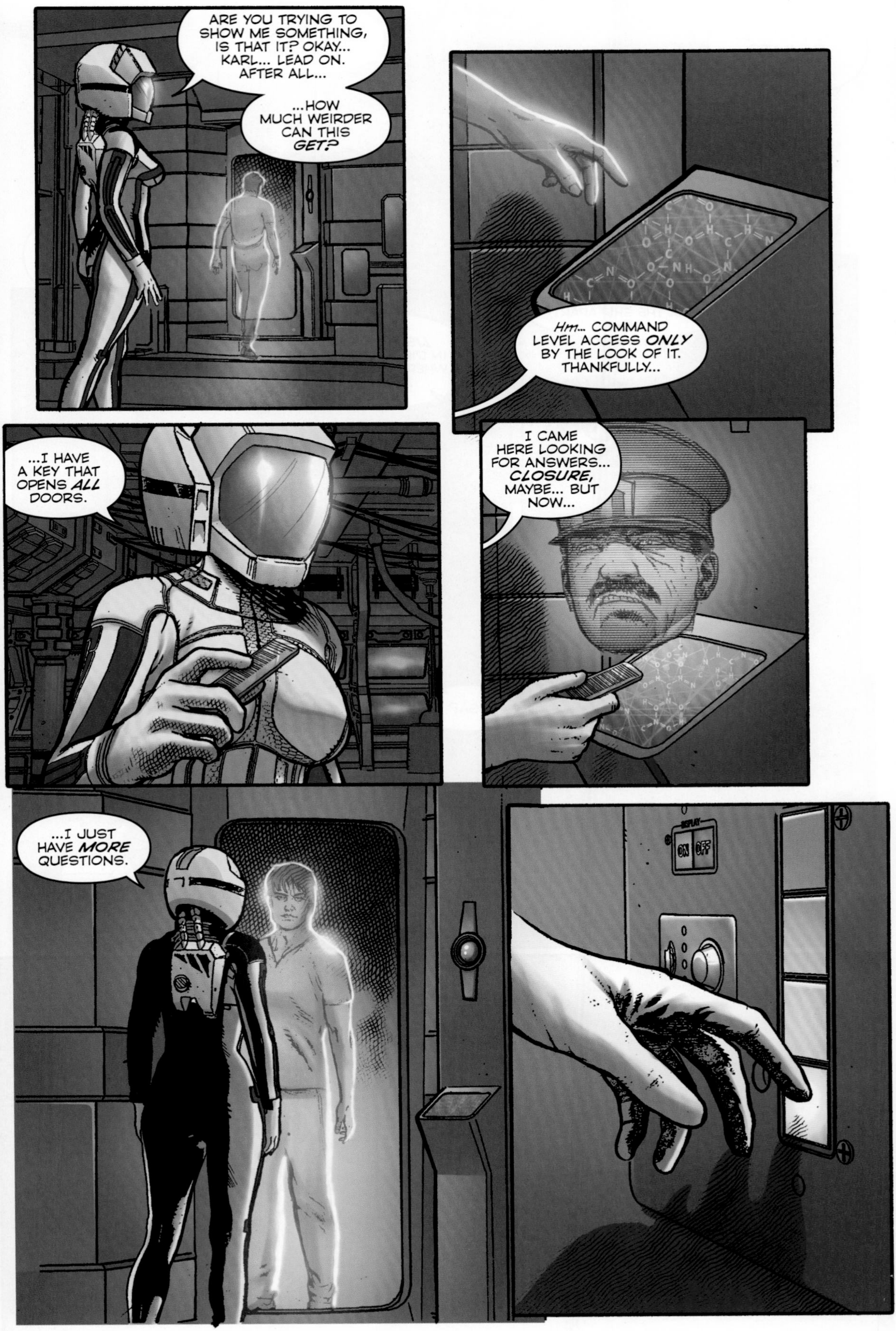
ARE YOU TRYING TO SHOW ME SOMETHING, IS THAT IT? OKAY... KARL... LEAD ON. AFTER ALL...
...HOW MUCH WEIRDER CAN THIS *GET?*
Hm... COMMAND LEVEL ACCESS *ONLY* BY THE LOOK OF IT. THANKFULLY...
...I HAVE A KEY THAT OPENS *ALL* DOORS.
I CAME HERE LOOKING FOR ANSWERS... *CLOSURE,* MAYBE... BUT NOW...
...I JUST HAVE *MORE* QUESTIONS.
DISPLAY
ON OFF

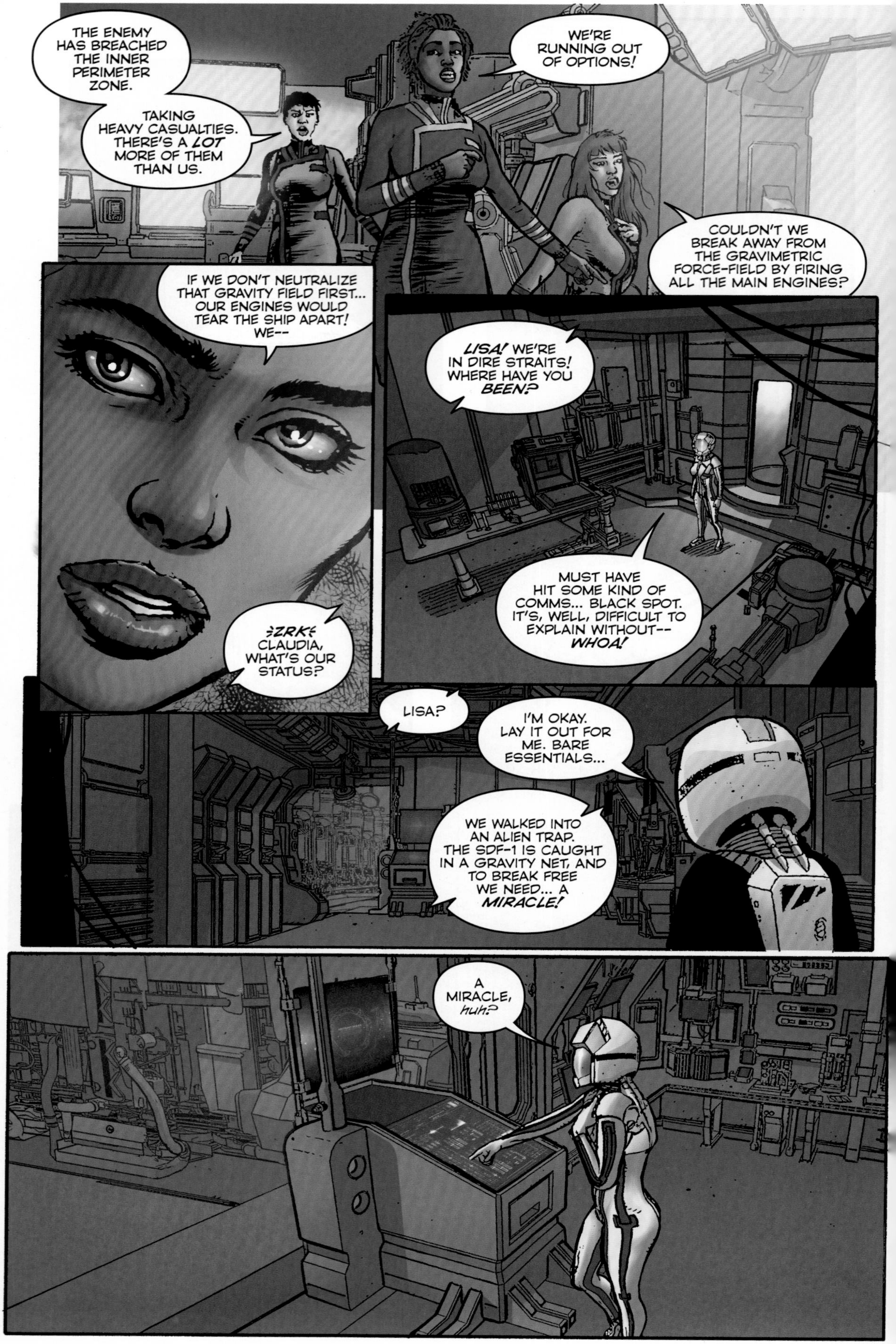
THE ENEMY HAS BREACHED THE INNER PERIMETER ZONE.
TAKING HEAVY CASUALTIES. THERE'S A *LOT* MORE OF THEM THAN US.
WE'RE RUNNING OUT OF OPTIONS!
COULDN'T WE BREAK AWAY FROM THE GRAVIMETRIC FORCE-FIELD BY FIRING ALL THE MAIN ENGINES?
IF WE DON'T NEUTRALIZE THAT GRAVITY FIELD FIRST... OUR ENGINES WOULD TEAR THE SHIP APART! WE--
ZRK CLAUDIA, WHAT'S OUR STATUS?
LISA! WE'RE IN DIRE STRAITS! WHERE HAVE YOU *BEEN?*
MUST HAVE HIT SOME KIND OF COMMS... BLACK SPOT. IT'S, WELL, DIFFICULT TO EXPLAIN WITHOUT-- *WHOA!*
LISA?
I'M OKAY. LAY IT OUT FOR ME. BARE ESSENTIALS...
WE WALKED INTO AN ALIEN TRAP. THE SDF-1 IS CAUGHT IN A GRAVITY NET, AND TO BREAK FREE WE NEED... A *MIRACLE!*
A MIRACLE, *huh?*

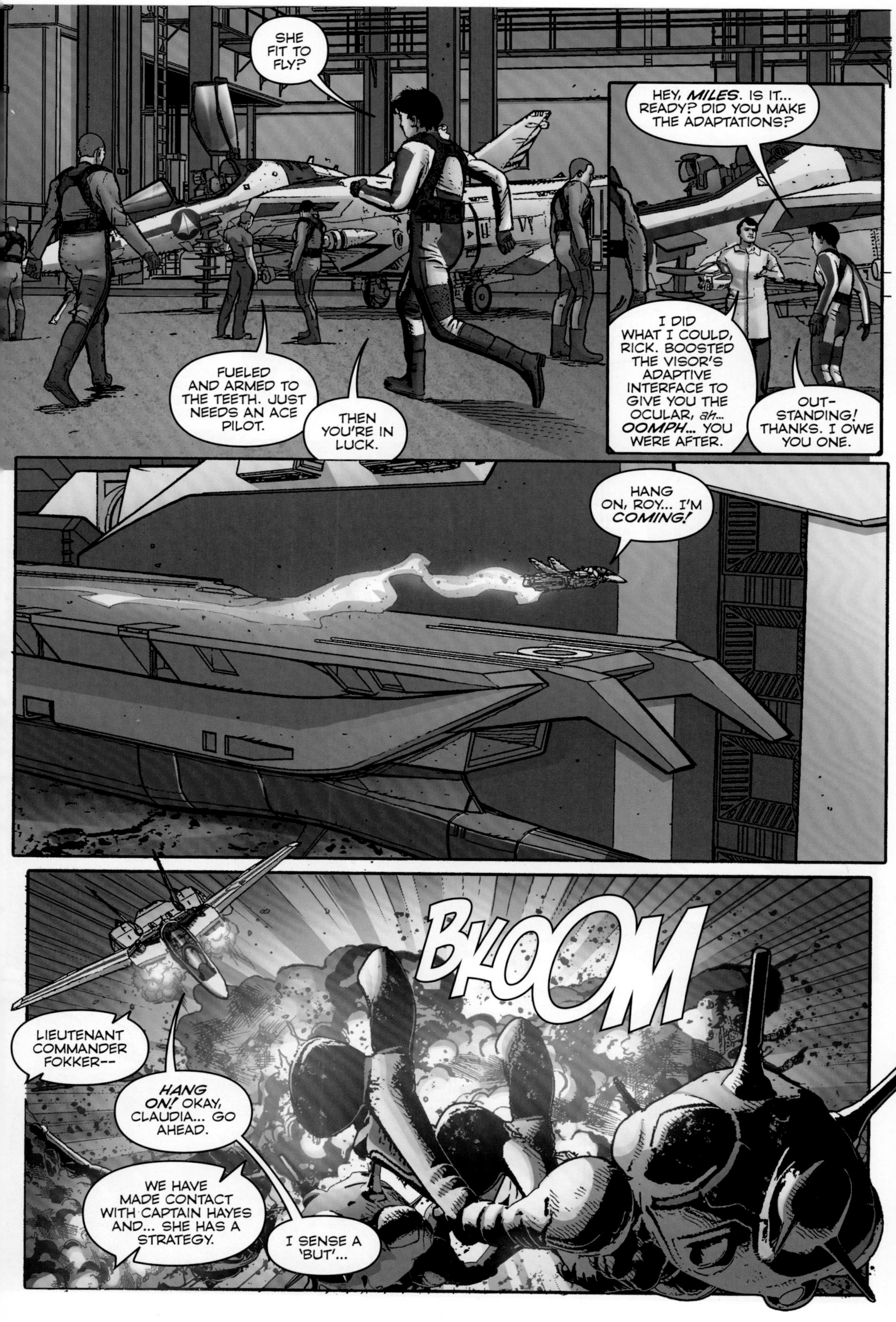
SHE FIT TO FLY?
FUELED AND ARMED TO THE TEETH. JUST NEEDS AN ACE PILOT.
THEN YOU'RE IN LUCK.
HEY, MILES. IS IT... READY? DID YOU MAKE THE ADAPTATIONS?
I DID WHAT I COULD, RICK. BOOSTED THE VISOR'S ADAPTIVE INTERFACE TO GIVE YOU THE OCULAR, ah... OOMPH... YOU WERE AFTER.
OUT-STANDING! THANKS. I OWE YOU ONE.
HANG ON, ROY... I'M COMING!
BKOOM
LIEUTENANT COMMANDER FOKKER--
HANG ON! OKAY, CLAUDIA... GO AHEAD.
WE HAVE MADE CONTACT WITH CAPTAIN HAYES AND... SHE HAS A STRATEGY.
I SENSE A 'BUT'...

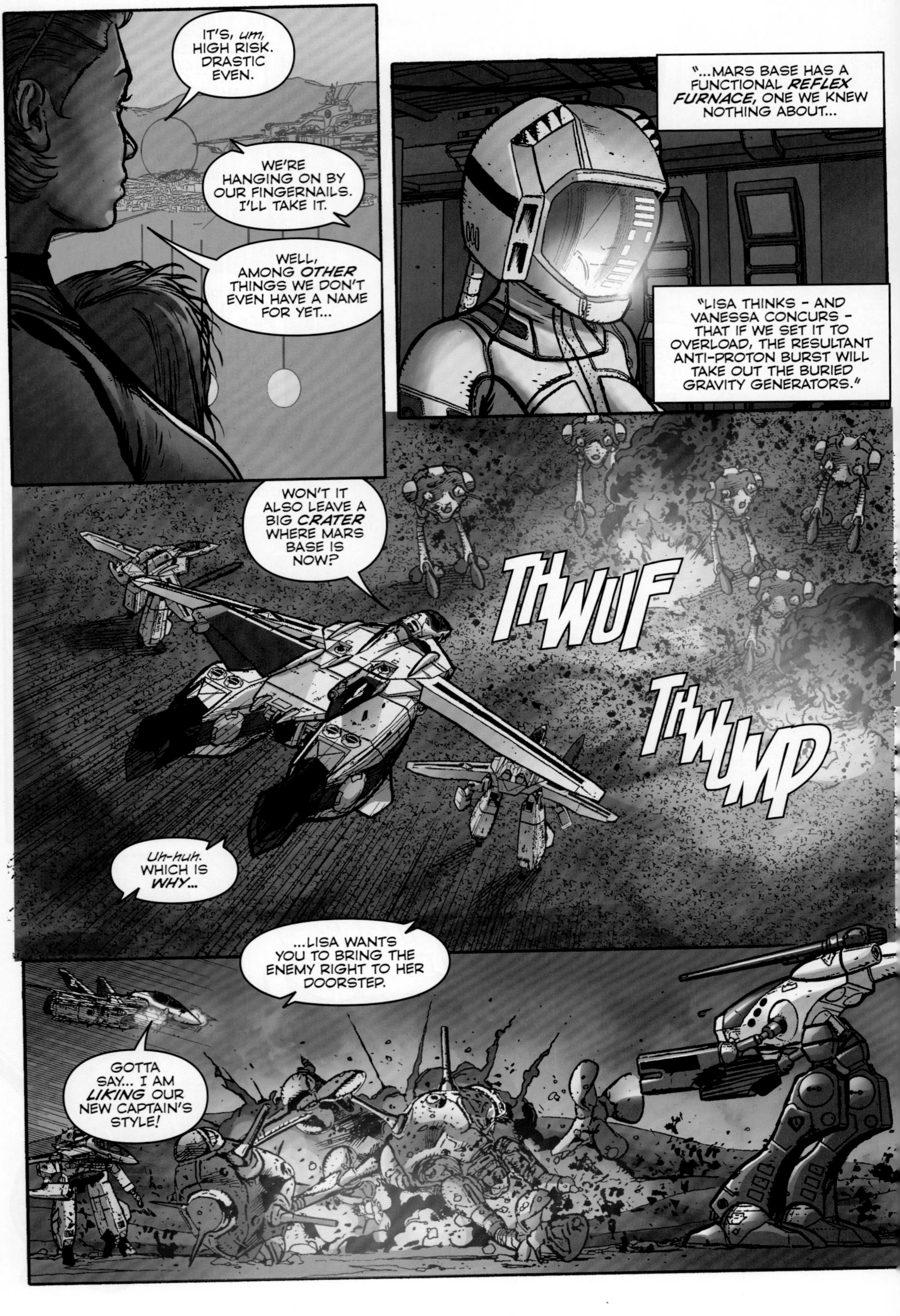
IT'S, *um,* HIGH RISK. DRASTIC EVEN.
WE'RE HANGING ON BY OUR FINGERNAILS. I'LL TAKE IT.
WELL, AMONG *OTHER* THINGS WE DON'T EVEN HAVE A NAME FOR YET...
"...MARS BASE HAS A FUNCTIONAL *REFLEX FURNACE,* ONE WE KNEW NOTHING ABOUT...
"LISA THINKS – AND VANESSA CONCURS – THAT IF WE SET IT TO OVERLOAD, THE RESULTANT ANTI-PROTON BURST WILL TAKE OUT THE BURIED GRAVITY GENERATORS."
WON'T IT ALSO LEAVE A BIG *CRATER* WHERE MARS BASE IS NOW?
THWUF
THWUMP
Uh-huh. WHICH IS *WHY...*
...LISA WANTS YOU TO BRING THE ENEMY RIGHT TO HER DOORSTEP.
GOTTA SAY... I AM *LIKING* OUR NEW CAPTAIN'S STYLE!

THE ALIEN FLAGSHIP...

ANYTHING FROM KHYRON?

JUST THE SAME, RATHER DISMISSIVE, RECORDING, INVITING US TO, *ah*, LEAVE A *"VERY BRIEF"* MESSAGE OF OUR OWN.

LONG-RANGE SCANS?

SUGGEST KHYRON HAS - AGAINST OUR MOST SPECIFIC WISHES - DEPLOYED GRAVITY MINES TO CONTAIN ZOR'S BATTLEFORTRESS. POTENTIALLY COMPROMISING ITS STRUCTURAL INTEGRITY.

RHAAAGH!

KLOOOM

THIS IS SKULL LEADER... ALL VERITECH SQUADRONS FALL BACK TO MARS BASE.

REGROUP, AND WAIT FOR 'EM TO COME TO US.

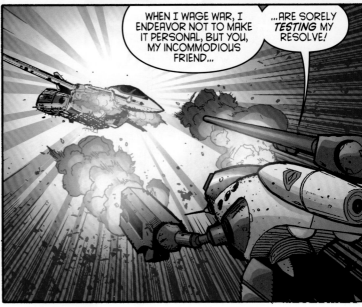

WHEN I WAGE WAR, I ENDEAVOR NOT TO MAKE IT PERSONAL, BUT YOU, MY INCOMMODIOUS FRIEND...

...ARE SORELY *TESTING* MY RESOLVE!

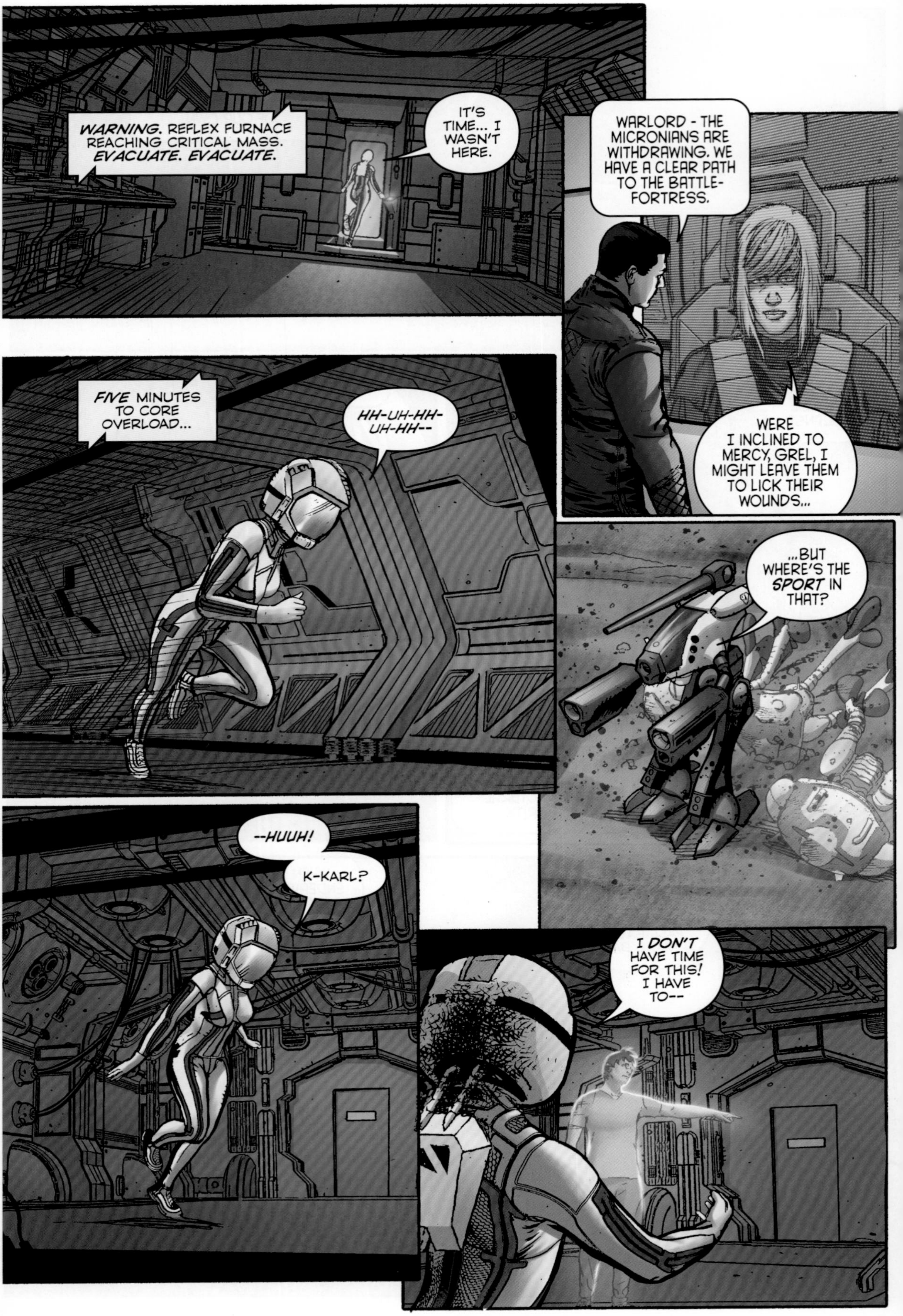

WARNING. REFLEX FURNACE REACHING CRITICAL MASS. EVACUATE. EVACUATE.
IT'S TIME... I WASN'T HERE.
WARLORD - THE MICRONIANS ARE WITHDRAWING. WE HAVE A CLEAR PATH TO THE BATTLE-FORTRESS.
WERE I INCLINED TO MERCY, GREL, I MIGHT LEAVE THEM TO LICK THEIR WOUNDS...
FIVE MINUTES TO CORE OVERLOAD...
HH-UH-HH-UH-HH--
...BUT WHERE'S THE SPORT IN THAT?
--HUUH!
K-KARL?
I DON'T HAVE TIME FOR THIS! I HAVE TO--

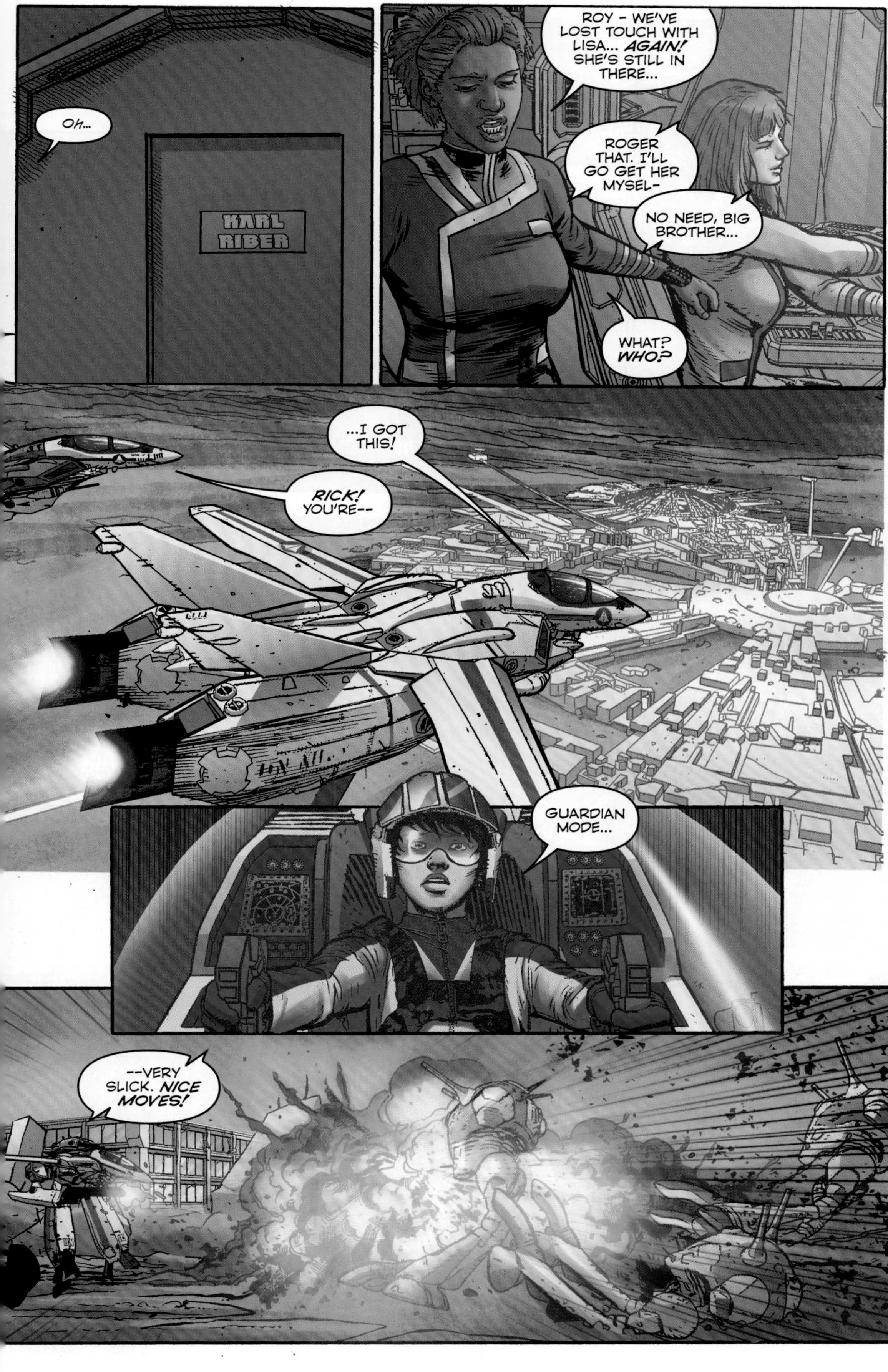
Oh...
KARL RIBER
ROY - WE'VE LOST TOUCH WITH LISA... AGAIN! SHE'S STILL IN THERE...
ROGER THAT. I'LL GO GET HER MYSEL-
NO NEED, BIG BROTHER...
WHAT? WHO?
...I GOT THIS!
RICK! YOU'RE--
GUARDIAN MODE...
--VERY SLICK. NICE MOVES!

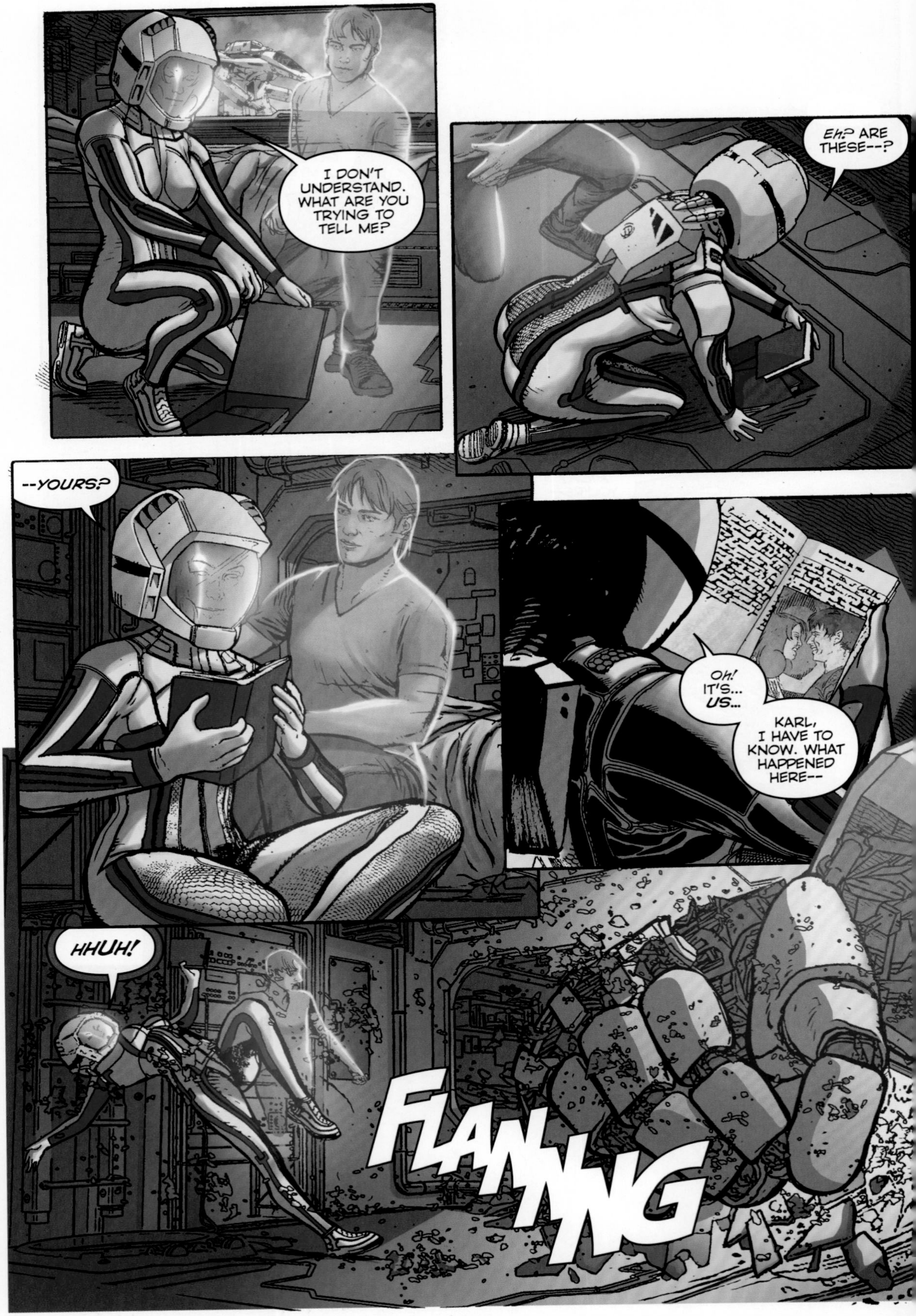
I DON'T UNDERSTAND. WHAT ARE YOU TRYING TO TELL ME?
Eh? ARE THESE--?
--YOURS?
Oh! IT'S... US...
KARL, I HAVE TO KNOW. WHAT HAPPENED HERE--
HHUH!
FLANNNG

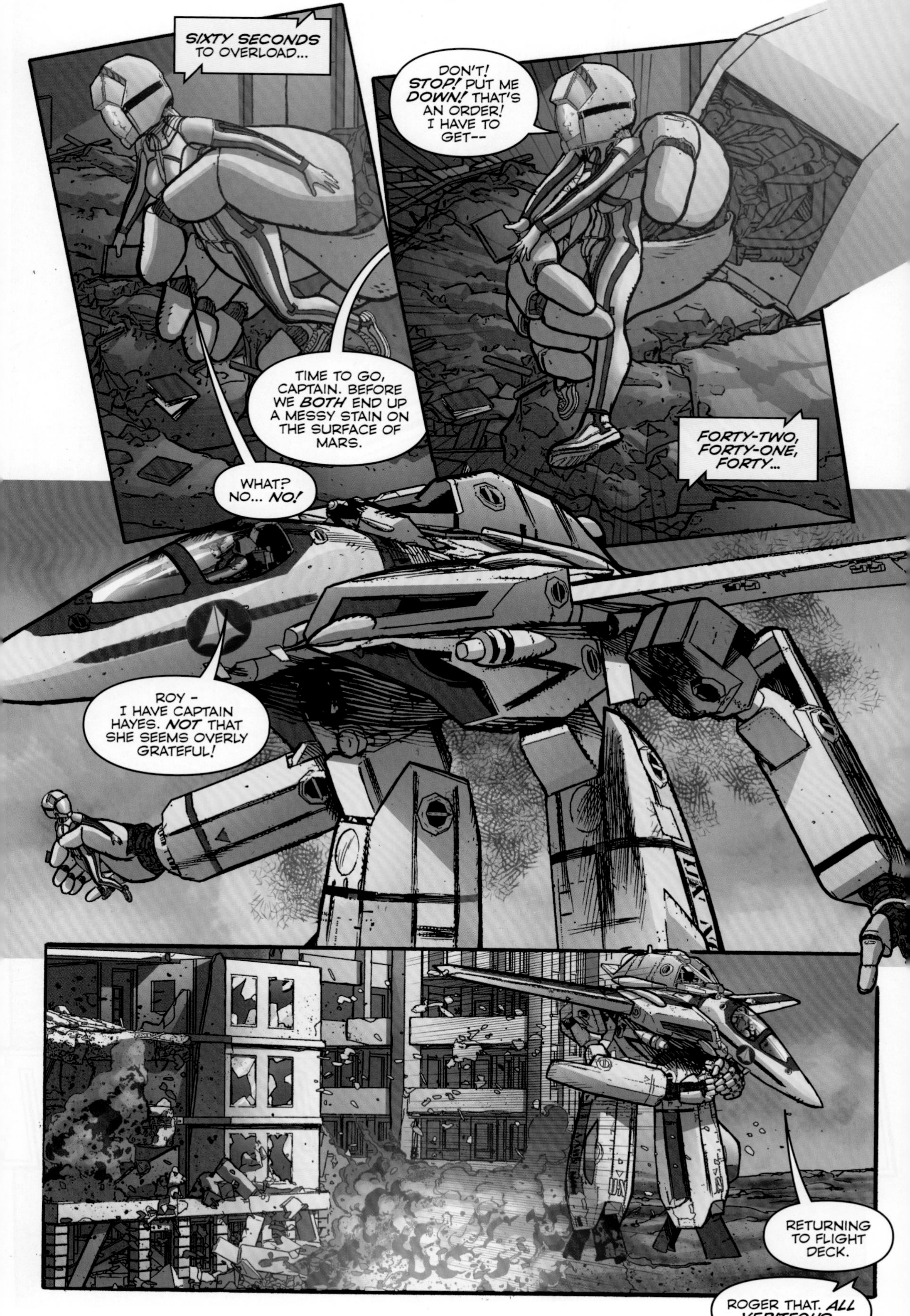
SIXTY SECONDS TO OVERLOAD...
DON'T! STOP! PUT ME DOWN! THAT'S AN ORDER! I HAVE TO GET--
TIME TO GO, CAPTAIN. BEFORE WE BOTH END UP A MESSY STAIN ON THE SURFACE OF MARS.
WHAT? NO... NO!
FORTY-TWO, FORTY-ONE, FORTY...
ROY - I HAVE CAPTAIN HAYES. NOT THAT SHE SEEMS OVERLY GRATEFUL!
RETURNING TO FLIGHT DECK.
ROGER THAT. ALL VERITECHS...

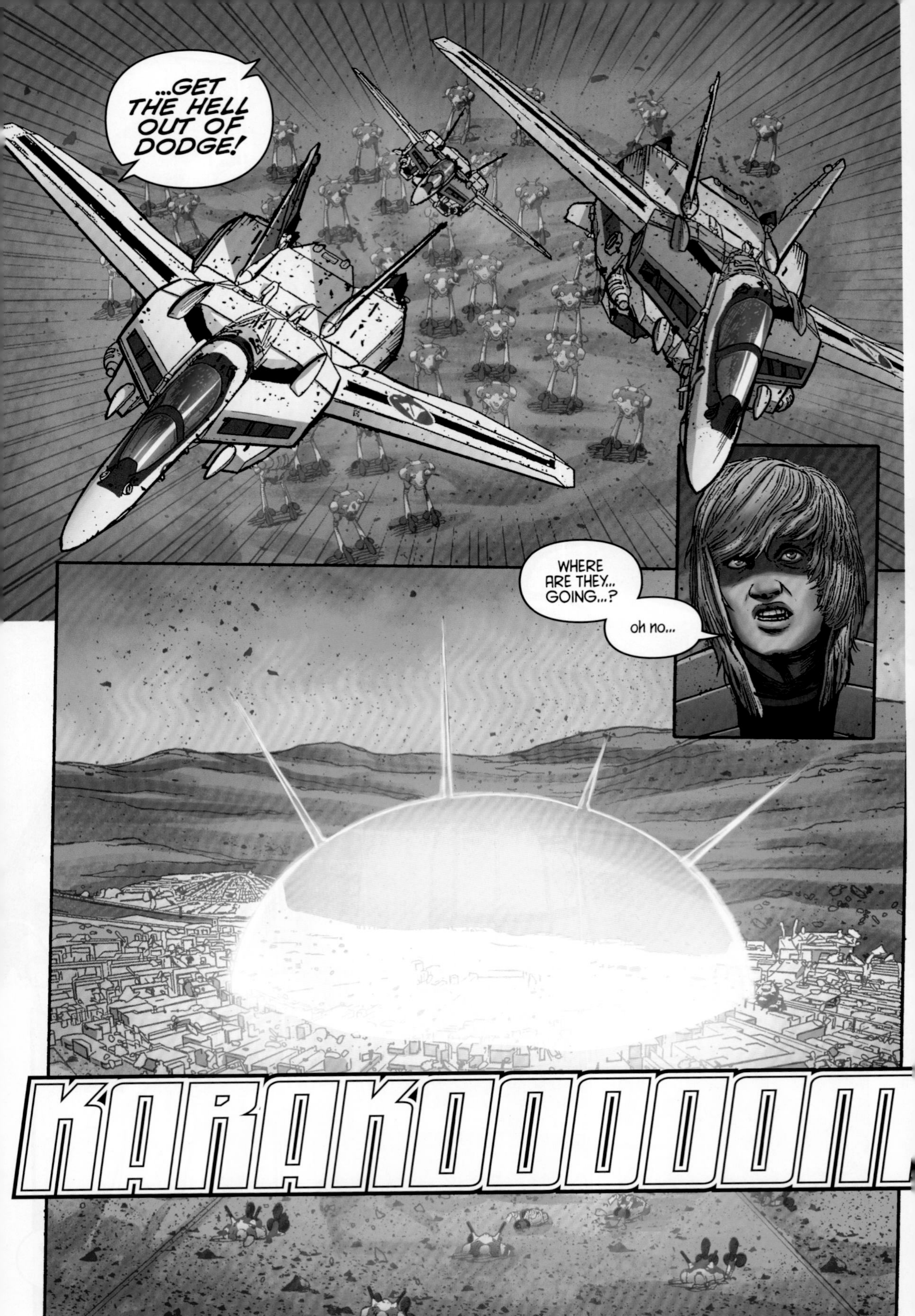
...GET THE HELL OUT OF DODGE!
WHERE ARE THEY... GOING...?
oh no...
KARAKOOOOOOM

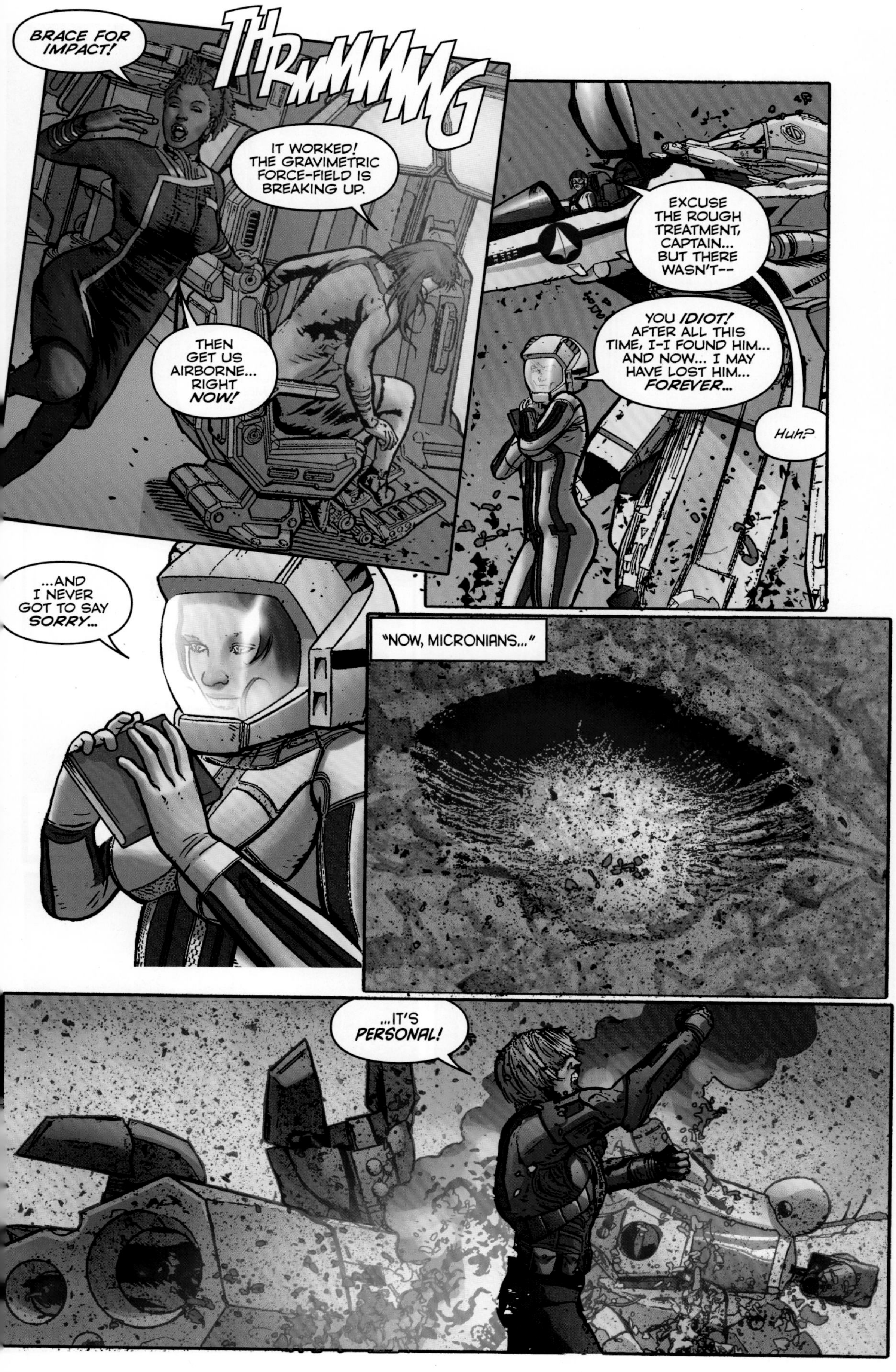
BRACE FOR IMPACT!
THRMMMMG
IT WORKED! THE GRAVIMETRIC FORCE-FIELD IS BREAKING UP.
THEN GET US AIRBORNE... RIGHT NOW!
EXCUSE THE ROUGH TREATMENT, CAPTAIN... BUT THERE WASN'T--
YOU IDIOT! AFTER ALL THIS TIME, I-I FOUND HIM... AND NOW... I MAY HAVE LOST HIM... FOREVER...
Huh?
...AND I NEVER GOT TO SAY SORRY...
"NOW, MICRONIANS..."
...IT'S PERSONAL!

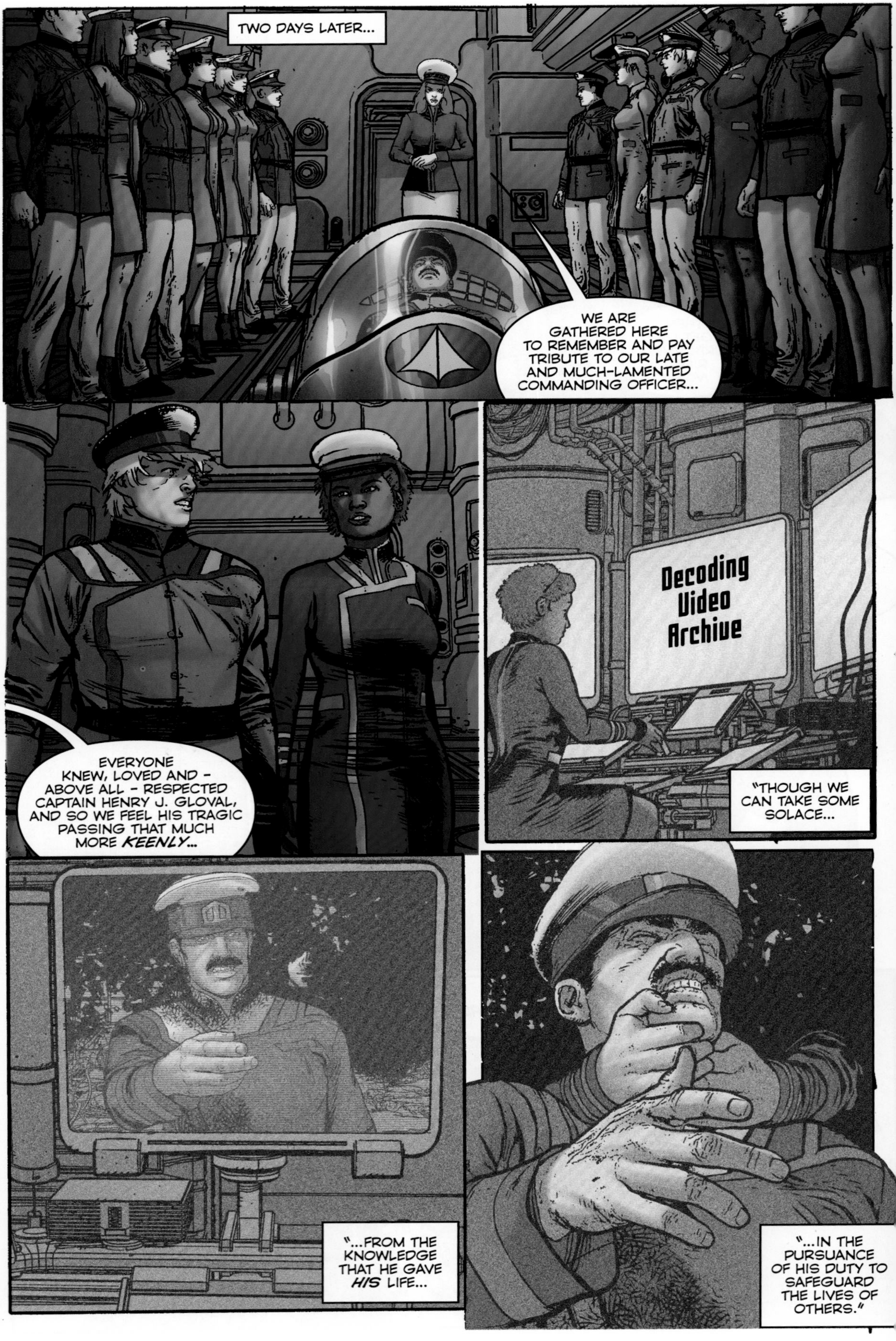
TWO DAYS LATER...
WE ARE GATHERED HERE TO REMEMBER AND PAY TRIBUTE TO OUR LATE AND MUCH-LAMENTED COMMANDING OFFICER...
EVERYONE KNEW, LOVED AND - ABOVE ALL - RESPECTED CAPTAIN HENRY J. GLOVAL, AND SO WE FEEL HIS TRAGIC PASSING THAT MUCH MORE *KEENLY*...
Decoding Video Archive
"THOUGH WE CAN TAKE SOME SOLACE...
"...FROM THE KNOWLEDGE THAT HE GAVE *HIS* LIFE...
"...IN THE PURSUANCE OF HIS DUTY TO SAFEGUARD THE LIVES OF OTHERS."

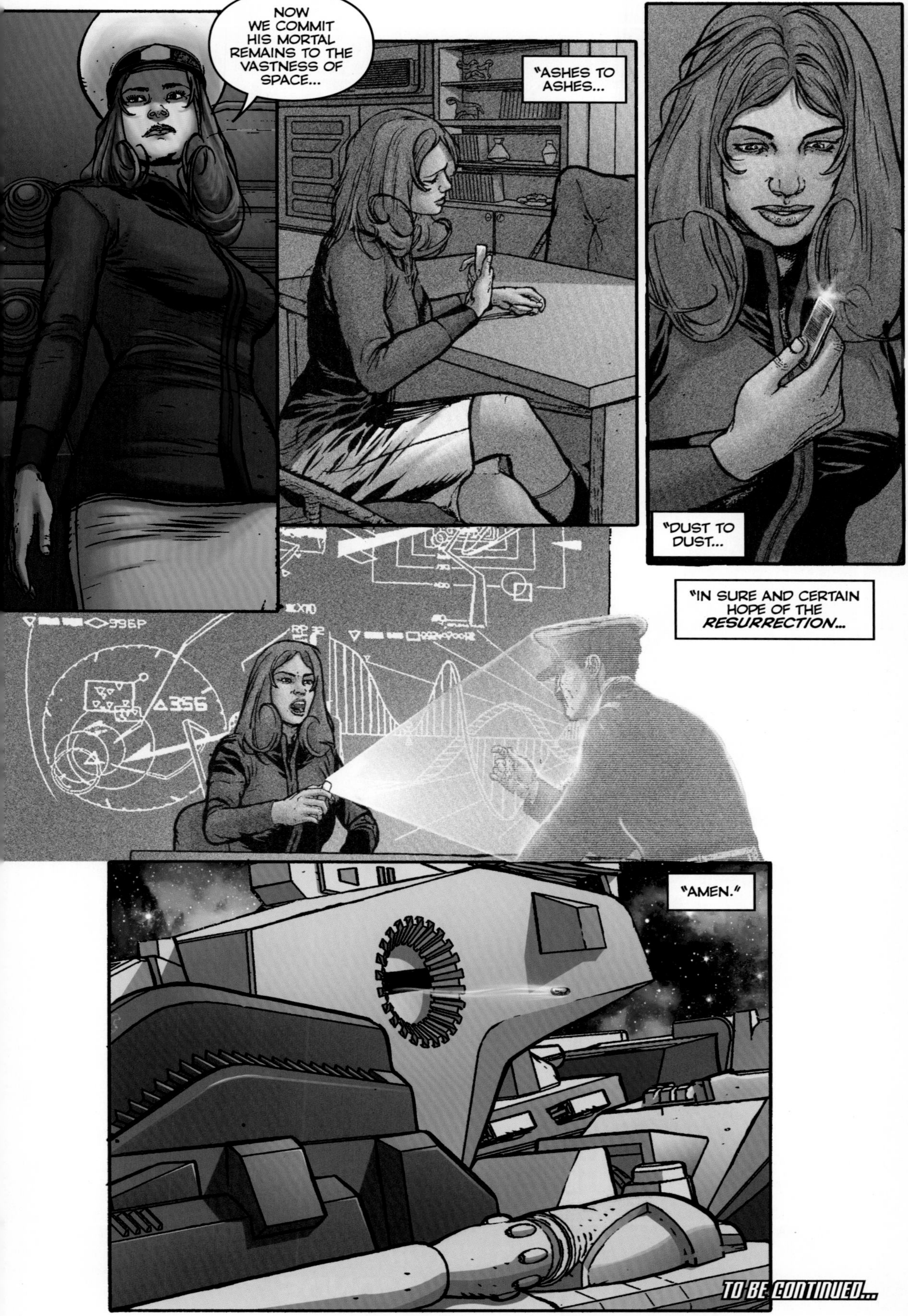
NOW WE COMMIT HIS MORTAL REMAINS TO THE VASTNESS OF SPACE...
"ASHES TO ASHES...
"DUST TO DUST...
"IN SURE AND CERTAIN HOPE OF THE *RESURRECTION*...
"AMEN."
TO BE CONTINUED...

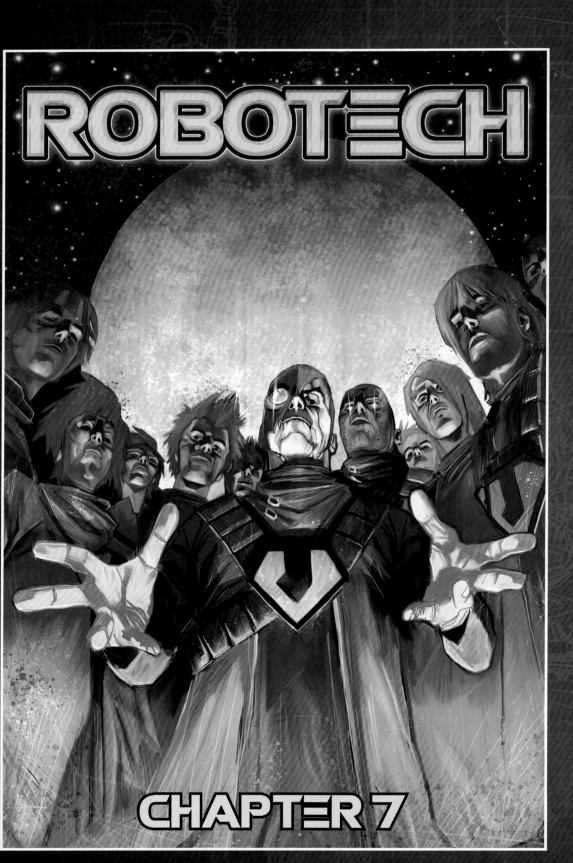

ROBOTECH

CHAPTER 7

ILLUSTRATION BY
MARTIN SIMMONDS

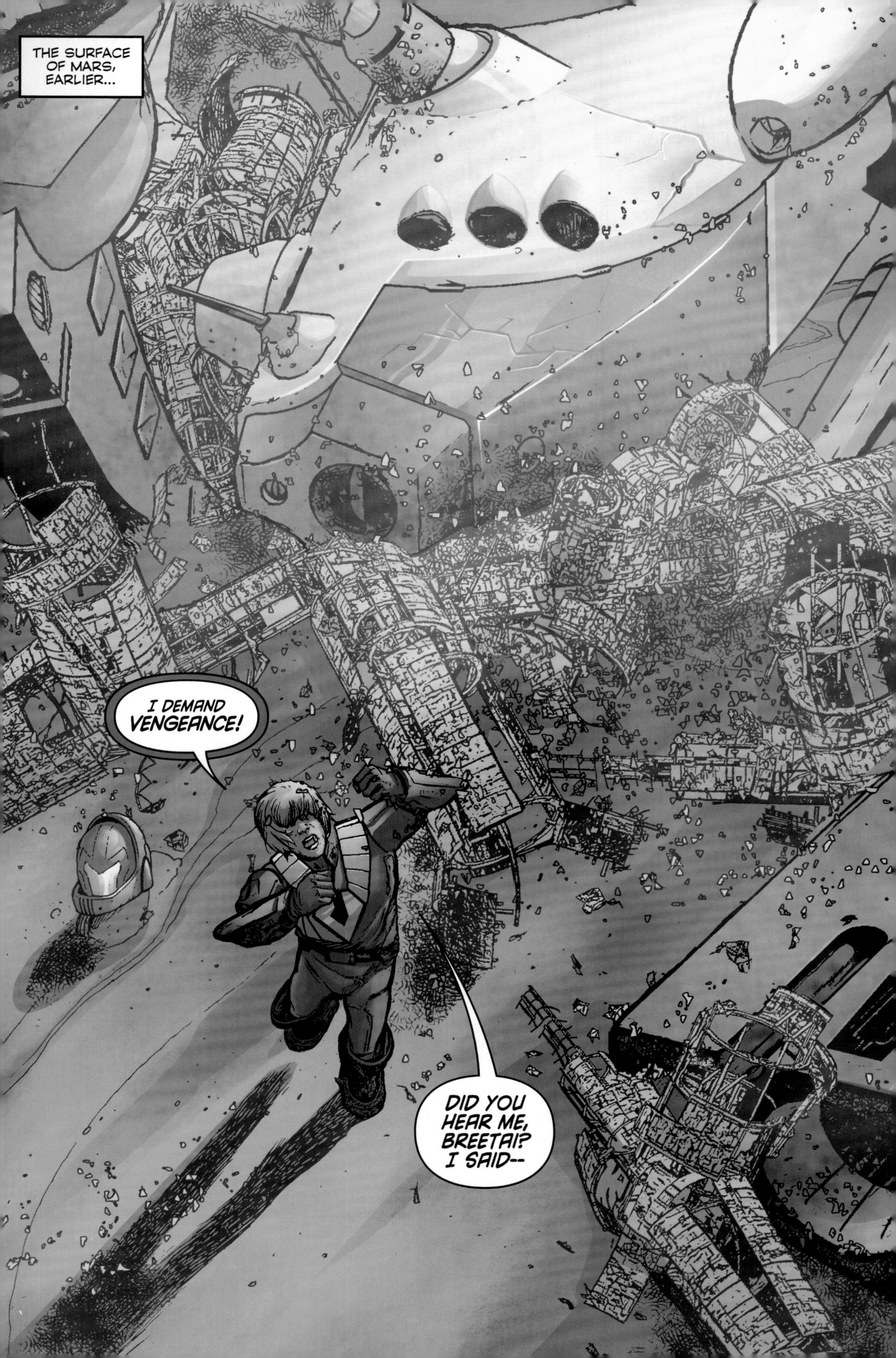
THE SURFACE OF MARS, EARLIER...
I DEMAND VENGEANCE!
DID YOU HEAR ME, BREETAI? I SAID--

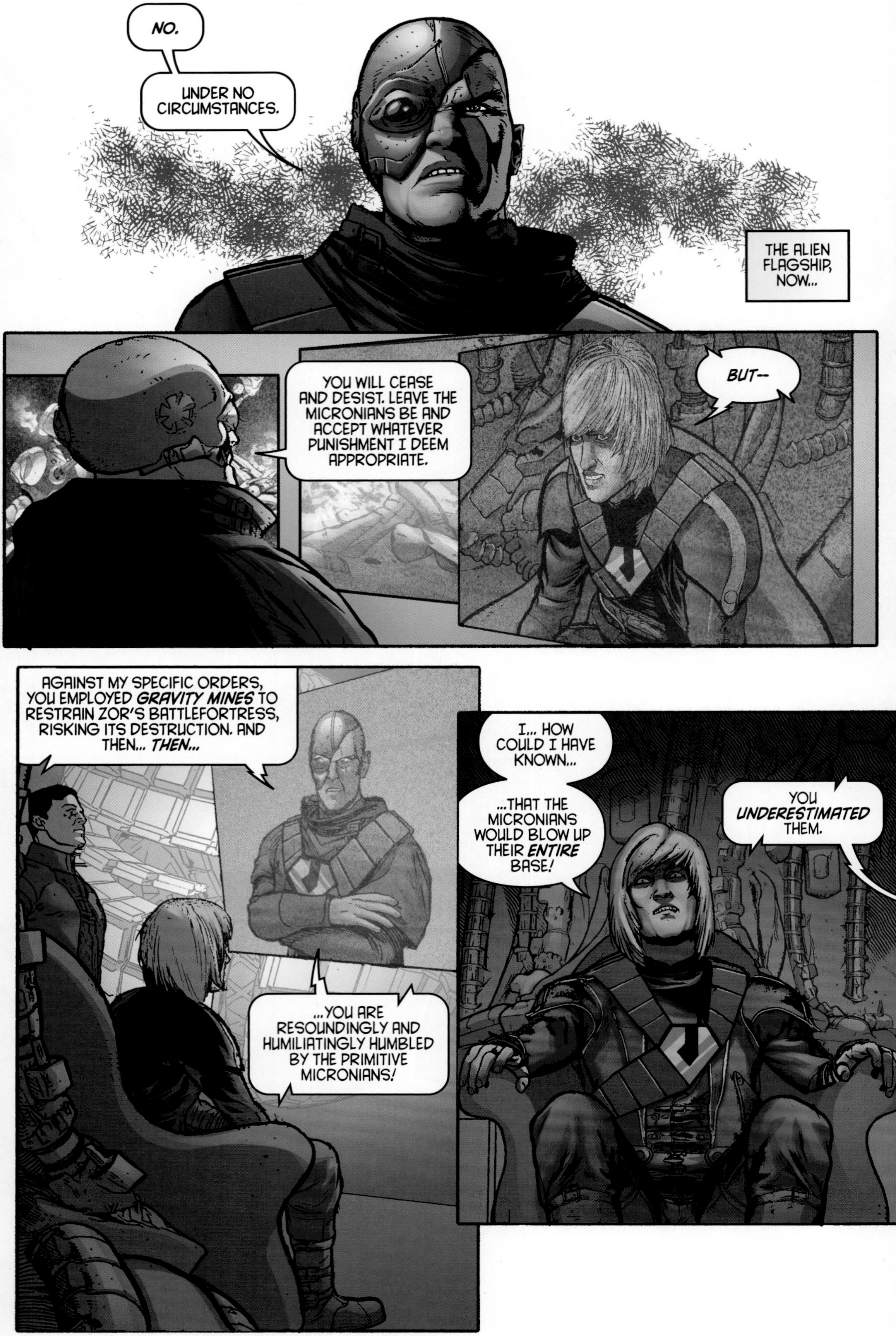
NO.
UNDER NO CIRCUMSTANCES.
THE ALIEN FLAGSHIP, NOW...
YOU WILL CEASE AND DESIST. LEAVE THE MICRONIANS BE AND ACCEPT WHATEVER PUNISHMENT I DEEM APPROPRIATE.
BUT--
AGAINST MY SPECIFIC ORDERS, YOU EMPLOYED GRAVITY MINES TO RESTRAIN ZOR'S BATTLEFORTRESS, RISKING ITS DESTRUCTION. AND THEN... THEN...
...YOU ARE RESOUNDINGLY AND HUMILIATINGLY HUMBLED BY THE PRIMITIVE MICRONIANS!
I... HOW COULD I HAVE KNOWN...
...THAT THE MICRONIANS WOULD BLOW UP THEIR ENTIRE BASE!
YOU UNDERESTIMATED THEM.

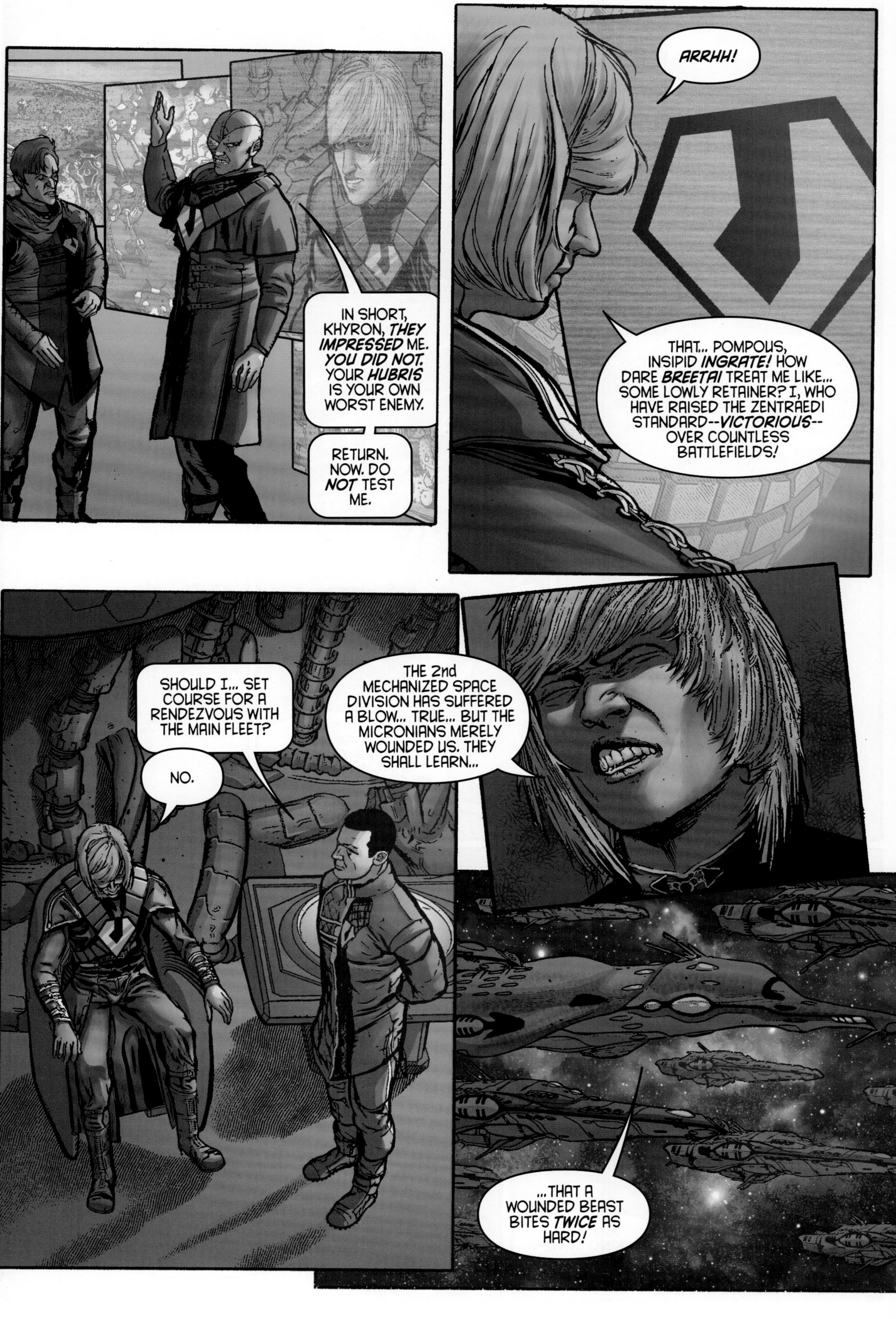

IN SHORT, KHYRON, THEY IMPRESSED ME. YOU DID NOT. YOUR HUBRIS IS YOUR OWN WORST ENEMY.
RETURN. NOW. DO NOT TEST ME.
ARRHH!
THAT... POMPOUS, INSIPID INGRATE! HOW DARE BREETAI TREAT ME LIKE... SOME LOWLY RETAINER? I, WHO HAVE RAISED THE ZENTRAEDI STANDARD--VICTORIOUS--OVER COUNTLESS BATTLEFIELDS!
SHOULD I... SET COURSE FOR A RENDEZVOUS WITH THE MAIN FLEET?
NO.
THE 2nd MECHANIZED SPACE DIVISION HAS SUFFERED A BLOW... TRUE... BUT THE MICRONIANS MERELY WOUNDED US. THEY SHALL LEARN...
...THAT A WOUNDED BEAST BITES TWICE AS HARD!

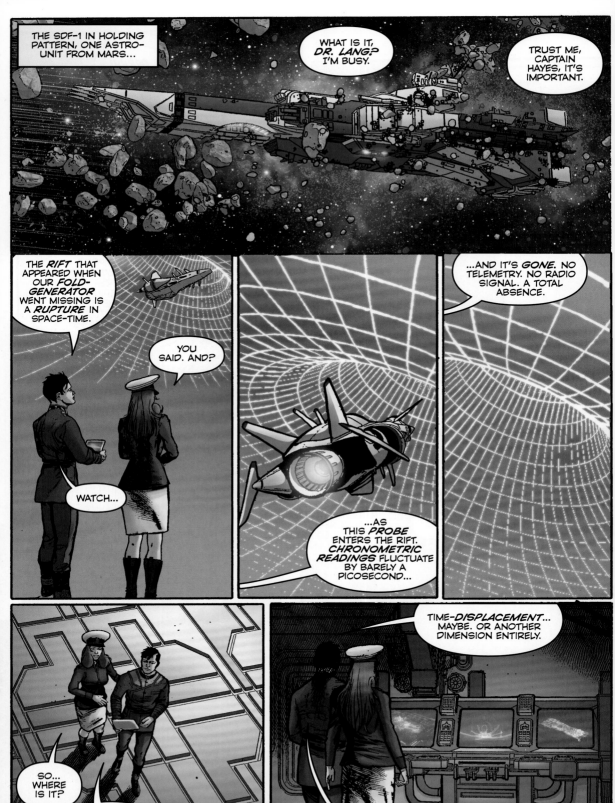

THE SDF-1 IN HOLDING PATTERN, ONE ASTRO-UNIT FROM MARS...

WHAT IS IT, *DR. LANG?* I'M BUSY.

TRUST ME, CAPTAIN HAYES, IT'S IMPORTANT.

THE *RIFT* THAT APPEARED WHEN OUR *FOLD-GENERATOR* WENT MISSING IS A *RUPTURE* IN SPACE-TIME.

YOU SAID. AND?

WATCH...

...AS THIS *PROBE* ENTERS THE RIFT. *CHRONOMETRIC READINGS* FLUCTUATE BY BARELY A PICOSECOND...

...AND IT'S *GONE.* NO TELEMETRY. NO RADIO SIGNAL. A TOTAL ABSENCE.

SO... WHERE IS IT?

MY EDUCATED GUESS IS SOME-*WHEN*... RATHER THAN SOMEWHERE.

ARE WE TALKING *TIME-TRAVEL?* IT'S JUST... NO, NEVER MIND.

TIME-*DISPLACEMENT*... MAYBE. OR ANOTHER DIMENSION ENTIRELY.

AMONG THE DATA RETRIEVED FROM MARS BASE, I FOUND REFERENCE TO *SHADOW WARFARE.*

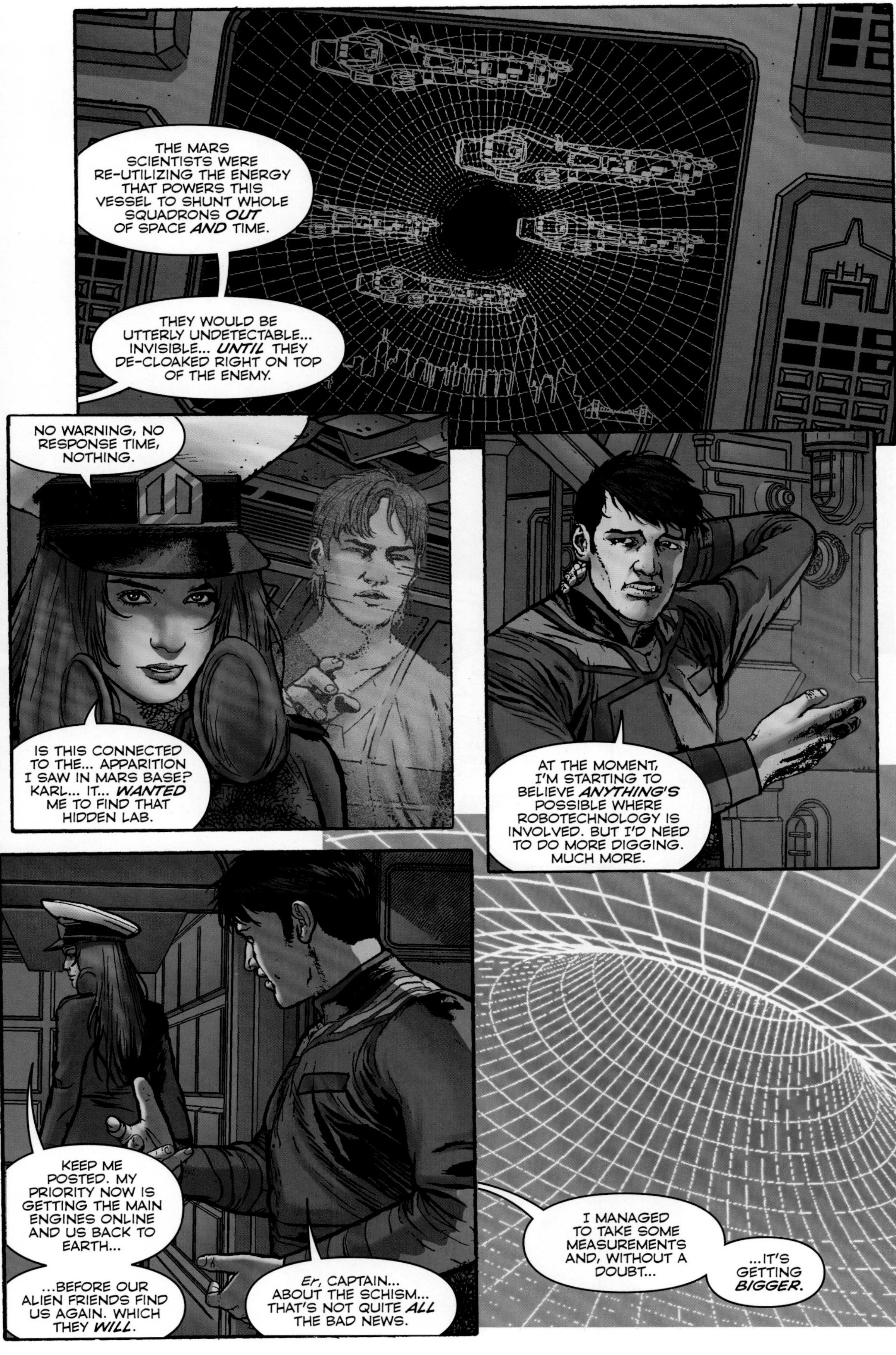
THE MARS SCIENTISTS WERE RE-UTILIZING THE ENERGY THAT POWERS THIS VESSEL TO SHUNT WHOLE SQUADRONS OUT OF SPACE AND TIME.
THEY WOULD BE UTTERLY UNDETECTABLE... INVISIBLE... UNTIL THEY DE-CLOAKED RIGHT ON TOP OF THE ENEMY.
NO WARNING, NO RESPONSE TIME, NOTHING.
IS THIS CONNECTED TO THE... APPARITION I SAW IN MARS BASE? KARL... IT... WANTED ME TO FIND THAT HIDDEN LAB.
AT THE MOMENT, I'M STARTING TO BELIEVE ANYTHING'S POSSIBLE WHERE ROBOTECHNOLOGY IS INVOLVED. BUT I'D NEED TO DO MORE DIGGING. MUCH MORE.
KEEP ME POSTED. MY PRIORITY NOW IS GETTING THE MAIN ENGINES ONLINE AND US BACK TO EARTH...
...BEFORE OUR ALIEN FRIENDS FIND US AGAIN. WHICH THEY WILL.
Er, CAPTAIN... ABOUT THE SCHISM... THAT'S NOT QUITE ALL THE BAD NEWS.
I MANAGED TO TAKE SOME MEASUREMENTS AND, WITHOUT A DOUBT...
...IT'S GETTING BIGGER.

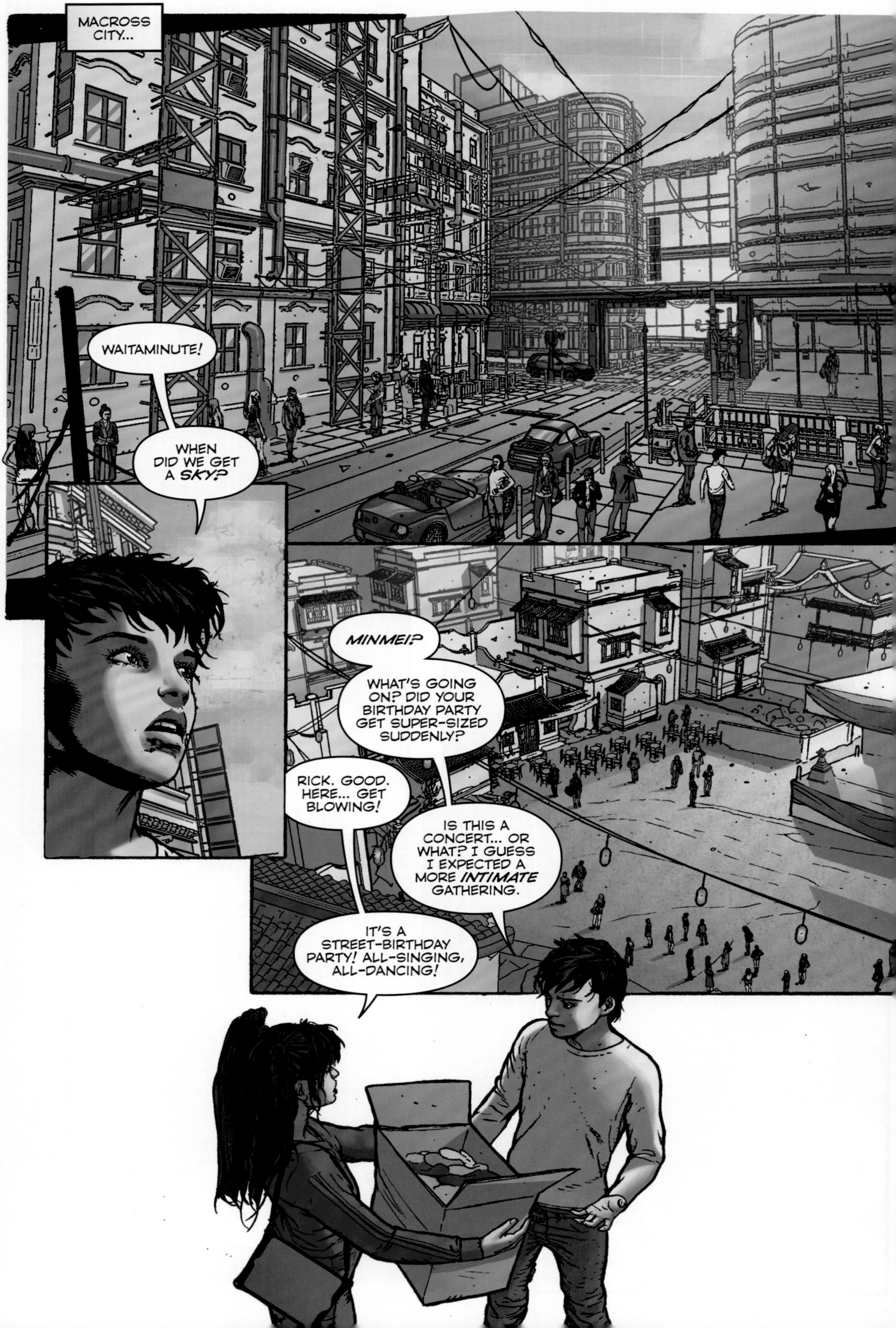
MACROSS CITY...
WAITAMINUTE!
WHEN DID WE GET A SKY?
MINMEI?
WHAT'S GOING ON? DID YOUR BIRTHDAY PARTY GET SUPER-SIZED SUDDENLY?
RICK. GOOD. HERE... GET BLOWING!
IS THIS A CONCERT... OR WHAT? I GUESS I EXPECTED A MORE INTIMATE GATHERING.
IT'S A STREET-BIRTHDAY PARTY! ALL-SINGING, ALL-DANCING!

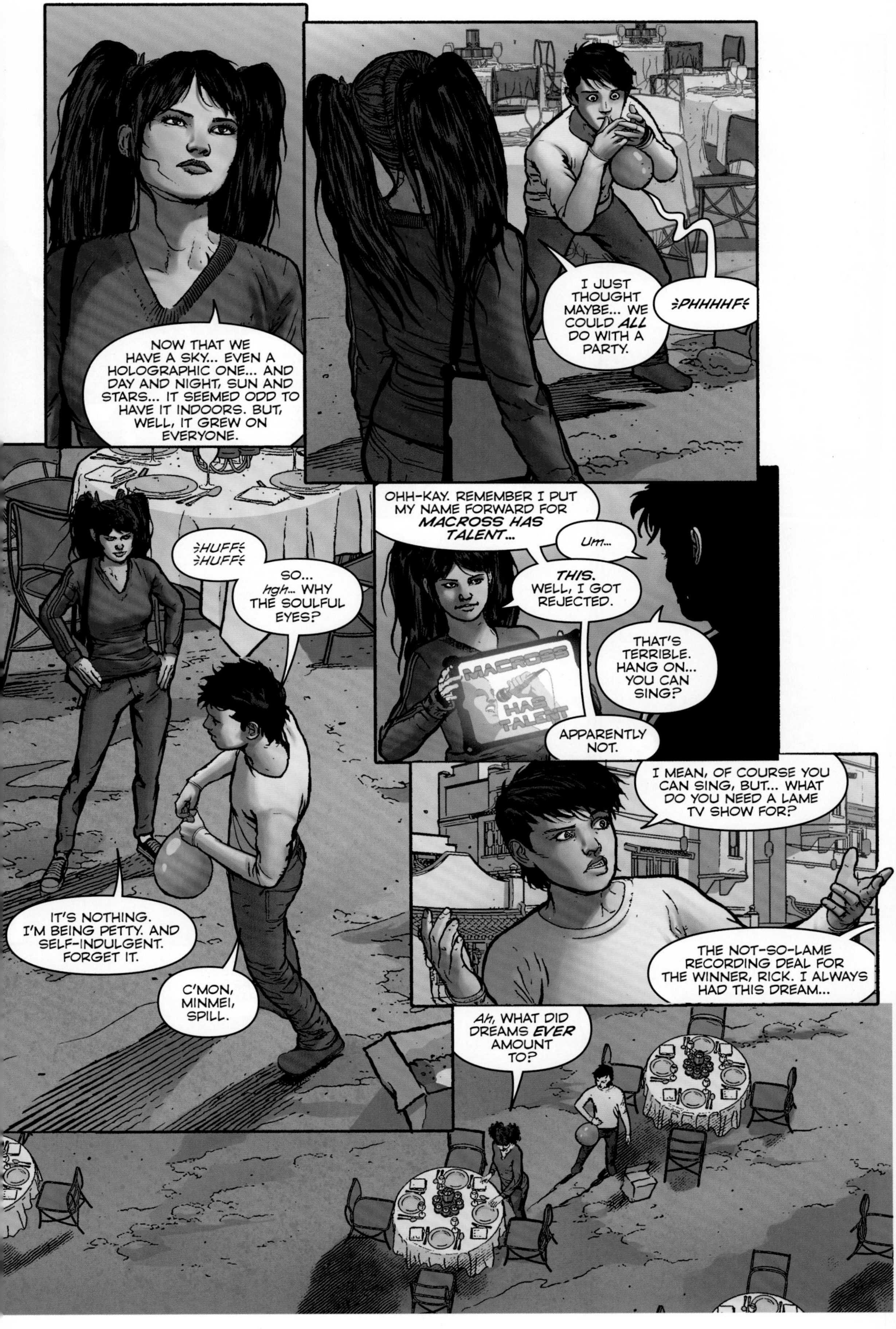

NOW THAT WE HAVE A SKY... EVEN A HOLOGRAPHIC ONE... AND DAY AND NIGHT, SUN AND STARS... IT SEEMED ODD TO HAVE IT INDOORS. BUT, WELL, IT GREW ON EVERYONE.
I JUST THOUGHT MAYBE... WE COULD ALL DO WITH A PARTY.
PHHHHF
HUFF HUFF
SO... hgh... WHY THE SOULFUL EYES?
IT'S NOTHING. I'M BEING PETTY. AND SELF-INDULGENT. FORGET IT.
C'MON, MINMEI, SPILL.
OHH-KAY. REMEMBER I PUT MY NAME FORWARD FOR MACROSS HAS TALENT...
Um...
THIS. WELL, I GOT REJECTED.
MACROSS HAS TALENT
THAT'S TERRIBLE. HANG ON... YOU CAN SING?
APPARENTLY NOT.
I MEAN, OF COURSE YOU CAN SING, BUT... WHAT DO YOU NEED A LAME TV SHOW FOR?
THE NOT-SO-LAME RECORDING DEAL FOR THE WINNER, RICK. I ALWAYS HAD THIS DREAM...
Ah, WHAT DID DREAMS EVER AMOUNT TO?

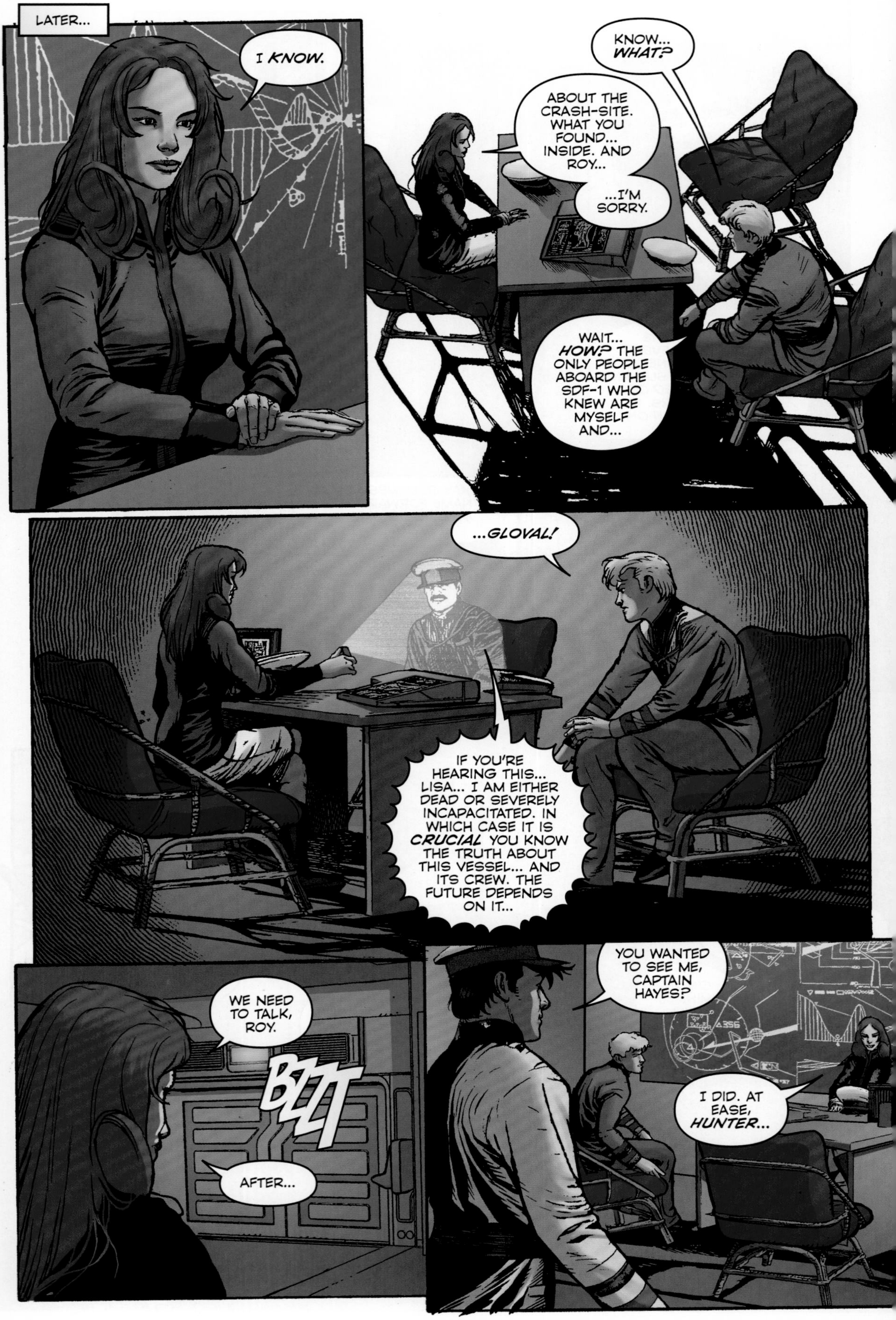
LATER...
I *KNOW.*
KNOW... *WHAT?*
ABOUT THE CRASH-SITE. WHAT YOU FOUND... INSIDE. AND ROY...
...I'M SORRY.
WAIT... *HOW?* THE ONLY PEOPLE ABOARD THE SDF-1 WHO KNEW ARE MYSELF AND...
...*GLOVAL!*
IF YOU'RE HEARING THIS... LISA... I AM EITHER DEAD OR SEVERELY INCAPACITATED. IN WHICH CASE IT IS *CRUCIAL* YOU KNOW THE TRUTH ABOUT THIS VESSEL... AND ITS CREW. THE FUTURE DEPENDS ON IT...
WE NEED TO TALK, ROY.
BZZT
AFTER...
YOU WANTED TO SEE ME, CAPTAIN HAYES?
I DID. AT EASE, *HUNTER...*

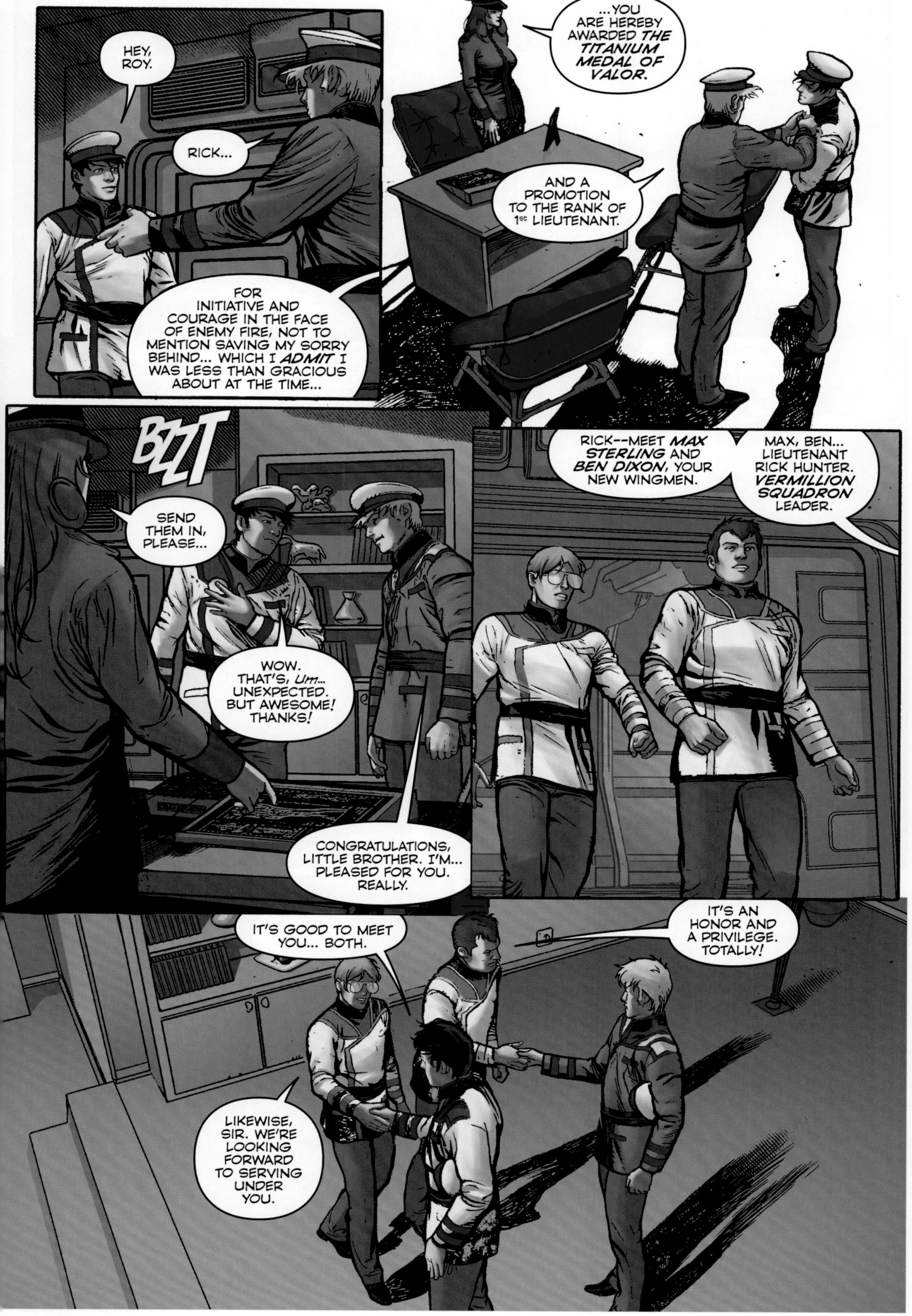
HEY, ROY.
RICK...
FOR INITIATIVE AND COURAGE IN THE FACE OF ENEMY FIRE, NOT TO MENTION SAVING MY SORRY BEHIND... WHICH I *ADMIT* I WAS LESS THAN GRACIOUS ABOUT AT THE TIME...
...YOU ARE HEREBY AWARDED ***THE TITANIUM MEDAL OF VALOR***.
AND A PROMOTION TO THE RANK OF 1st LIEUTENANT.
BZZT
SEND THEM IN, PLEASE...
WOW. THAT'S, *Um*... UNEXPECTED. BUT AWESOME! THANKS!
CONGRATULATIONS, LITTLE BROTHER. I'M... PLEASED FOR YOU. REALLY.
RICK--MEET ***MAX STERLING*** AND ***BEN DIXON***, YOUR NEW WINGMEN.
MAX, BEN... LIEUTENANT RICK HUNTER. ***VERMILLION SQUADRON*** LEADER.
IT'S GOOD TO MEET YOU... BOTH.
IT'S AN HONOR AND A PRIVILEGE. TOTALLY!
LIKEWISE, SIR. WE'RE LOOKING FORWARD TO SERVING UNDER YOU.

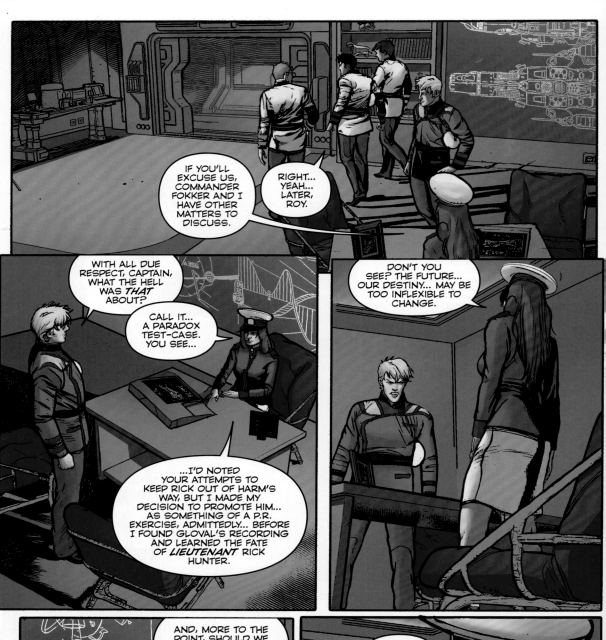

IF YOU'LL EXCUSE US, COMMANDER FOKKER AND I HAVE OTHER MATTERS TO DISCUSS.

RIGHT... YEAH... LATER, ROY.

WITH ALL DUE RESPECT, CAPTAIN, WHAT THE HELL WAS *THAT* ABOUT?

CALL IT... A PARADOX TEST-CASE. YOU SEE...

...I'D NOTED YOUR ATTEMPTS TO KEEP RICK OUT OF HARM'S WAY, BUT I MADE MY DECISION TO PROMOTE HIM... AS SOMETHING OF A P.R. EXERCISE, ADMITTEDLY... BEFORE I FOUND GLOVAL'S RECORDING AND LEARNED THE FATE OF *LIEUTENANT* RICK HUNTER.

DON'T YOU SEE? THE FUTURE... OUR DESTINY... MAY BE TOO INFLEXIBLE TO CHANGE.

AND, MORE TO THE POINT, SHOULD WE EVEN TRY? TAMPERING MAY CREATE AN EVEN WORSE OUTLOOK FOR *US*...

...WORSE FOR *ALL*.

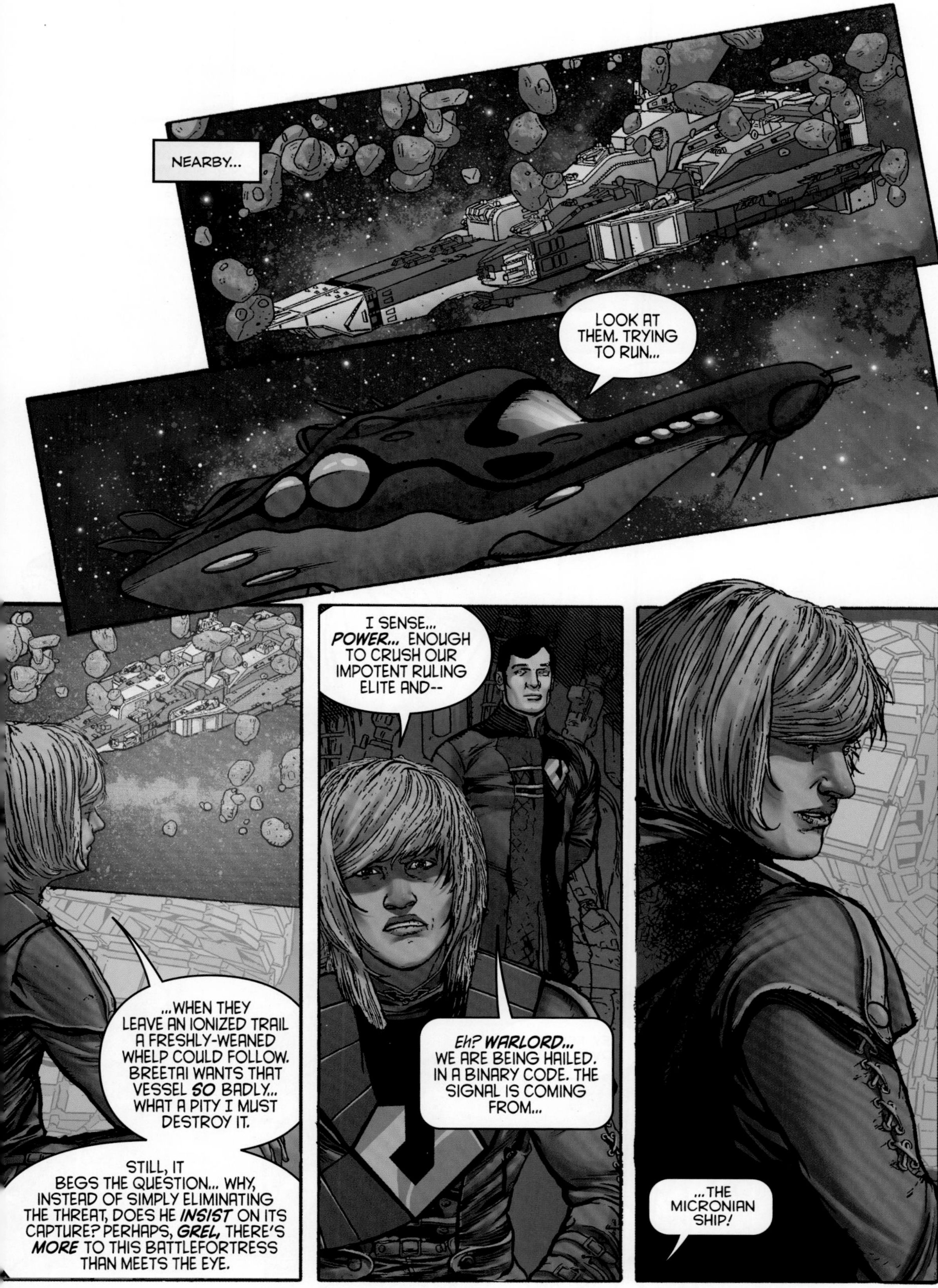
NEARBY...
LOOK AT THEM. TRYING TO RUN...
...WHEN THEY LEAVE AN IONIZED TRAIL A FRESHLY-WEANED WHELP COULD FOLLOW. BREETAI WANTS THAT VESSEL *SO* BADLY... WHAT A PITY I MUST DESTROY IT.
STILL, IT BEGS THE QUESTION... WHY, INSTEAD OF SIMPLY ELIMINATING THE THREAT, DOES HE *INSIST* ON ITS CAPTURE? PERHAPS, *GREL,* THERE'S *MORE* TO THIS BATTLEFORTRESS THAN MEETS THE EYE.
I SENSE... *POWER...* ENOUGH TO CRUSH OUR IMPOTENT RULING ELITE AND--
Eh? WARLORD... WE ARE BEING HAILED. IN A BINARY CODE. THE SIGNAL IS COMING FROM...
...THE MICRONIAN SHIP!

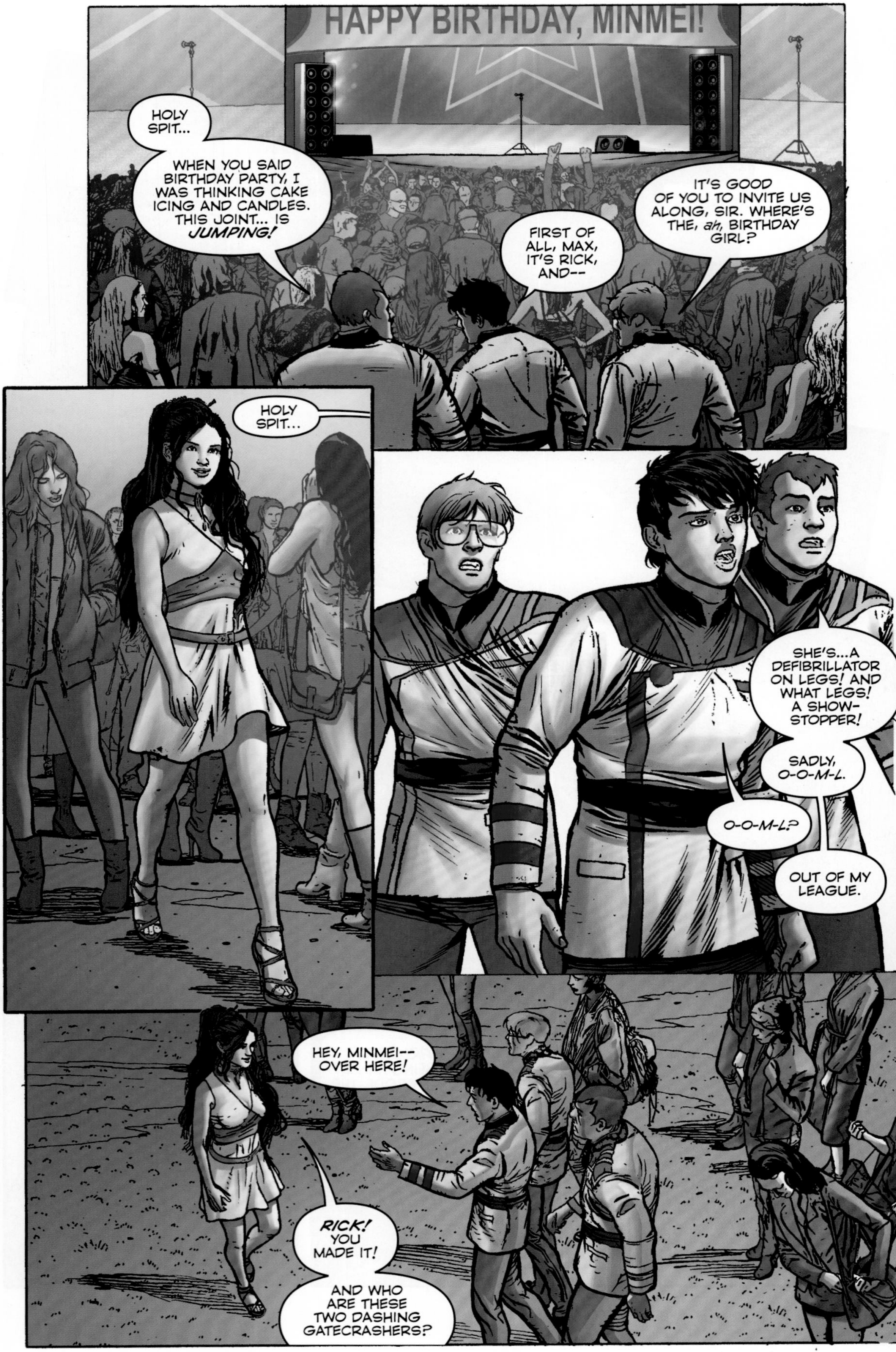
HAPPY BIRTHDAY, MINMEI!
HOLY SPIT...
WHEN YOU SAID BIRTHDAY PARTY, I WAS THINKING CAKE ICING AND CANDLES. THIS JOINT... IS *JUMPING!*
FIRST OF ALL, MAX, IT'S RICK, AND--
IT'S GOOD OF YOU TO INVITE US ALONG, SIR. WHERE'S THE, *ah*, BIRTHDAY GIRL?
HOLY SPIT...
SHE'S...A DEFIBRILLATOR ON LEGS! AND WHAT LEGS! A SHOW-STOPPER!
SADLY, *O-O-M-L.*
O-O-M-L?
OUT OF MY LEAGUE.
HEY, MINMEI-- OVER HERE!
RICK! YOU MADE IT!
AND WHO ARE THESE TWO DASHING GATECRASHERS?

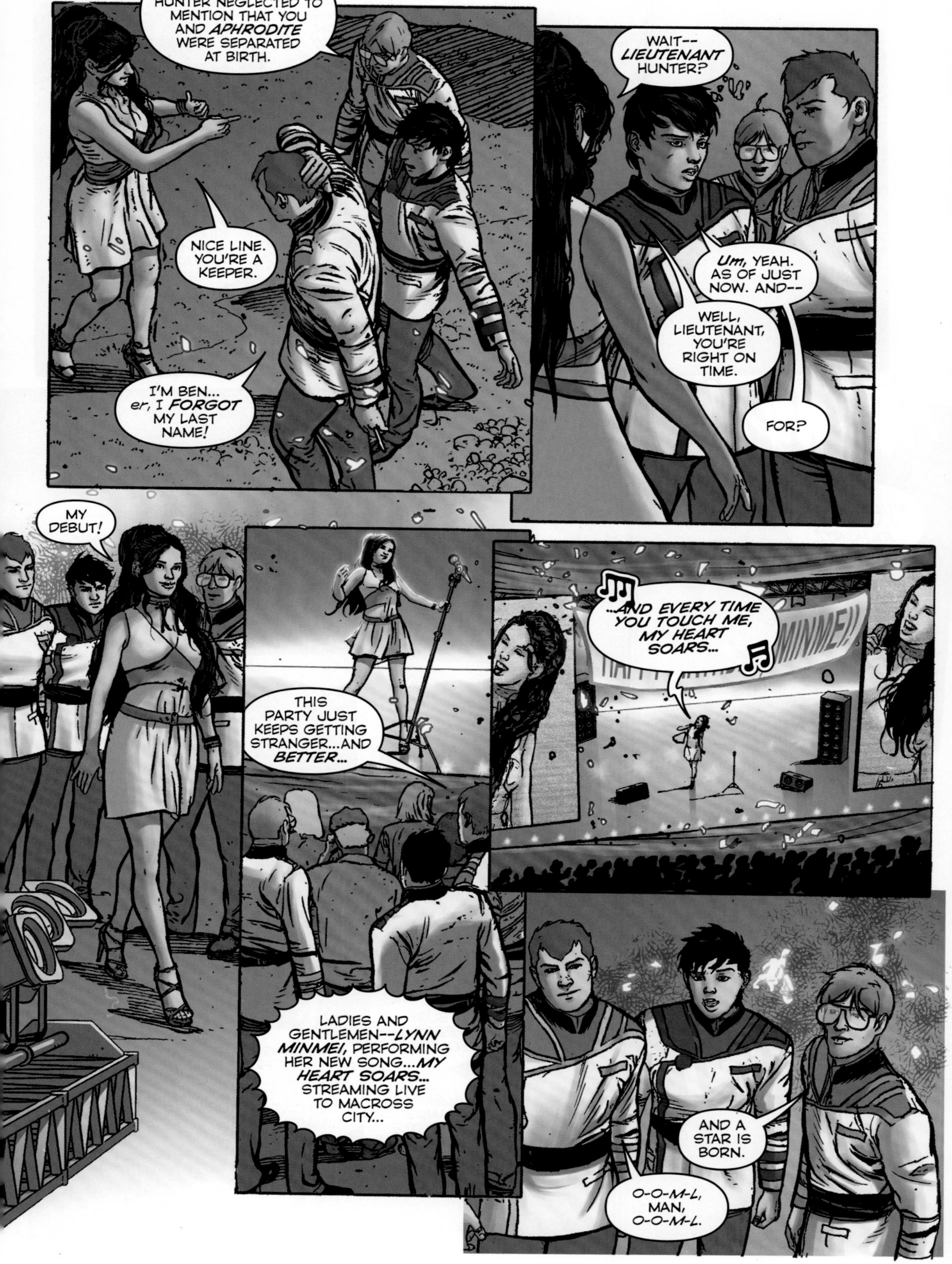
MAX STERLING. CLEARLY, LIEUTENANT HUNTER NEGLECTED TO MENTION THAT YOU AND *APHRODITE* WERE SEPARATED AT BIRTH.
NICE LINE. YOU'RE A KEEPER.
I'M BEN... *er*, I *FORGOT* MY LAST NAME!
WAIT-- *LIEUTENANT* HUNTER?
Um, YEAH. AS OF JUST NOW. AND--
WELL, LIEUTENANT, YOU'RE RIGHT ON TIME.
FOR?
MY DEBUT!
THIS PARTY JUST KEEPS GETTING STRANGER...AND *BETTER*...
LADIES AND GENTLEMEN--*LYNN MINMEI*, PERFORMING HER NEW SONG...*MY HEART SOARS*... STREAMING LIVE TO MACROSS CITY...
...*AND EVERY TIME YOU TOUCH ME, MY HEART SOARS*...
AND A STAR IS BORN.
O-O-M-L, MAN, O-O-M-L.

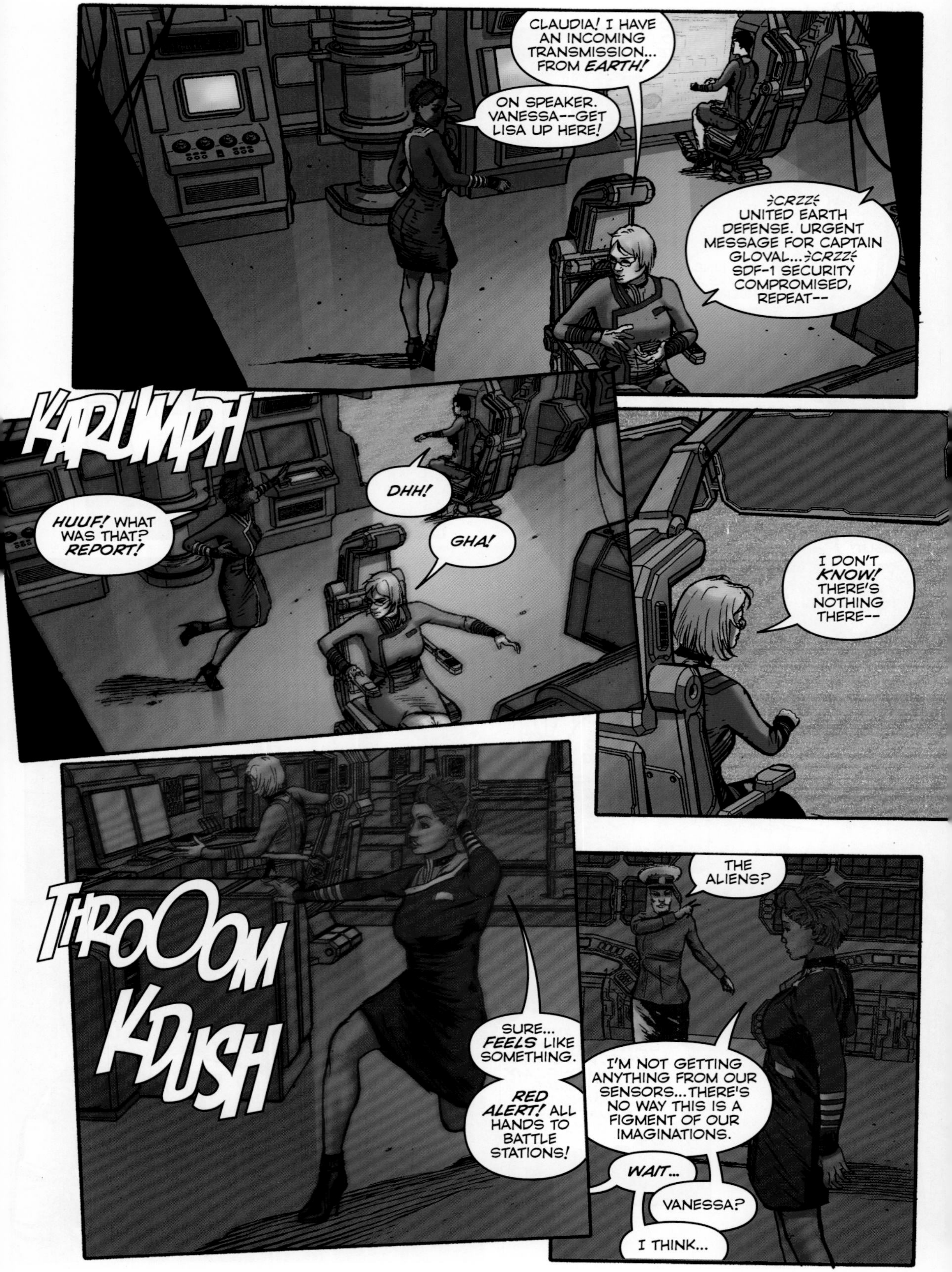
CLAUDIA! I HAVE AN INCOMING TRANSMISSION... FROM EARTH!
ON SPEAKER. VANESSA--GET LISA UP HERE!
CRZZ UNITED EARTH DEFENSE. URGENT MESSAGE FOR CAPTAIN GLOVAL... CRZZ SDF-1 SECURITY COMPROMISED, REPEAT--
KARUMPH
HUUF! WHAT WAS THAT? REPORT!
DHH!
GHA!
I DON'T KNOW! THERE'S NOTHING THERE--
THROOOM
KDUSH
SURE... FEELS LIKE SOMETHING.
RED ALERT! ALL HANDS TO BATTLE STATIONS!
THE ALIENS?
I'M NOT GETTING ANYTHING FROM OUR SENSORS... THERE'S NO WAY THIS IS A FIGMENT OF OUR IMAGINATIONS.
WAIT...
VANESSA?
I THINK...

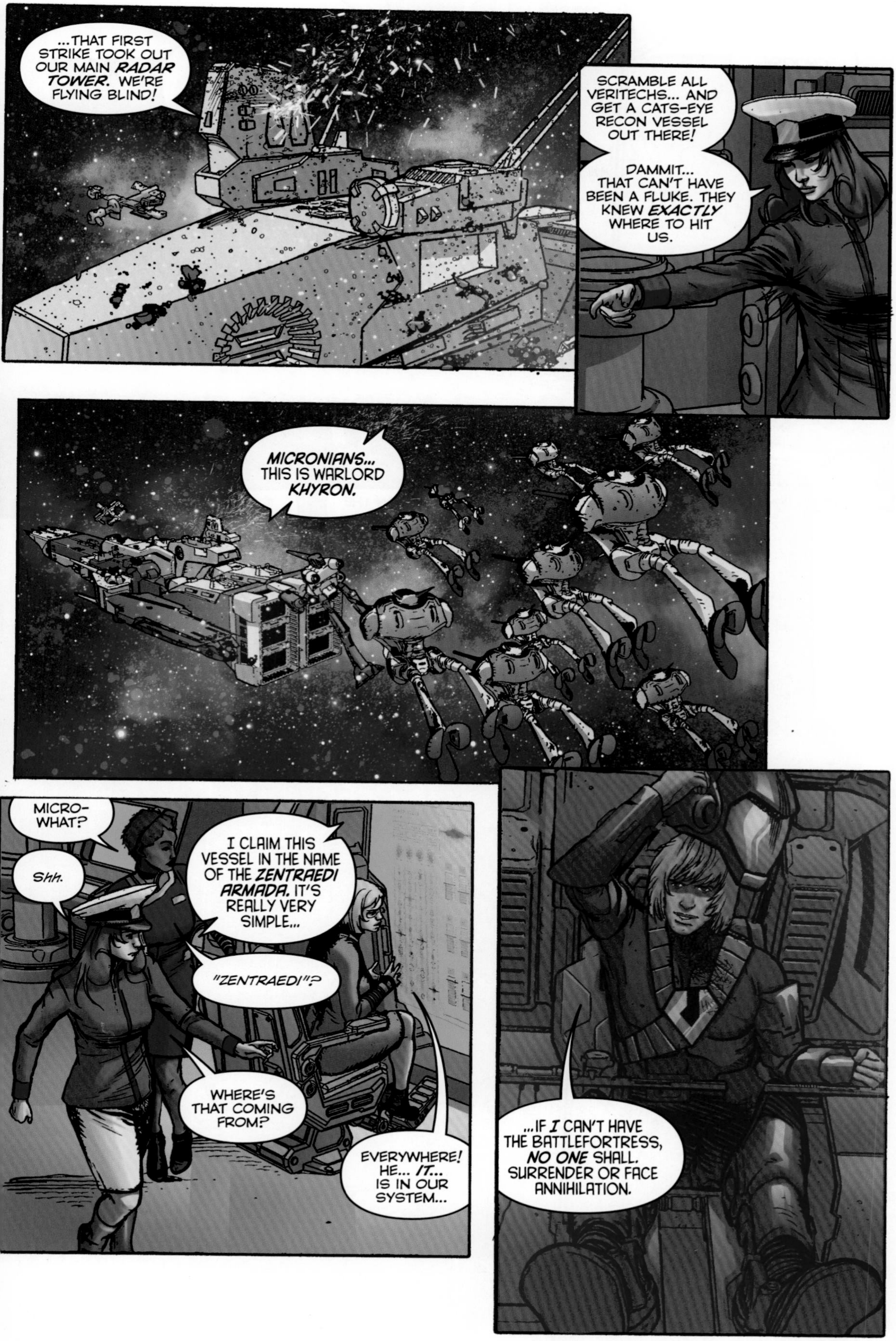
...THAT FIRST STRIKE TOOK OUT OUR MAIN *RADAR TOWER.* WE'RE FLYING BLIND!
SCRAMBLE ALL VERITECHS... AND GET A CATS-EYE RECON VESSEL OUT THERE!
DAMMIT... THAT CAN'T HAVE BEEN A FLUKE. THEY KNEW *EXACTLY* WHERE TO HIT US.
MICRONIANS... THIS IS WARLORD *KHYRON.*
MICRO-WHAT?
Shh.
I CLAIM THIS VESSEL IN THE NAME OF THE *ZENTRAEDI ARMADA.* IT'S REALLY VERY SIMPLE...
"ZENTRAEDI"?
WHERE'S THAT COMING FROM?
EVERYWHERE! HE... *IT...* IS IN OUR SYSTEM...
...IF *I* CAN'T HAVE THE BATTLEFORTRESS, *NO ONE* SHALL. SURRENDER OR FACE ANNIHILATION.

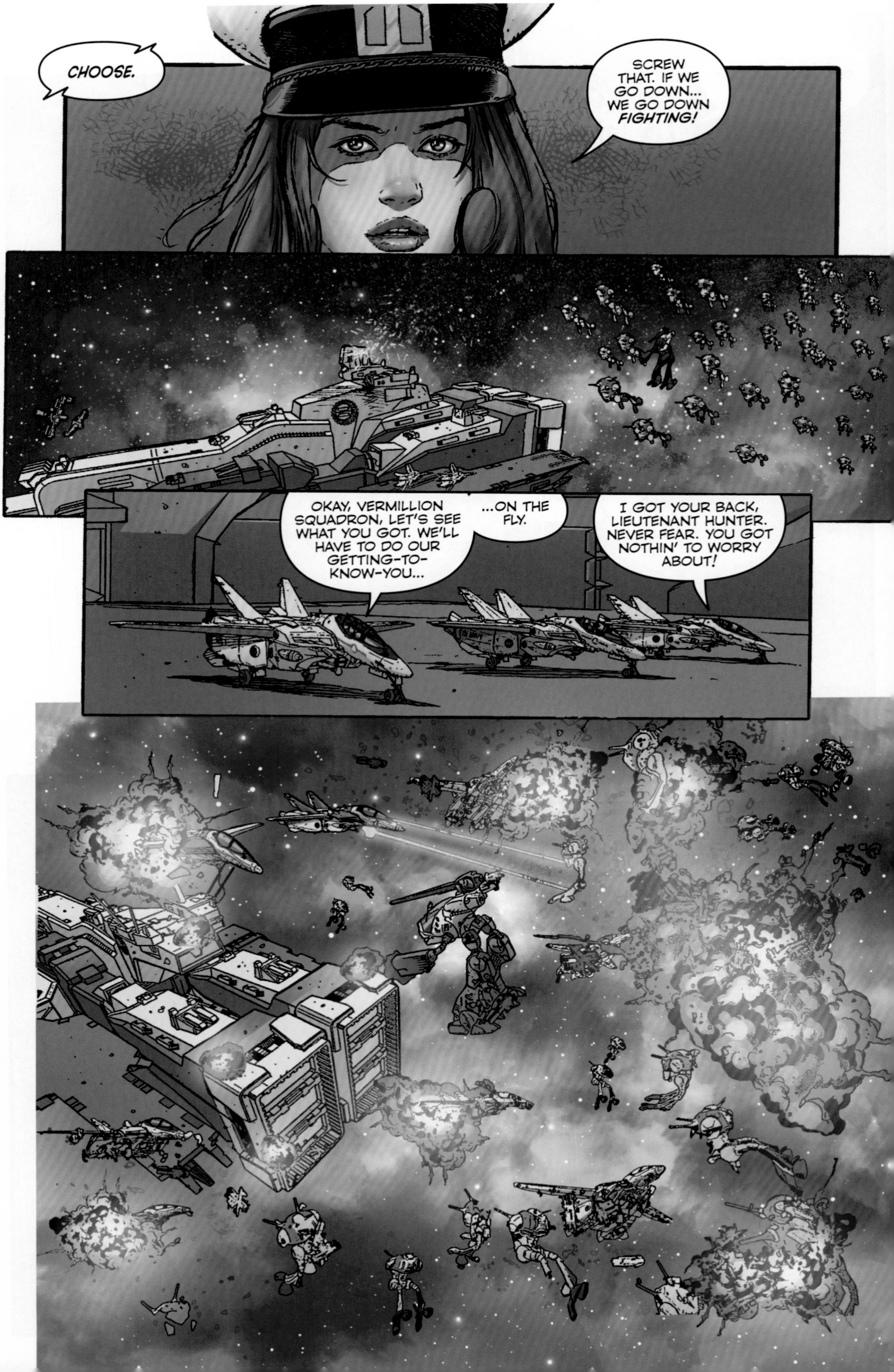
CHOOSE.
SCREW THAT. IF WE GO DOWN... WE GO DOWN FIGHTING!
OKAY, VERMILLION SQUADRON, LET'S SEE WHAT YOU GOT. WE'LL HAVE TO DO OUR GETTING-TO-KNOW-YOU...
...ON THE FLY.
I GOT YOUR BACK, LIEUTENANT HUNTER. NEVER FEAR. YOU GOT NOTHIN' TO WORRY ABOUT!
!

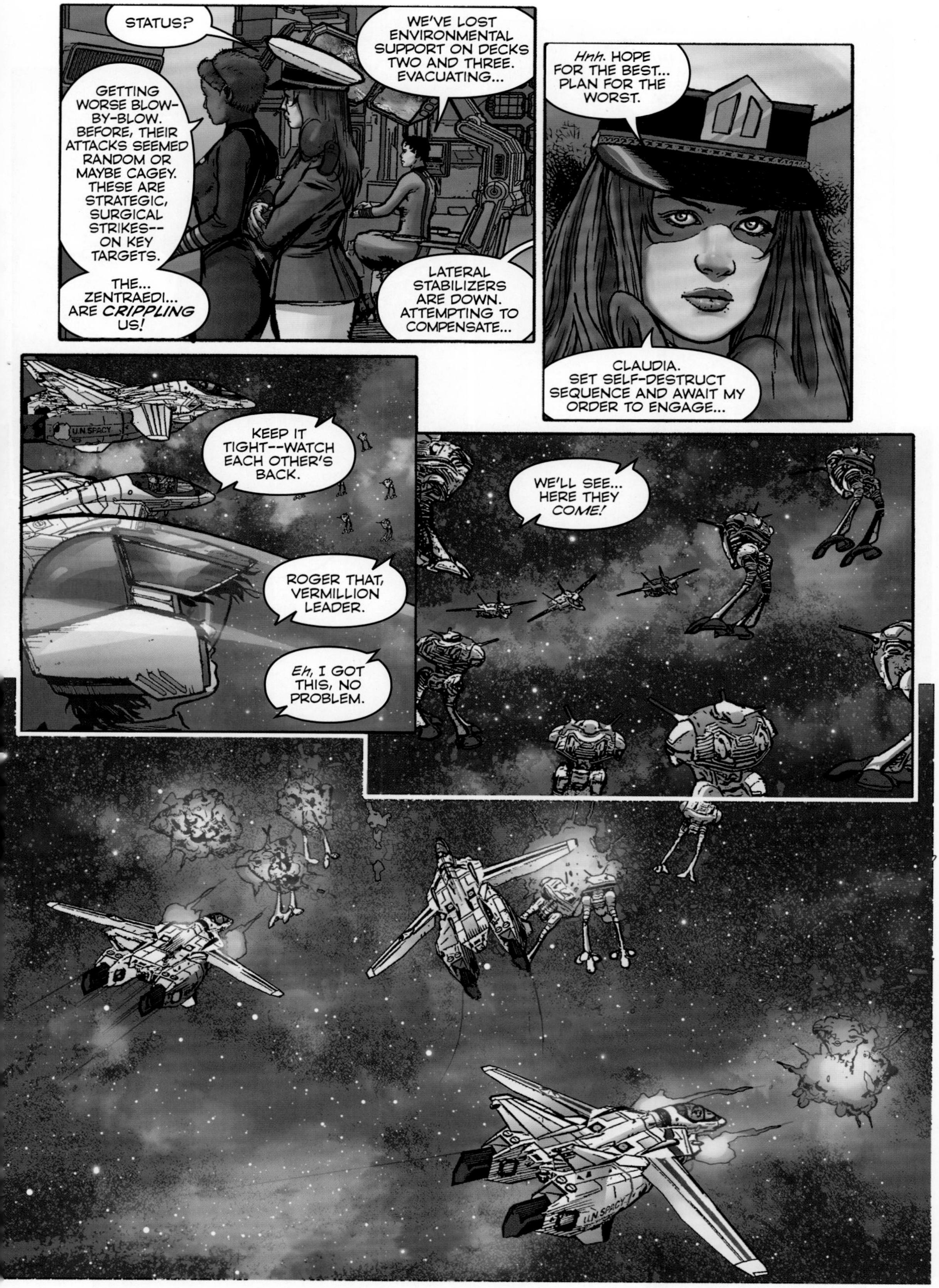
STATUS?
GETTING WORSE BLOW-BY-BLOW. BEFORE, THEIR ATTACKS SEEMED RANDOM OR MAYBE CAGEY. THESE ARE STRATEGIC, SURGICAL STRIKES--ON KEY TARGETS.
THE... ZENTRAEDI... ARE *CRIPPLING* US!
WE'VE LOST ENVIRONMENTAL SUPPORT ON DECKS TWO AND THREE. EVACUATING...
LATERAL STABILIZERS ARE DOWN. ATTEMPTING TO COMPENSATE...
Hnh. HOPE FOR THE BEST... PLAN FOR THE WORST.
CLAUDIA. SET SELF-DESTRUCT SEQUENCE AND AWAIT MY ORDER TO ENGAGE...
U.N.SPACY
KEEP IT TIGHT--WATCH EACH OTHER'S BACK.
ROGER THAT, VERMILLION LEADER.
Eh, I GOT THIS, NO PROBLEM.
WE'LL SEE... HERE THEY *COME!*
U.N.SPACY

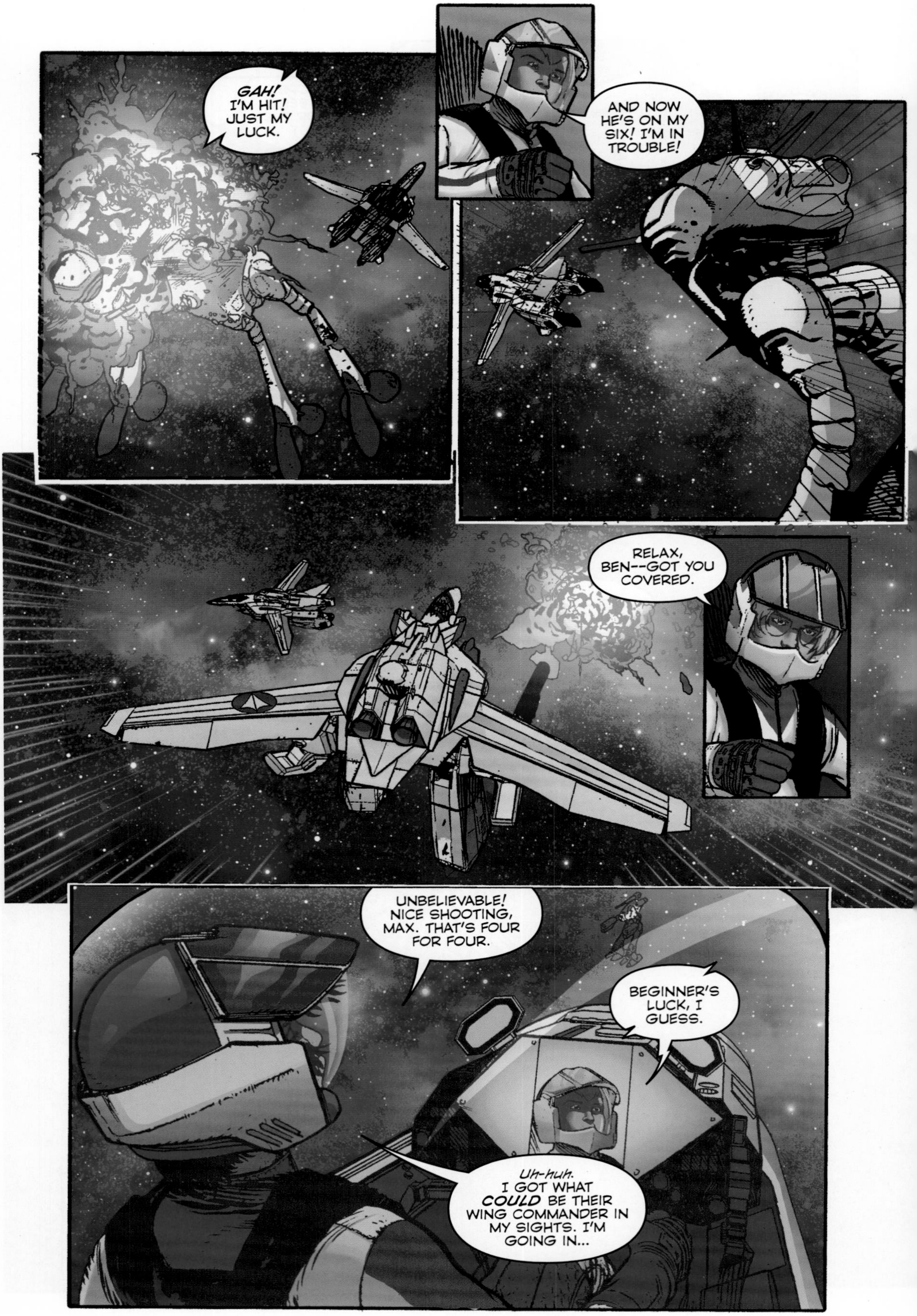
GAH! I'M HIT! JUST MY LUCK.
AND NOW HE'S ON MY SIX! I'M IN TROUBLE!
RELAX, BEN--GOT YOU COVERED.
UNBELIEVABLE! NICE SHOOTING, MAX. THAT'S FOUR FOR FOUR.
BEGINNER'S LUCK, I GUESS.
Uh-huh. I GOT WHAT **COULD** BE THEIR WING COMMANDER IN MY SIGHTS. I'M GOING IN...

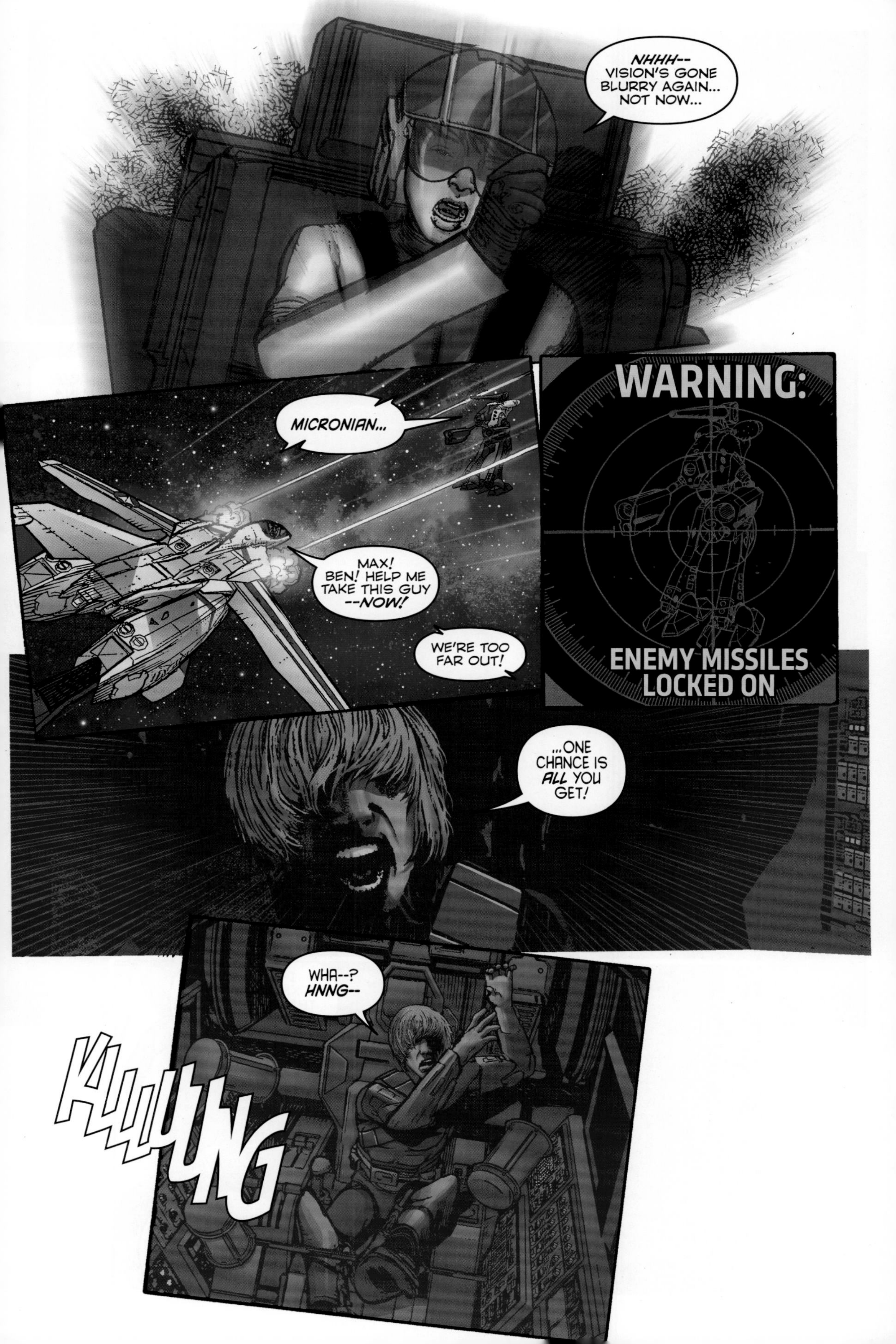
NHHH-- VISION'S GONE BLURRY AGAIN... NOT NOW...
MICRONIAN...
WARNING:
ENEMY MISSILES LOCKED ON
MAX! BEN! HELP ME TAKE THIS GUY --NOW!
WE'RE TOO FAR OUT!
...ONE CHANCE IS ALL YOU GET!
WHA--? HNNG--
KWUUNG

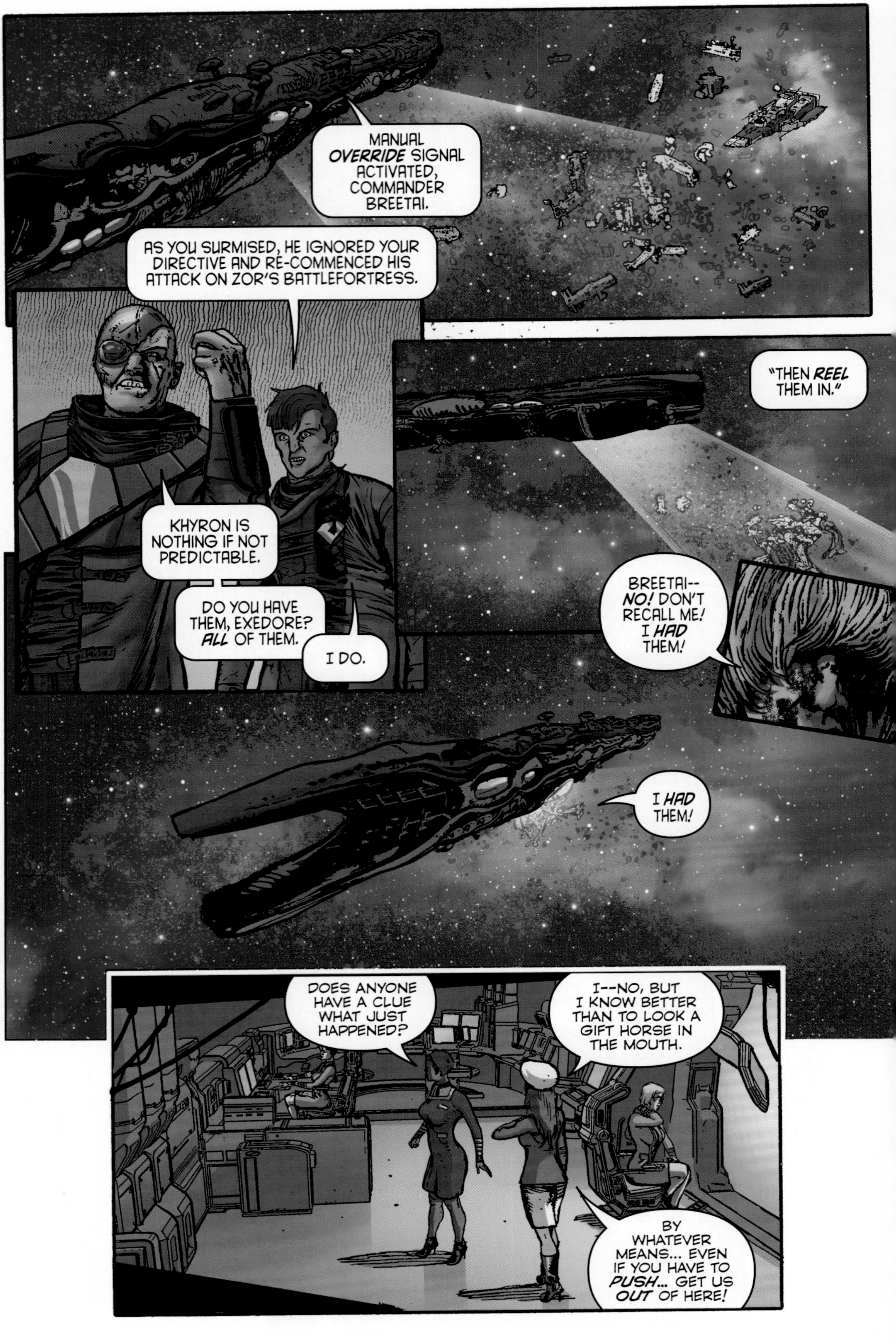
MANUAL OVERRIDE SIGNAL ACTIVATED, COMMANDER BREETAI.
AS YOU SURMISED, HE IGNORED YOUR DIRECTIVE AND RE-COMMENCED HIS ATTACK ON ZOR'S BATTLEFORTRESS.
KHYRON IS NOTHING IF NOT PREDICTABLE.
DO YOU HAVE THEM, EXEDORE? ALL OF THEM.
I DO.
"THEN REEL THEM IN."
BREETAI-- NO! DON'T RECALL ME! I HAD THEM!
I HAD THEM!
DOES ANYONE HAVE A CLUE WHAT JUST HAPPENED?
I--NO, BUT I KNOW BETTER THAN TO LOOK A GIFT HORSE IN THE MOUTH.
BY WHATEVER MEANS... EVEN IF YOU HAVE TO PUSH... GET US OUT OF HERE!

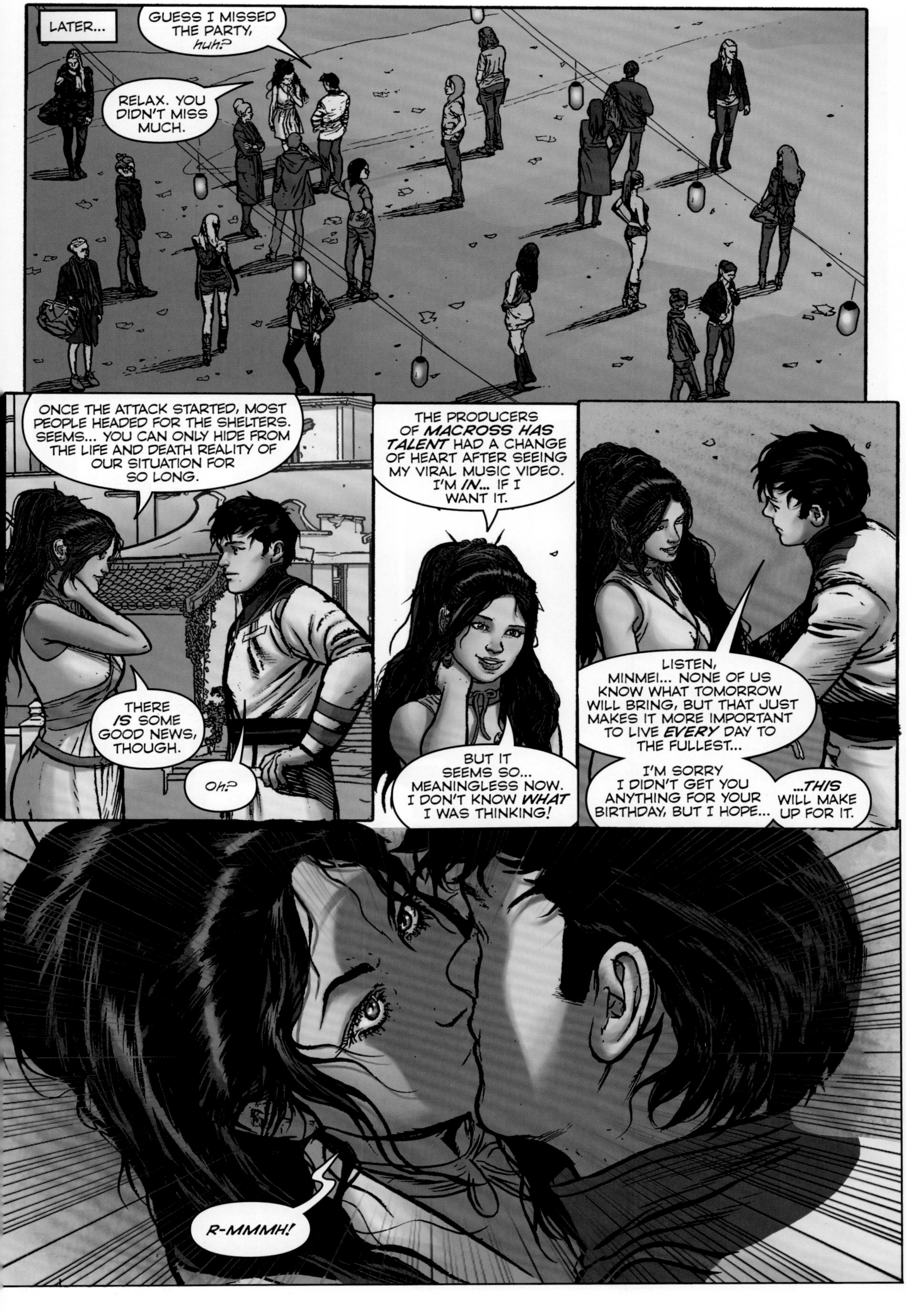
LATER...
GUESS I MISSED THE PARTY, *huh?*
RELAX. YOU DIDN'T MISS MUCH.
ONCE THE ATTACK STARTED, MOST PEOPLE HEADED FOR THE SHELTERS. SEEMS... YOU CAN ONLY HIDE FROM THE LIFE AND DEATH REALITY OF OUR SITUATION FOR SO LONG.
THERE *IS* SOME GOOD NEWS, THOUGH.
Oh?
THE PRODUCERS OF ***MACROSS HAS TALENT*** HAD A CHANGE OF HEART AFTER SEEING MY VIRAL MUSIC VIDEO. I'M *IN*... IF I WANT IT.
BUT IT SEEMS SO... MEANINGLESS NOW. I DON'T KNOW *WHAT* I WAS THINKING!
LISTEN, MINMEI... NONE OF US KNOW WHAT TOMORROW WILL BRING, BUT THAT JUST MAKES IT MORE IMPORTANT TO LIVE *EVERY* DAY TO THE FULLEST...
I'M SORRY I DIDN'T GET YOU ANYTHING FOR YOUR BIRTHDAY, BUT I HOPE...
...THIS WILL MAKE UP FOR IT.
R-MMMH!

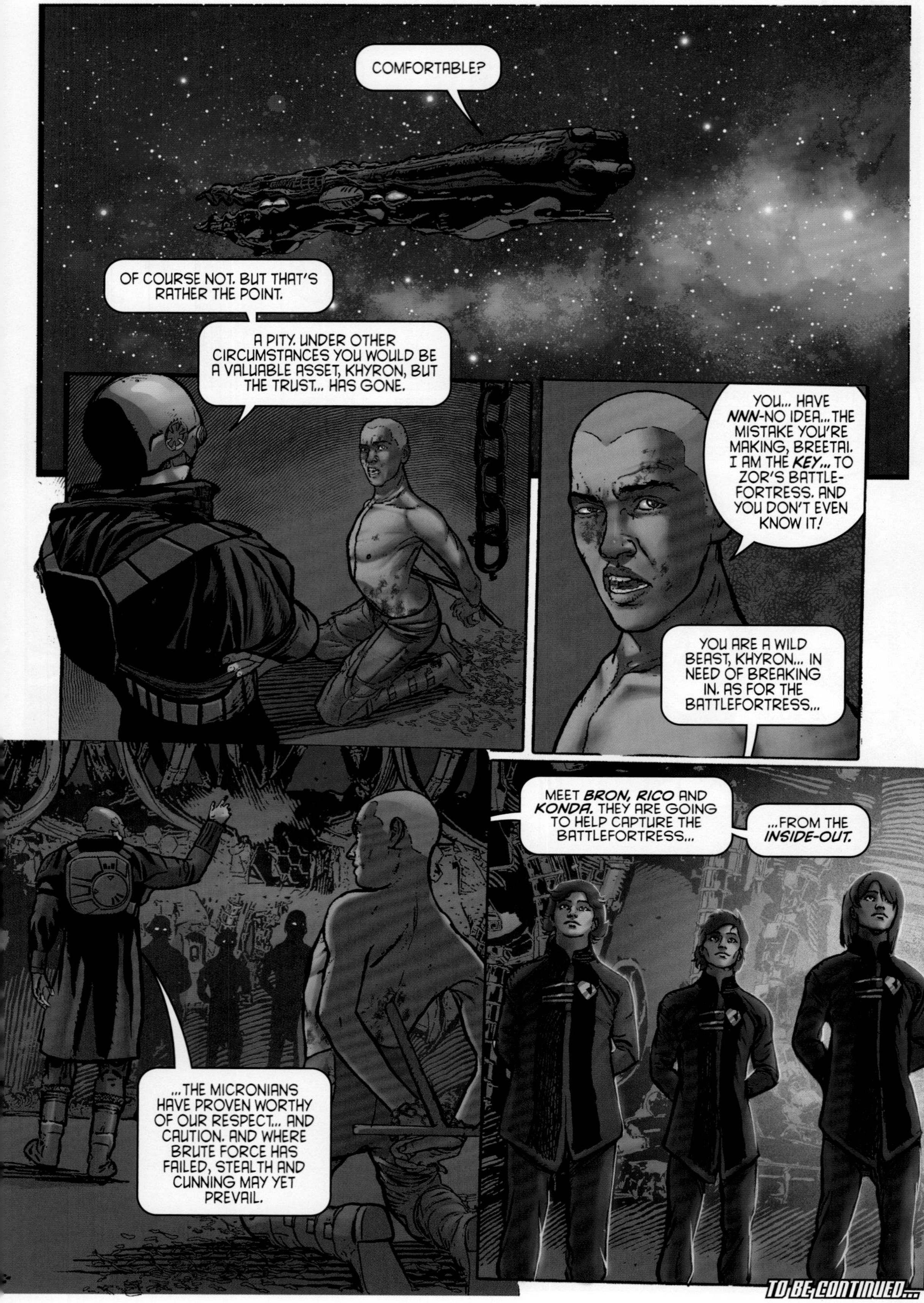
COMFORTABLE?
OF COURSE NOT. BUT THAT'S RATHER THE POINT.
A PITY. UNDER OTHER CIRCUMSTANCES YOU WOULD BE A VALUABLE ASSET, KHYRON, BUT THE TRUST... HAS GONE.
YOU... HAVE NNN-NO IDEA... THE MISTAKE YOU'RE MAKING, BREETAI. I AM THE KEY... TO ZOR'S BATTLE-FORTRESS. AND YOU DON'T EVEN KNOW IT!
YOU ARE A WILD BEAST, KHYRON... IN NEED OF BREAKING IN. AS FOR THE BATTLEFORTRESS...
...THE MICRONIANS HAVE PROVEN WORTHY OF OUR RESPECT... AND CAUTION. AND WHERE BRUTE FORCE HAS FAILED, STEALTH AND CUNNING MAY YET PREVAIL.
MEET BRON, RICO AND KONDA. THEY ARE GOING TO HELP CAPTURE THE BATTLEFORTRESS...
...FROM THE INSIDE-OUT.
TO BE CONTINUED...

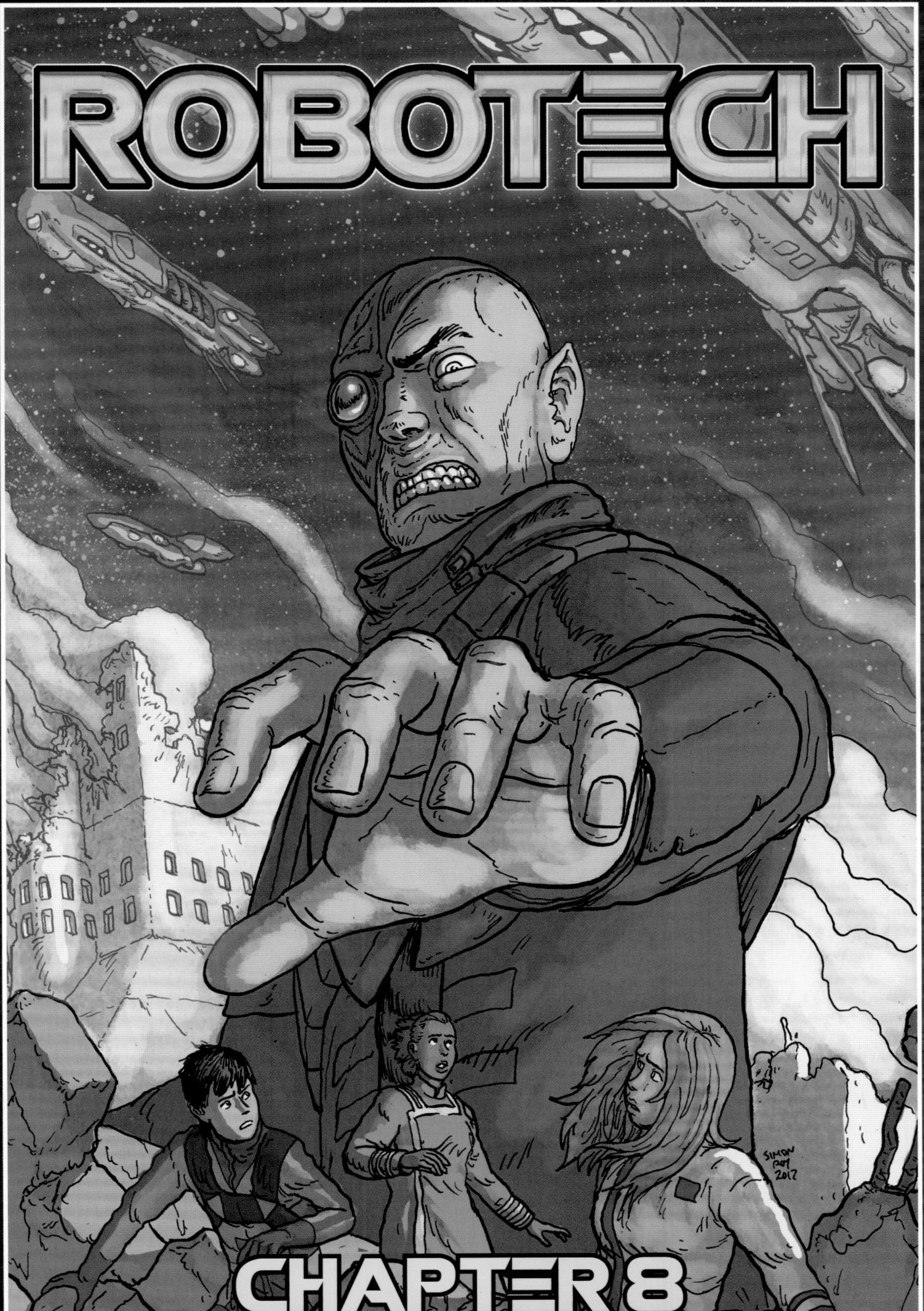
ROBOTECH
CHAPTER 8

ILLUSTRATION BY
SIMON ROY

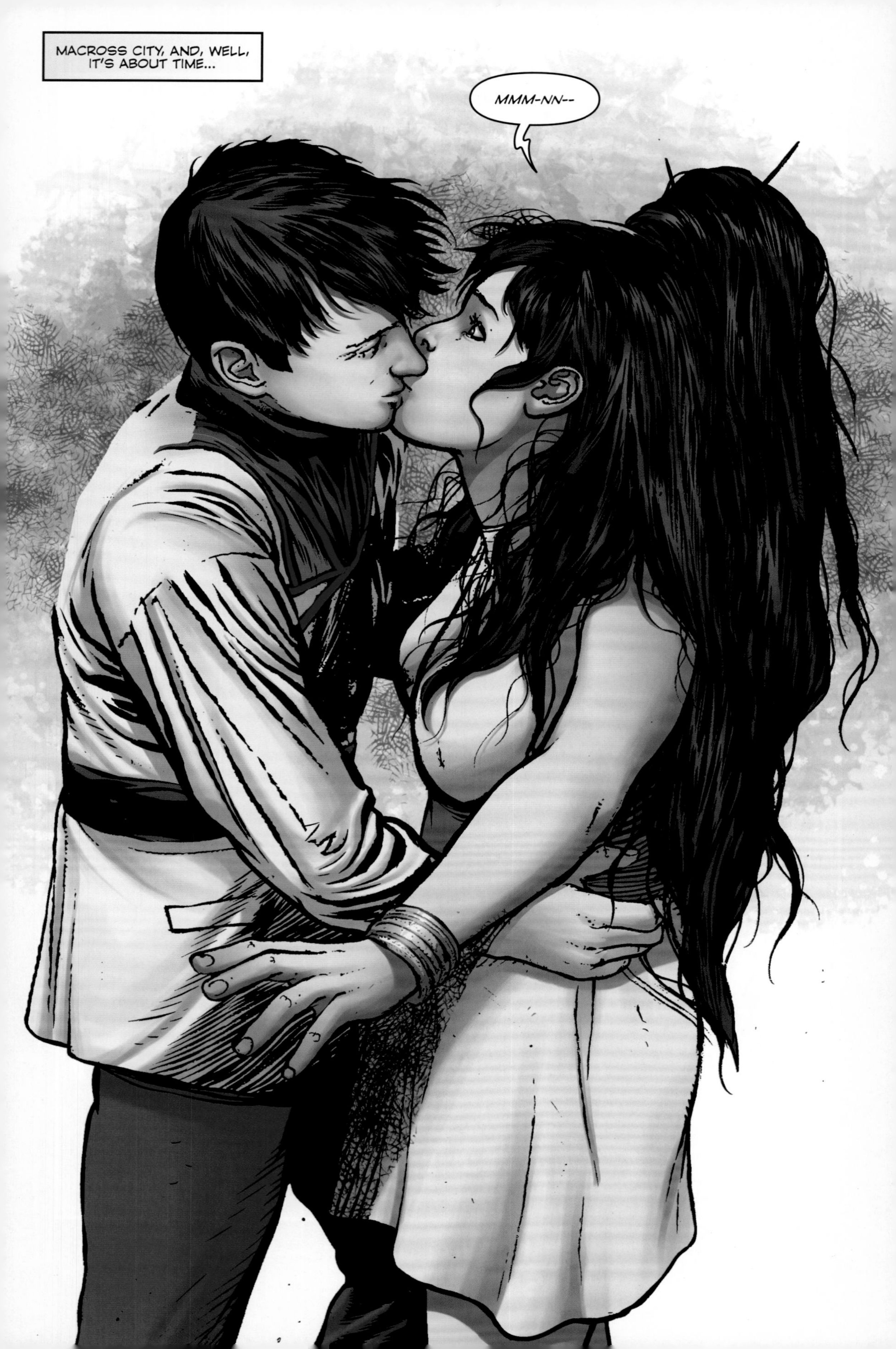
MACROSS CITY, AND, WELL, IT'S ABOUT TIME...
MMM-NN--

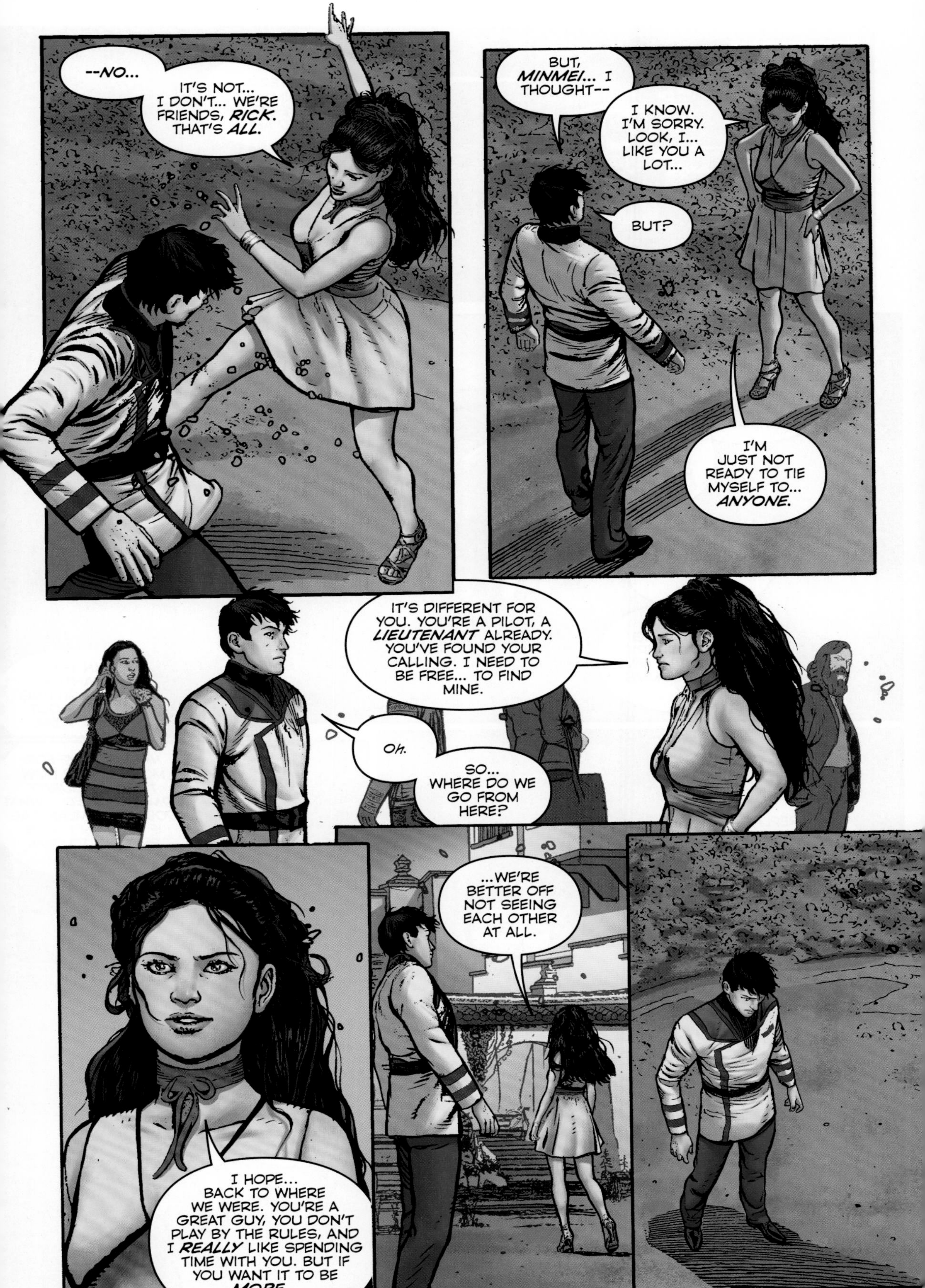
--NO...
IT'S NOT... I DON'T... WE'RE FRIENDS, RICK. THAT'S ALL.
BUT, MINMEI... I THOUGHT--
I KNOW. I'M SORRY. LOOK, I... LIKE YOU A LOT...
BUT?
I'M JUST NOT READY TO TIE MYSELF TO... ANYONE.
IT'S DIFFERENT FOR YOU. YOU'RE A PILOT, A LIEUTENANT ALREADY. YOU'VE FOUND YOUR CALLING. I NEED TO BE FREE... TO FIND MINE.
Oh.
SO... WHERE DO WE GO FROM HERE?
I HOPE... BACK TO WHERE WE WERE. YOU'RE A GREAT GUY, YOU DON'T PLAY BY THE RULES, AND I REALLY LIKE SPENDING TIME WITH YOU. BUT IF YOU WANT IT TO BE MORE...
...WE'RE BETTER OFF NOT SEEING EACH OTHER AT ALL.

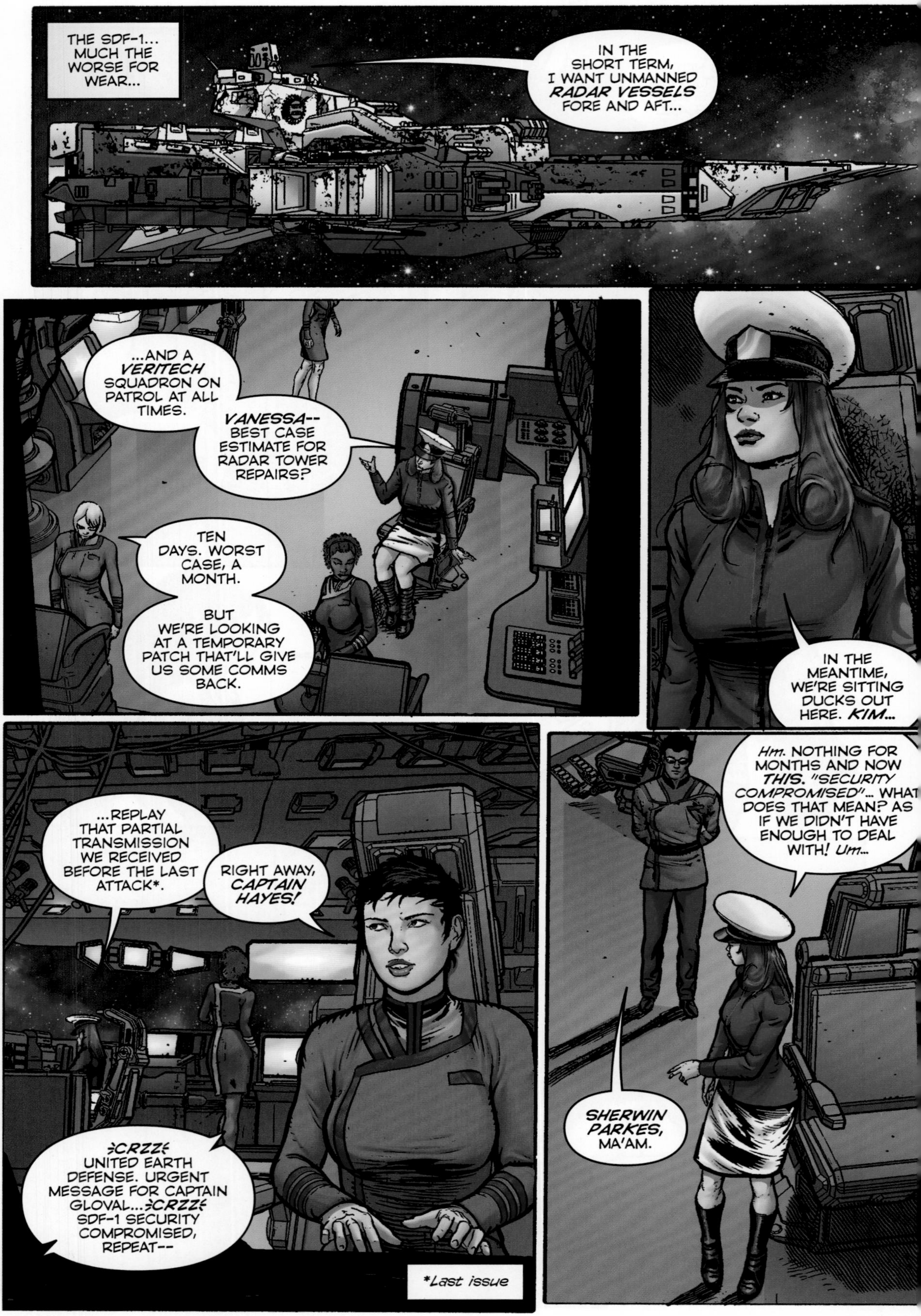
THE SDF-1... MUCH THE WORSE FOR WEAR...
IN THE SHORT TERM, I WANT UNMANNED RADAR VESSELS FORE AND AFT...
...AND A VERITECH SQUADRON ON PATROL AT ALL TIMES.
VANESSA-- BEST CASE ESTIMATE FOR RADAR TOWER REPAIRS?
TEN DAYS. WORST CASE, A MONTH.
BUT WE'RE LOOKING AT A TEMPORARY PATCH THAT'LL GIVE US SOME COMMS BACK.
IN THE MEANTIME, WE'RE SITTING DUCKS OUT HERE. KIM...
...REPLAY THAT PARTIAL TRANSMISSION WE RECEIVED BEFORE THE LAST ATTACK*.
RIGHT AWAY, CAPTAIN HAYES!
CRZZ UNITED EARTH DEFENSE. URGENT MESSAGE FOR CAPTAIN GLOVAL... CRZZ SDF-1 SECURITY COMPROMISED, REPEAT--
*Last issue
Hm. NOTHING FOR MONTHS AND NOW THIS. "SECURITY COMPROMISED"... WHAT DOES THAT MEAN? AS IF WE DIDN'T HAVE ENOUGH TO DEAL WITH! Um...
SHERWIN PARKES, MA'AM.

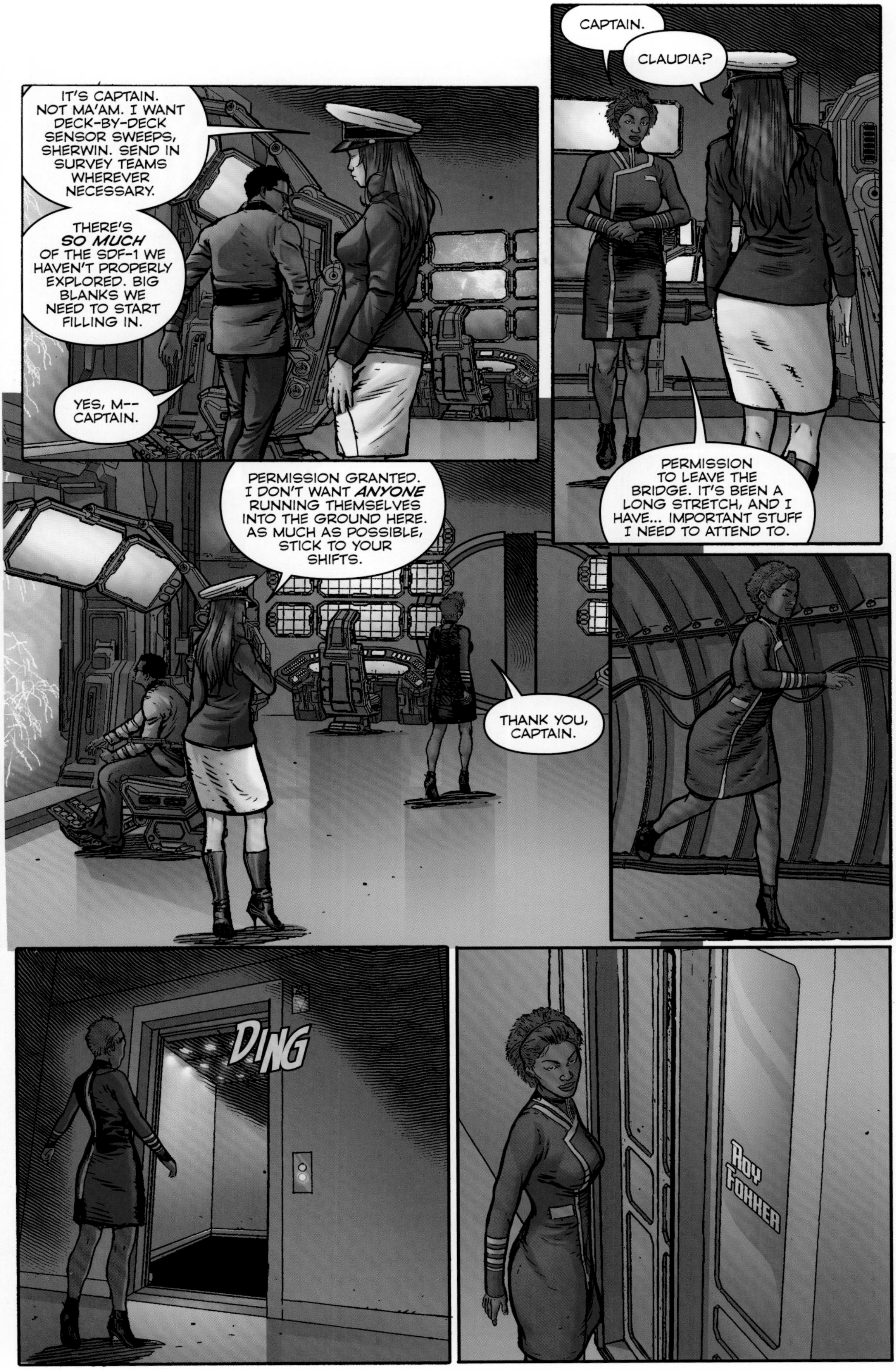
IT'S CAPTAIN. NOT MA'AM. I WANT DECK-BY-DECK SENSOR SWEEPS, SHERWIN. SEND IN SURVEY TEAMS WHEREVER NECESSARY.
THERE'S SO MUCH OF THE SDF-1 WE HAVEN'T PROPERLY EXPLORED. BIG BLANKS WE NEED TO START FILLING IN.
YES, M-- CAPTAIN.
CAPTAIN.
CLAUDIA?
PERMISSION TO LEAVE THE BRIDGE. IT'S BEEN A LONG STRETCH, AND I HAVE... IMPORTANT STUFF I NEED TO ATTEND TO.
PERMISSION GRANTED. I DON'T WANT ANYONE RUNNING THEMSELVES INTO THE GROUND HERE. AS MUCH AS POSSIBLE, STICK TO YOUR SHIFTS.
THANK YOU, CAPTAIN.
DING
ROY FOKKER

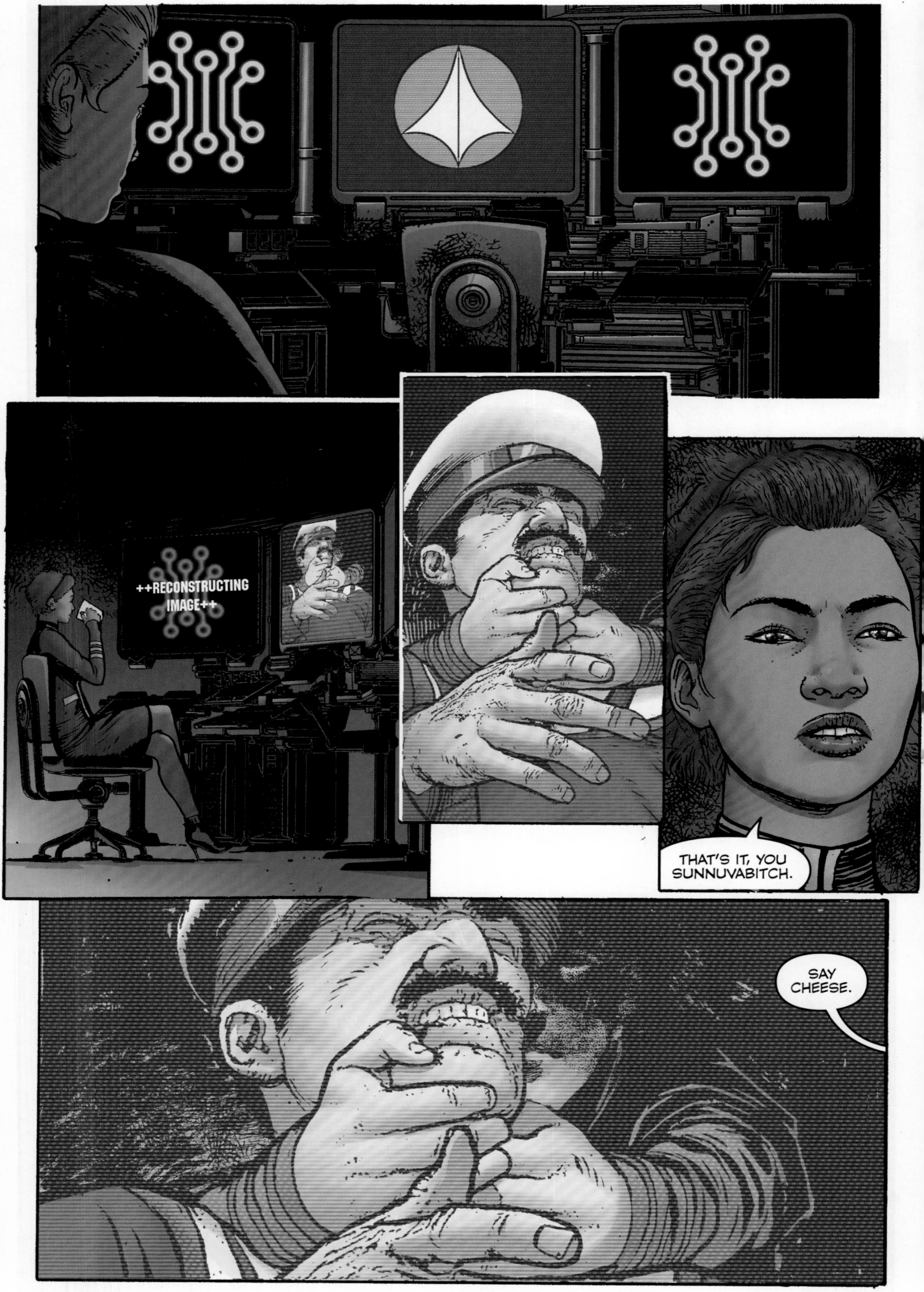
++RECONSTRUCTING IMAGE++
THAT'S IT, YOU SUNNUVABITCH.
SAY CHEESE.

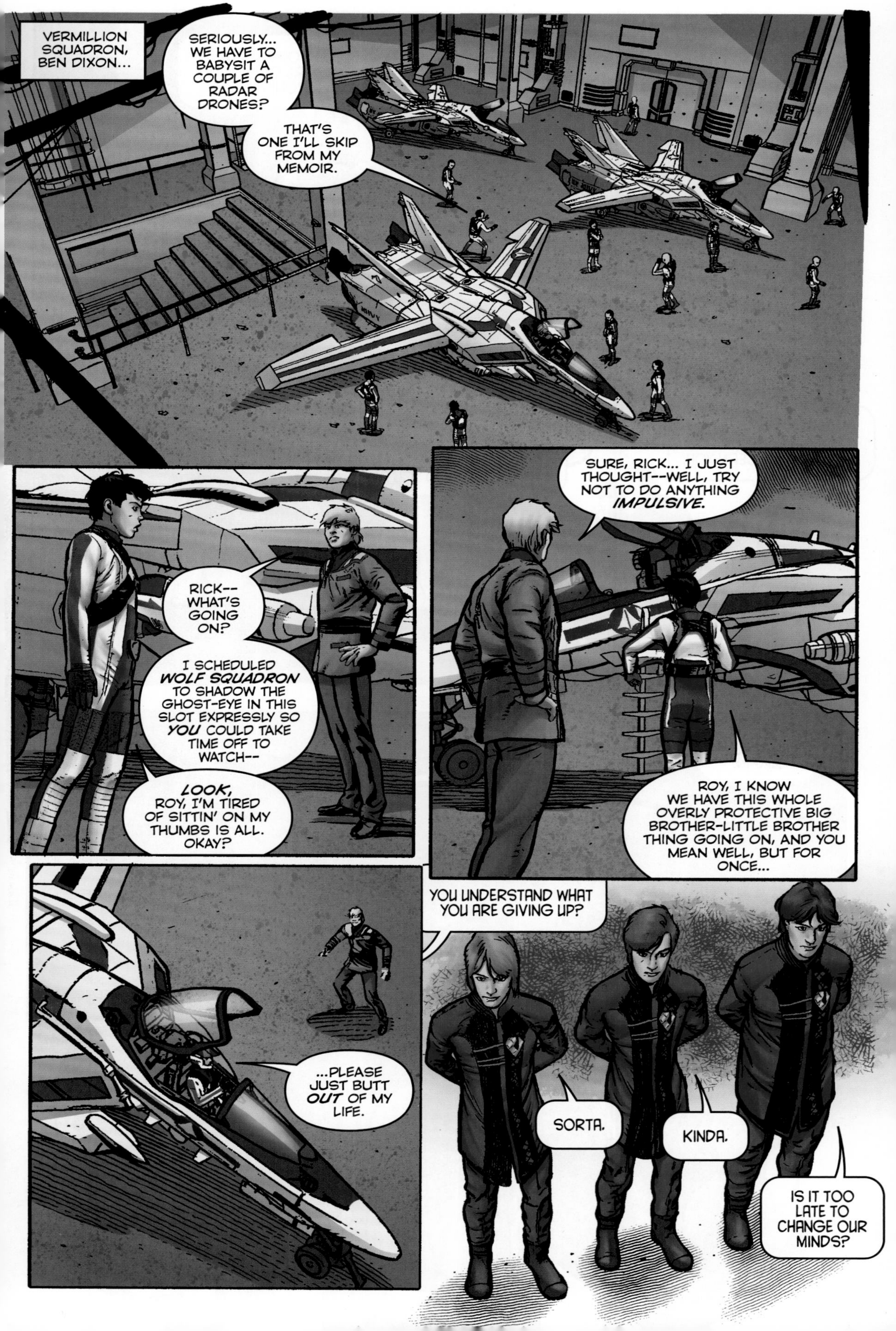
VERMILLION SQUADRON, BEN DIXON...
SERIOUSLY... WE HAVE TO BABYSIT A COUPLE OF RADAR DRONES?
THAT'S ONE I'LL SKIP FROM MY MEMOIR.
RICK-- WHAT'S GOING ON?
I SCHEDULED WOLF SQUADRON TO SHADOW THE GHOST-EYE IN THIS SLOT EXPRESSLY SO YOU COULD TAKE TIME OFF TO WATCH--
LOOK, ROY, I'M TIRED OF SITTIN' ON MY THUMBS IS ALL. OKAY?
SURE, RICK... I JUST THOUGHT--WELL, TRY NOT TO DO ANYTHING IMPULSIVE.
ROY, I KNOW WE HAVE THIS WHOLE OVERLY PROTECTIVE BIG BROTHER-LITTLE BROTHER THING GOING ON, AND YOU MEAN WELL, BUT FOR ONCE...
...PLEASE JUST BUTT OUT OF MY LIFE.
YOU UNDERSTAND WHAT YOU ARE GIVING UP?
SORTA.
KINDA.
IS IT TOO LATE TO CHANGE OUR MINDS?

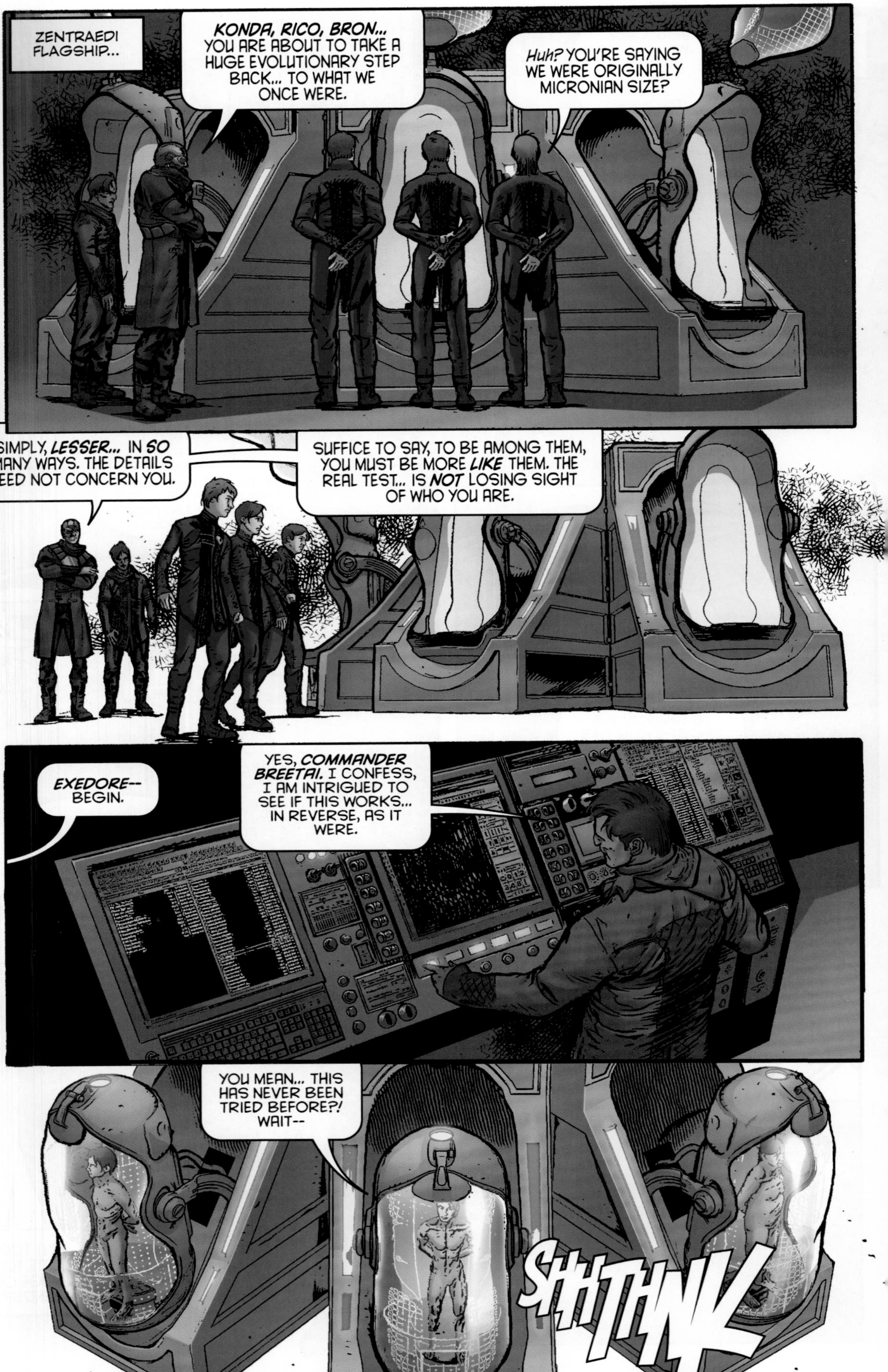
ZENTRAEDI FLAGSHIP...
KONDA, RICO, BRON... YOU ARE ABOUT TO TAKE A HUGE EVOLUTIONARY STEP BACK... TO WHAT WE ONCE WERE.
Huh? YOU'RE SAYING WE WERE ORIGINALLY MICRONIAN SIZE?
SIMPLY, LESSER... IN SO MANY WAYS. THE DETAILS NEED NOT CONCERN YOU.
SUFFICE TO SAY, TO BE AMONG THEM, YOU MUST BE MORE LIKE THEM. THE REAL TEST... IS NOT LOSING SIGHT OF WHO YOU ARE.
EXEDORE-- BEGIN.
YES, COMMANDER BREETAI. I CONFESS, I AM INTRIGUED TO SEE IF THIS WORKS... IN REVERSE, AS IT WERE.
YOU MEAN... THIS HAS NEVER BEEN TRIED BEFORE?! WAIT--
SHHTHNK

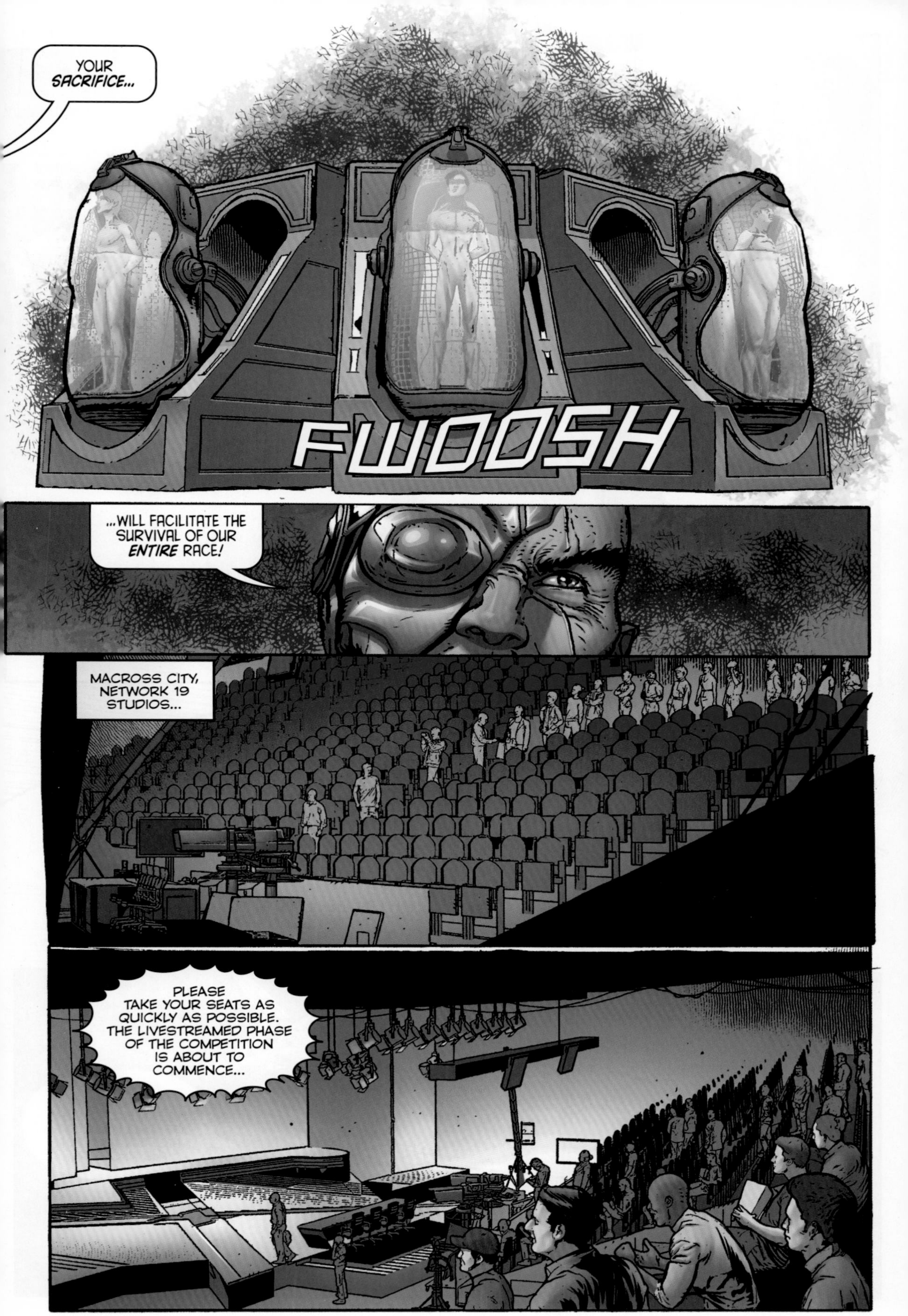
YOUR SACRIFICE...
FWOOSH
...WILL FACILITATE THE SURVIVAL OF OUR ENTIRE RACE!
MACROSS CITY, NETWORK 19 STUDIOS...
PLEASE TAKE YOUR SEATS AS QUICKLY AS POSSIBLE. THE LIVESTREAMED PHASE OF THE COMPETITION IS ABOUT TO COMMENCE...

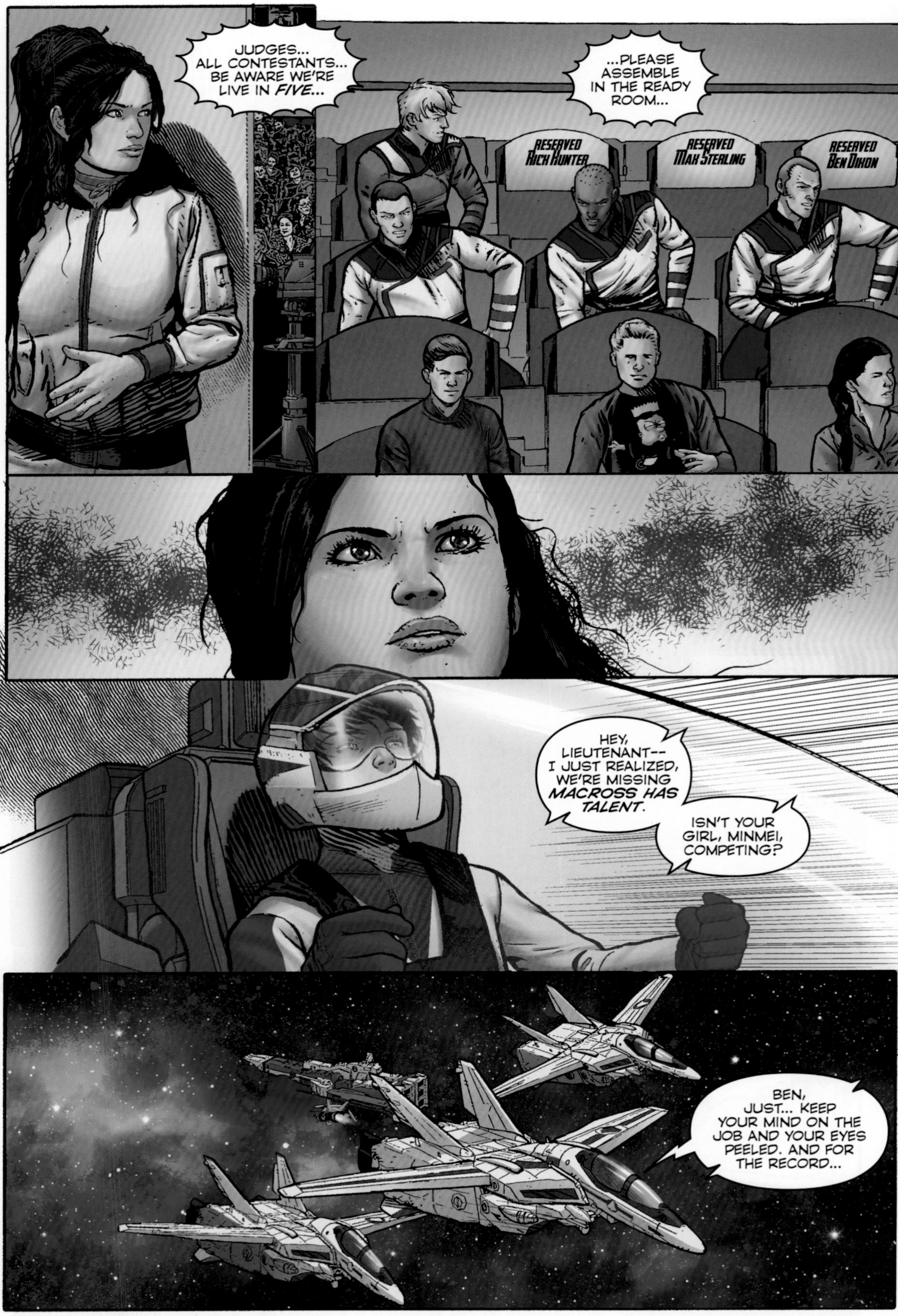
JUDGES... ALL CONTESTANTS... BE AWARE WE'RE LIVE IN FIVE...
...PLEASE ASSEMBLE IN THE READY ROOM...
RESERVED RICK HUNTER
RESERVED MAX STERLING
RESERVED BEN DIXON
HEY, LIEUTENANT-- I JUST REALIZED, WE'RE MISSING MACROSS HAS TALENT.
ISN'T YOUR GIRL, MINMEI, COMPETING?
BEN, JUST... KEEP YOUR MIND ON THE JOB AND YOUR EYES PEELED. AND FOR THE RECORD...

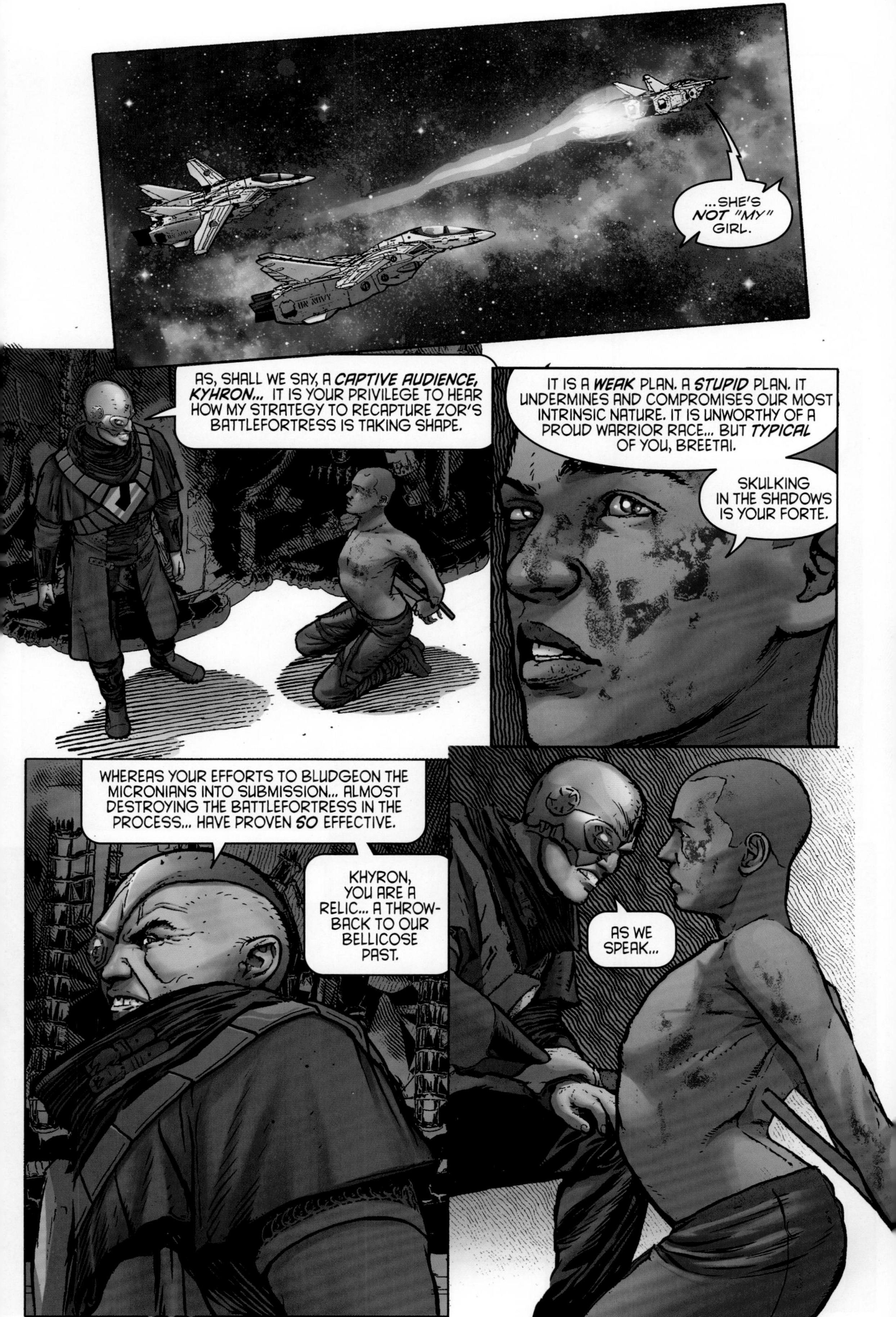
...SHE'S NOT "MY" GIRL.
AS, SHALL WE SAY, A CAPTIVE AUDIENCE, KYHRON... IT IS YOUR PRIVILEGE TO HEAR HOW MY STRATEGY TO RECAPTURE ZOR'S BATTLEFORTRESS IS TAKING SHAPE.
IT IS A WEAK PLAN. A STUPID PLAN. IT UNDERMINES AND COMPROMISES OUR MOST INTRINSIC NATURE. IT IS UNWORTHY OF A PROUD WARRIOR RACE... BUT TYPICAL OF YOU, BREETAI.
SKULKING IN THE SHADOWS IS YOUR FORTE.
WHEREAS YOUR EFFORTS TO BLUDGEON THE MICRONIANS INTO SUBMISSION... ALMOST DESTROYING THE BATTLEFORTRESS IN THE PROCESS... HAVE PROVEN SO EFFECTIVE.
KHYRON, YOU ARE A RELIC... A THROW-BACK TO OUR BELLICOSE PAST.
AS WE SPEAK...

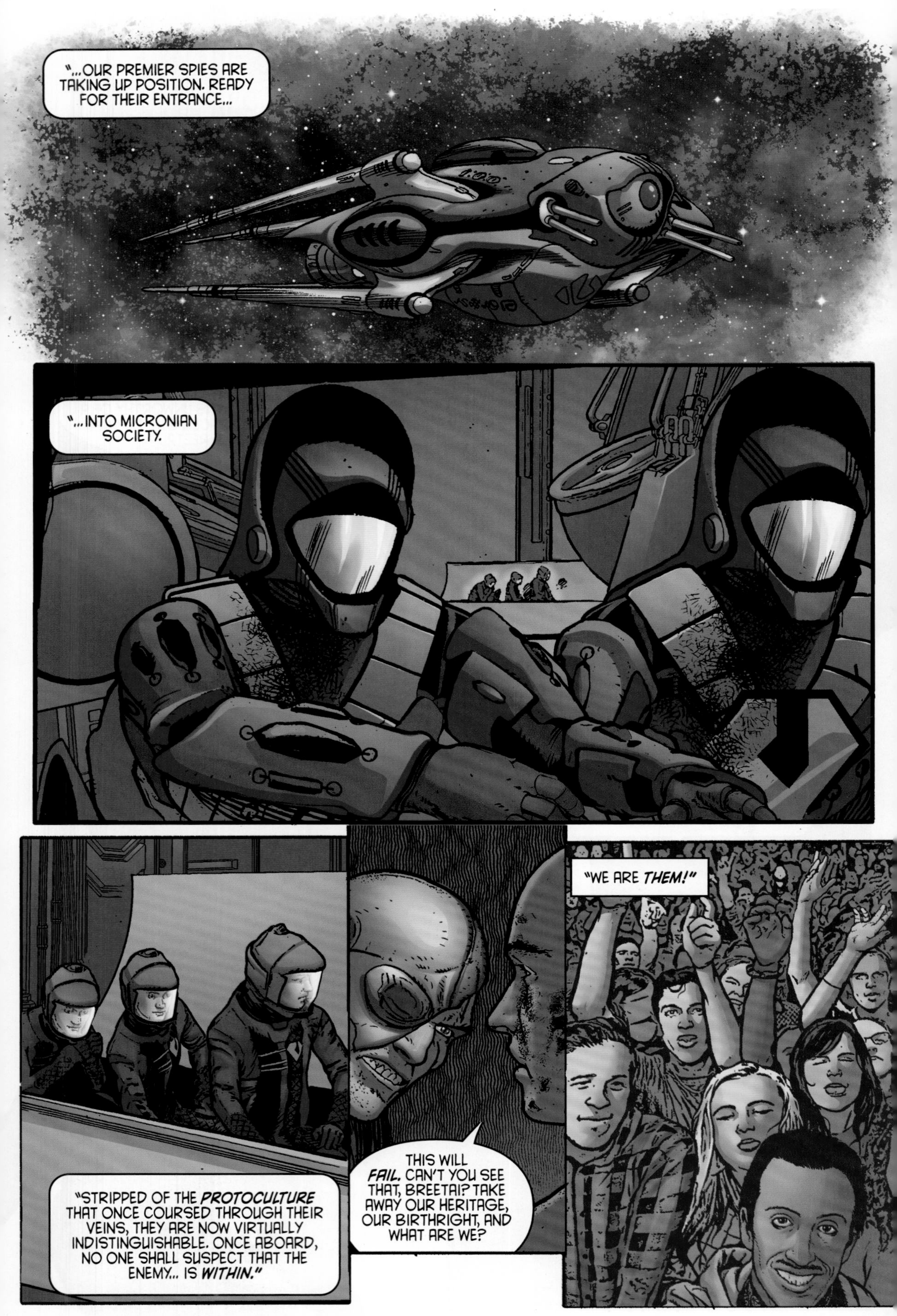
"...OUR PREMIER SPIES ARE TAKING UP POSITION. READY FOR THEIR ENTRANCE...
"...INTO MICRONIAN SOCIETY.
"STRIPPED OF THE *PROTOCULTURE* THAT ONCE COURSED THROUGH THEIR VEINS, THEY ARE NOW VIRTUALLY INDISTINGUISHABLE. ONCE ABOARD, NO ONE SHALL SUSPECT THAT THE ENEMY... IS *WITHIN.*"
THIS WILL *FAIL.* CAN'T YOU SEE THAT, BREETAI? TAKE AWAY OUR HERITAGE, OUR BIRTHRIGHT, AND WHAT ARE WE?
"WE ARE *THEM!*"

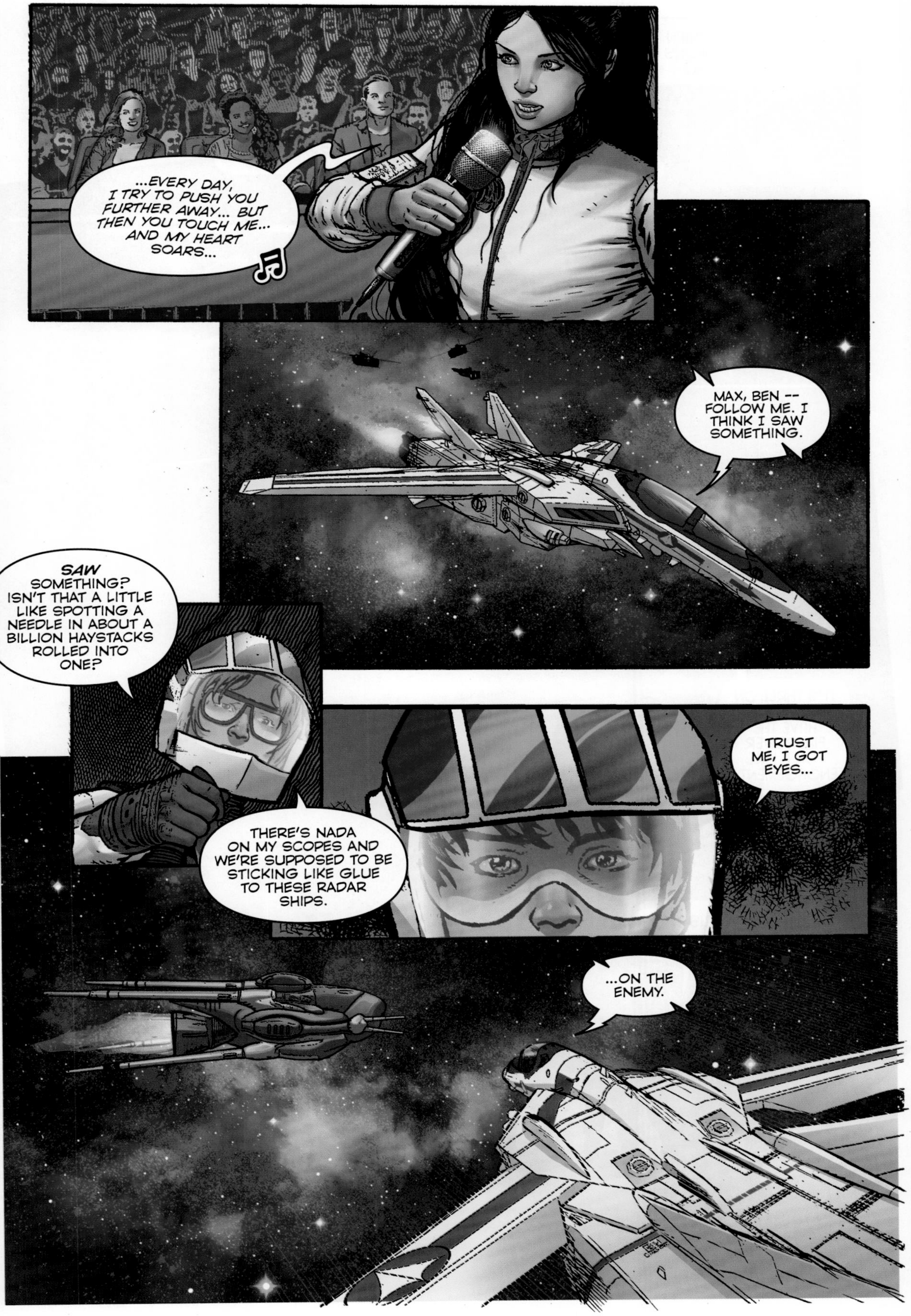
...EVERY DAY, I TRY TO PUSH YOU FURTHER AWAY... BUT THEN YOU TOUCH ME... AND MY HEART SOARS...
MAX, BEN -- FOLLOW ME. I THINK I SAW SOMETHING.
SAW SOMETHING? ISN'T THAT A LITTLE LIKE SPOTTING A NEEDLE IN ABOUT A BILLION HAYSTACKS ROLLED INTO ONE?
THERE'S NADA ON MY SCOPES AND WE'RE SUPPOSED TO BE STICKING LIKE GLUE TO THESE RADAR SHIPS.
TRUST ME, I GOT EYES...
...ON THE ENEMY.

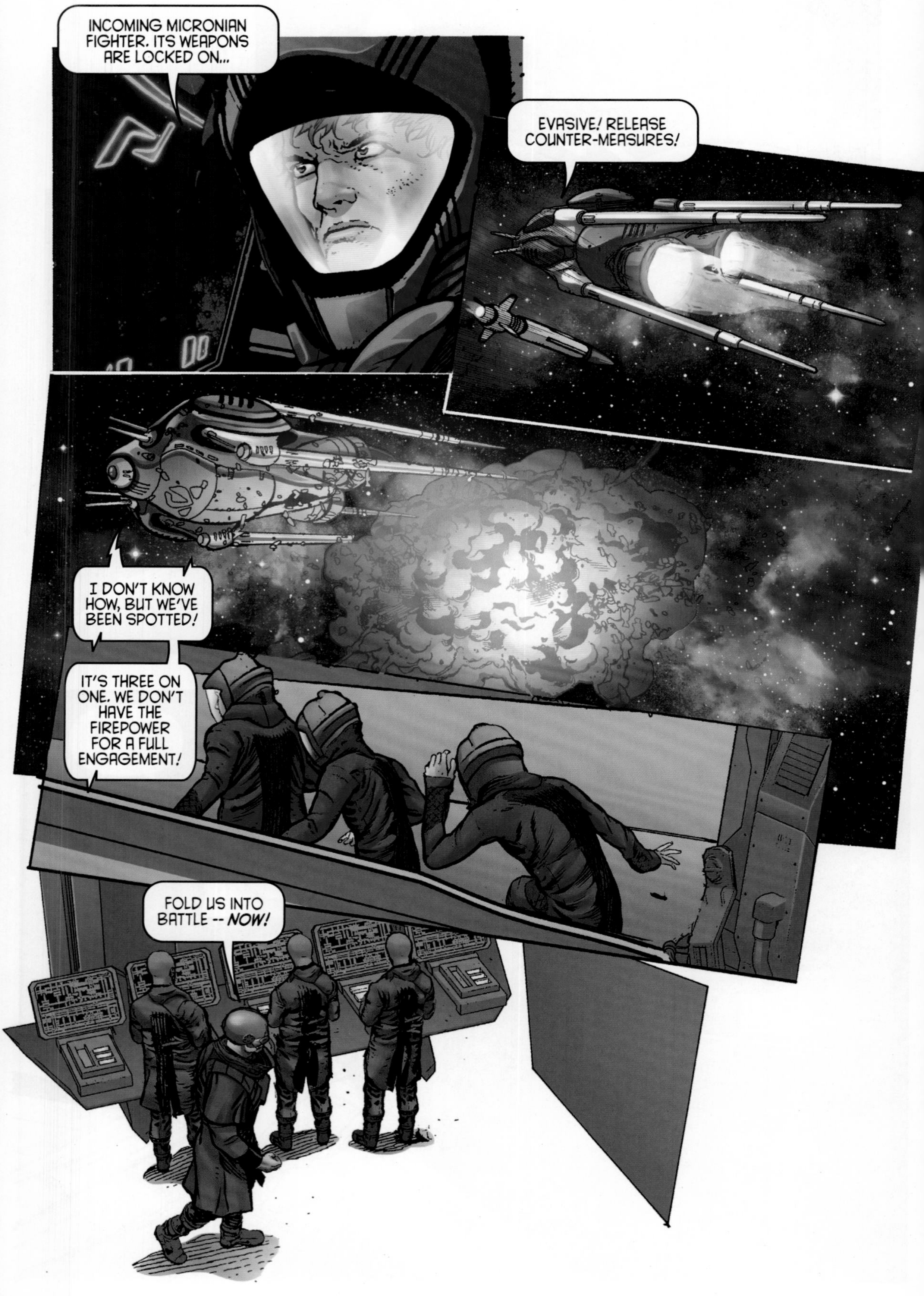
INCOMING MICRONIAN FIGHTER. ITS WEAPONS ARE LOCKED ON...
EVASIVE! RELEASE COUNTER-MEASURES!
I DON'T KNOW HOW, BUT WE'VE BEEN SPOTTED!
IT'S THREE ON ONE. WE DON'T HAVE THE FIREPOWER FOR A FULL ENGAGEMENT!
FOLD US INTO BATTLE -- *NOW!*

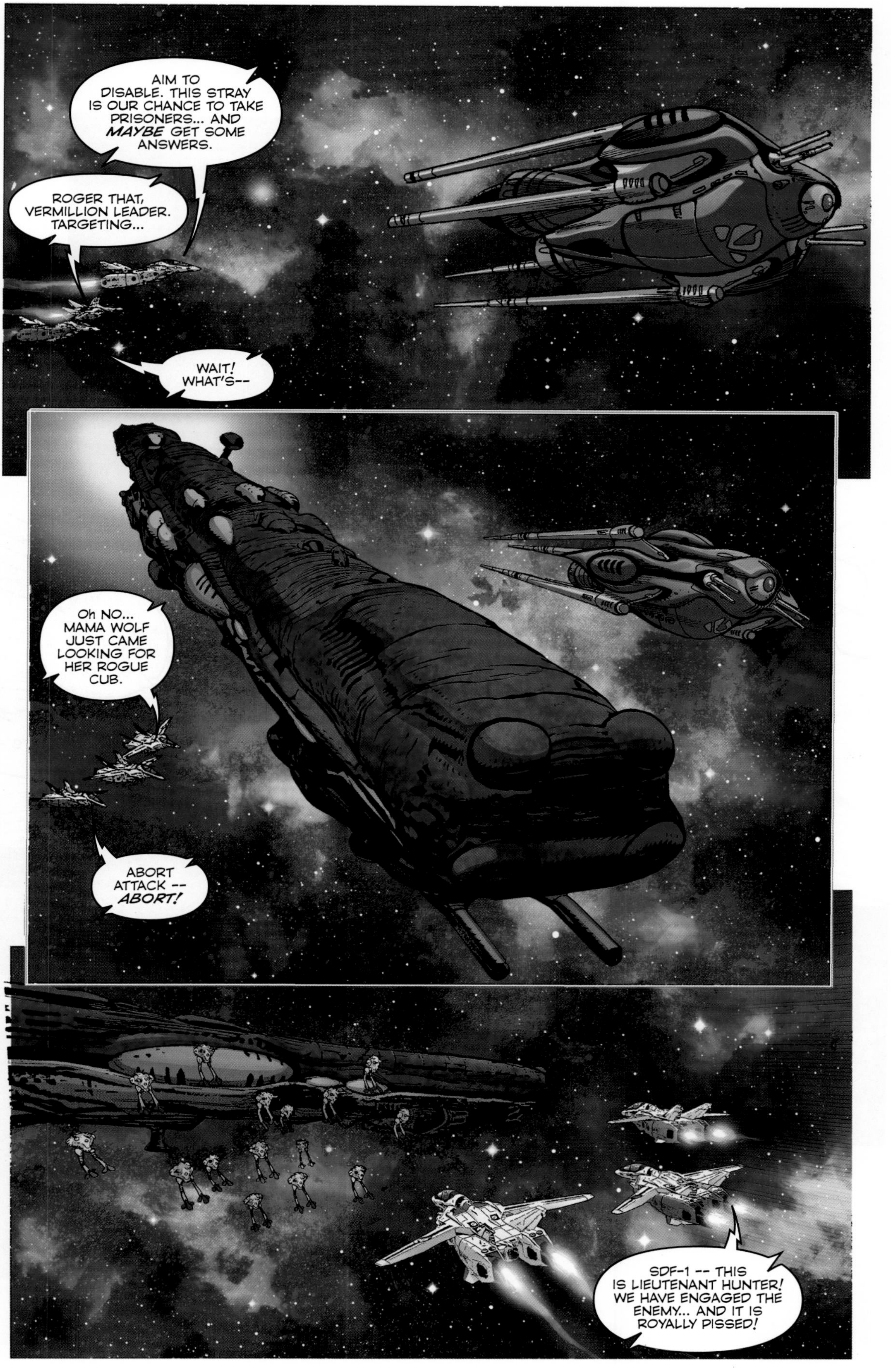
AIM TO DISABLE. THIS STRAY IS OUR CHANCE TO TAKE PRISONERS... AND *MAYBE* GET SOME ANSWERS.
ROGER THAT, VERMILLION LEADER. TARGETING...
WAIT! WHAT'S--
Oh NO... MAMA WOLF JUST CAME LOOKING FOR HER ROGUE CUB.
ABORT ATTACK -- *ABORT!*
SDF-1 -- THIS IS LIEUTENANT HUNTER! WE HAVE ENGAGED THE ENEMY... AND IT IS ROYALLY PISSED!

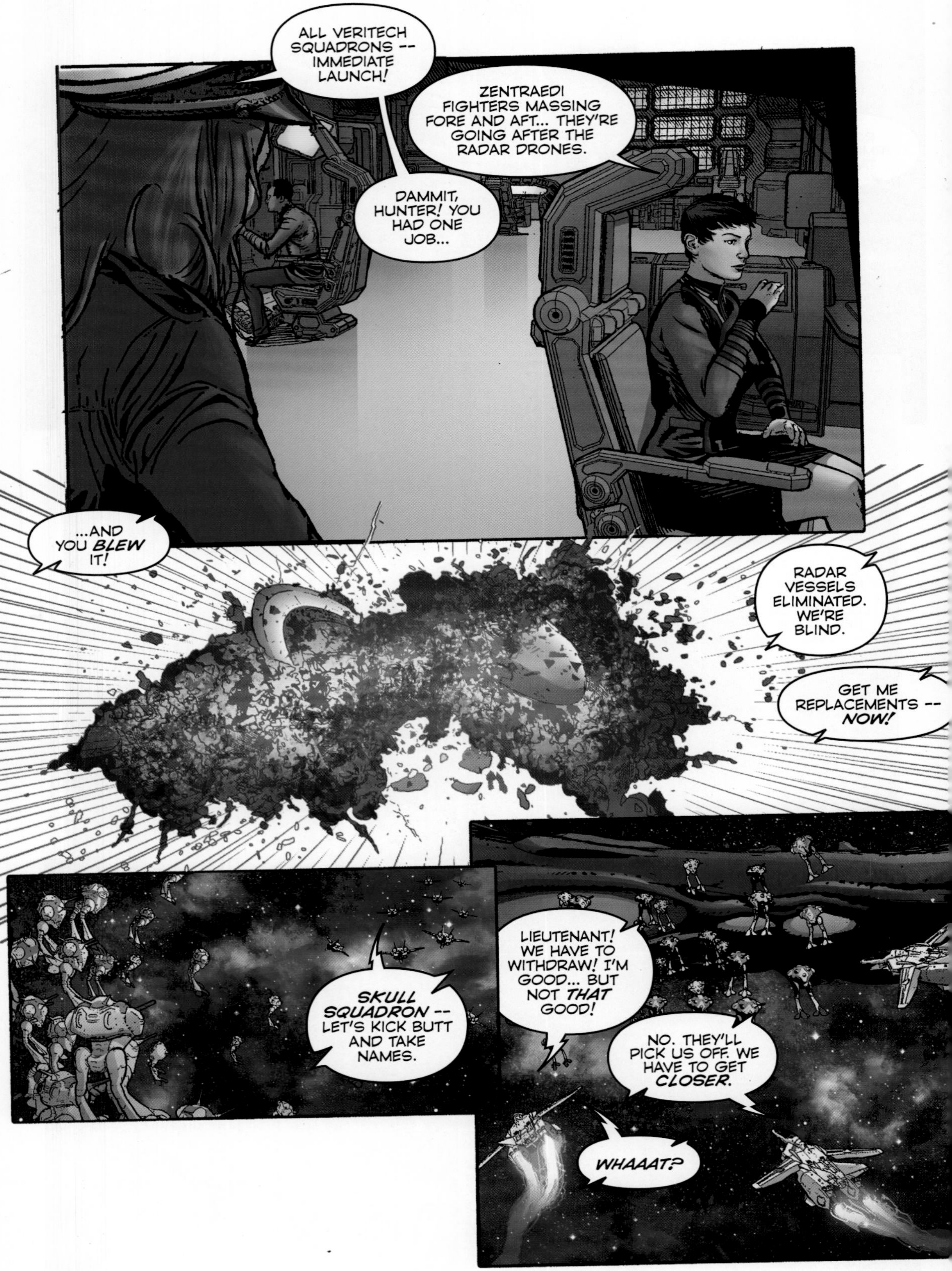

ALL VERITECH SQUADRONS -- IMMEDIATE LAUNCH!
ZENTRAEDI FIGHTERS MASSING FORE AND AFT... THEY'RE GOING AFTER THE RADAR DRONES.
DAMMIT, HUNTER! YOU HAD ONE JOB...
...AND YOU BLEW IT!
RADAR VESSELS ELIMINATED. WE'RE BLIND.
GET ME REPLACEMENTS -- NOW!
SKULL SQUADRON -- LET'S KICK BUTT AND TAKE NAMES.
LIEUTENANT! WE HAVE TO WITHDRAW! I'M GOOD... BUT NOT THAT GOOD!
NO. THEY'LL PICK US OFF. WE HAVE TO GET CLOSER.
WHAAAT?

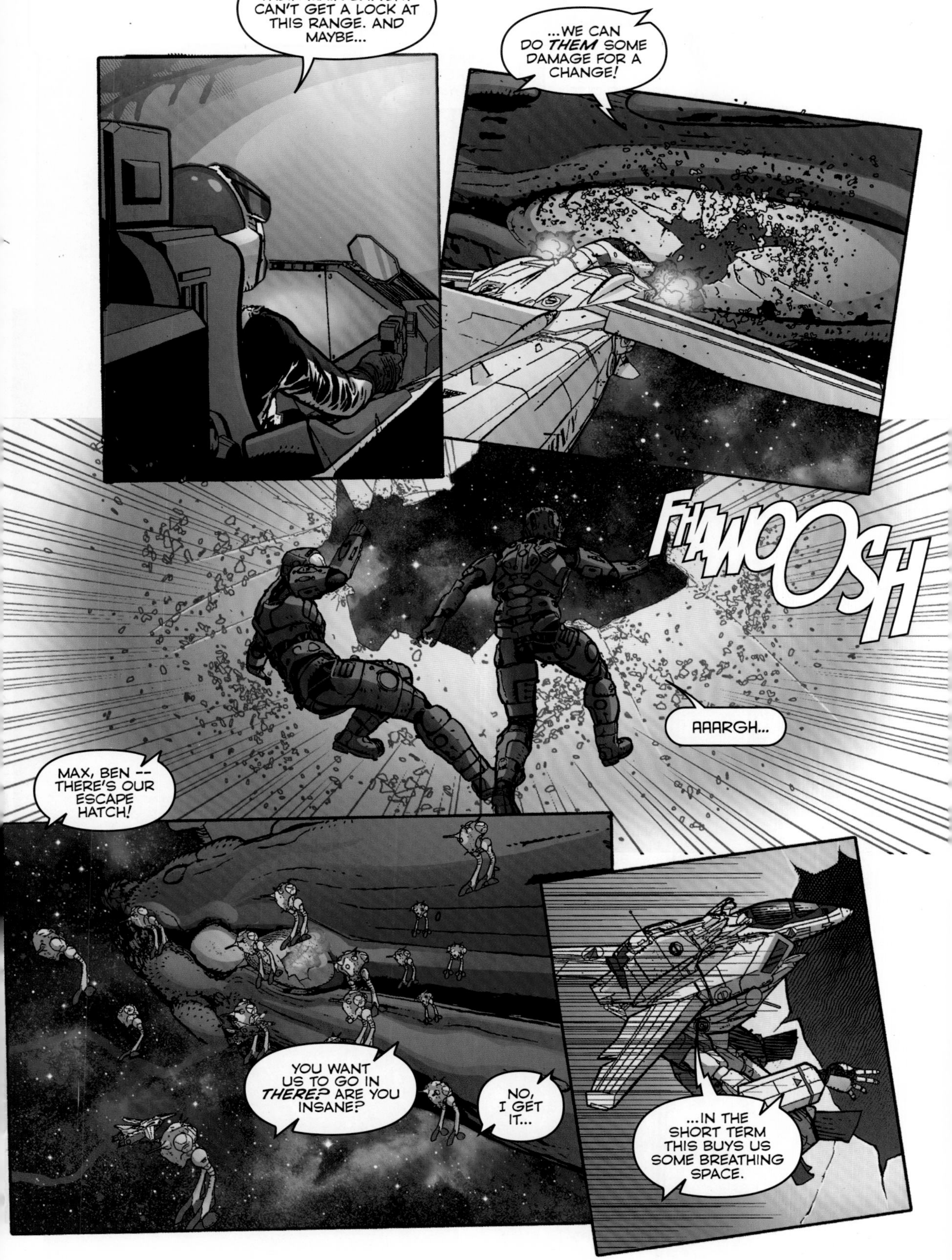

HOPEFULLY THEIR MAIN BATTERY CAN'T GET A LOCK AT THIS RANGE. AND MAYBE...
...WE CAN DO *THEM* SOME DAMAGE FOR A CHANGE!
FHAWOOSH
AAARGH...
MAX, BEN -- THERE'S OUR ESCAPE HATCH!
YOU WANT US TO GO IN *THERE?* ARE YOU INSANE?
NO, I GET IT...
...IN THE SHORT TERM THIS BUYS US SOME BREATHING SPACE.

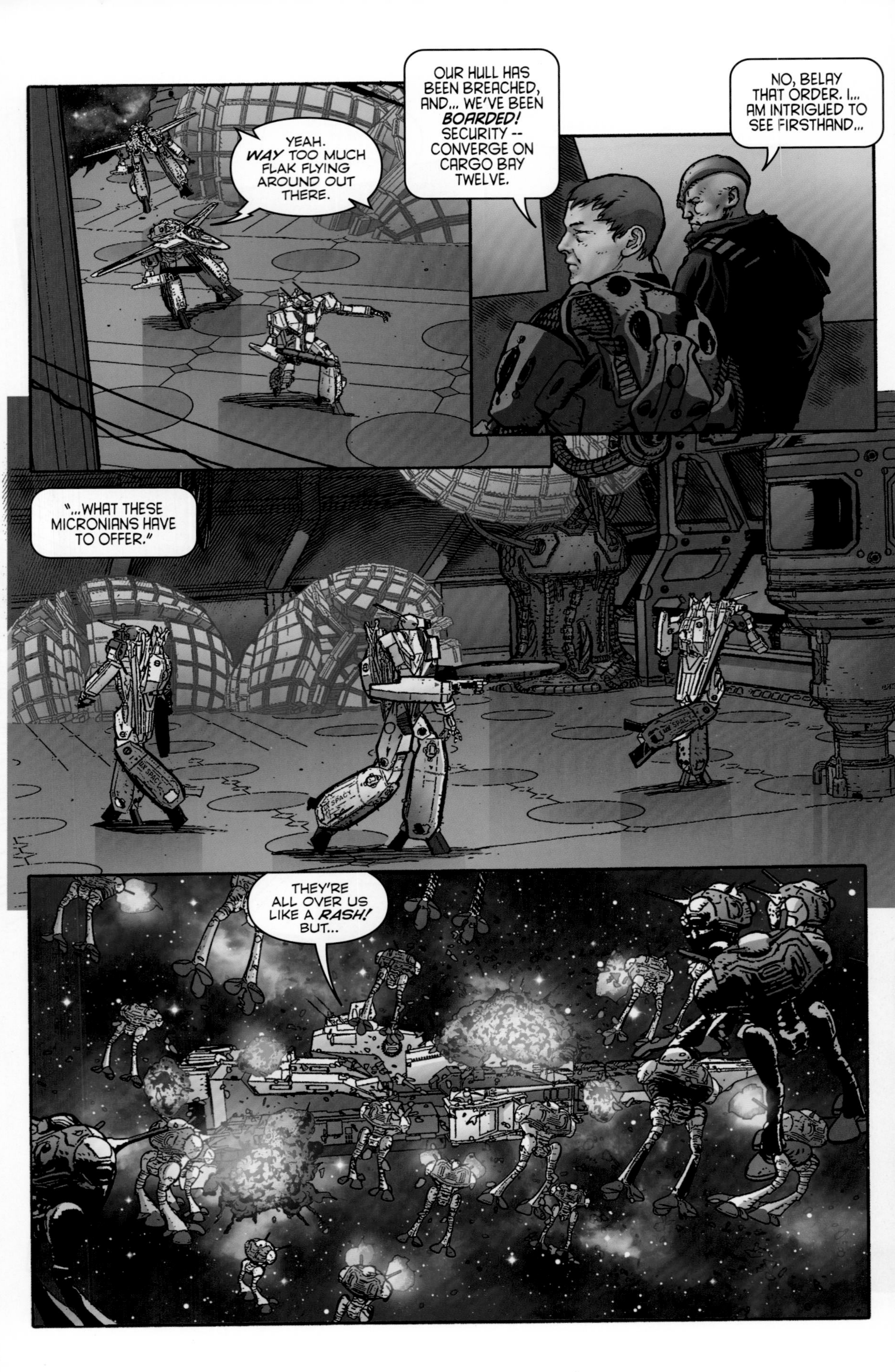
YEAH. WAY TOO MUCH FLAK FLYING AROUND OUT THERE.
OUR HULL HAS BEEN BREACHED, AND... WE'VE BEEN BOARDED! SECURITY -- CONVERGE ON CARGO BAY TWELVE.
NO, BELAY THAT ORDER. I... AM INTRIGUED TO SEE FIRSTHAND...
"...WHAT THESE MICRONIANS HAVE TO OFFER."
THEY'RE ALL OVER US LIKE A RASH! BUT...

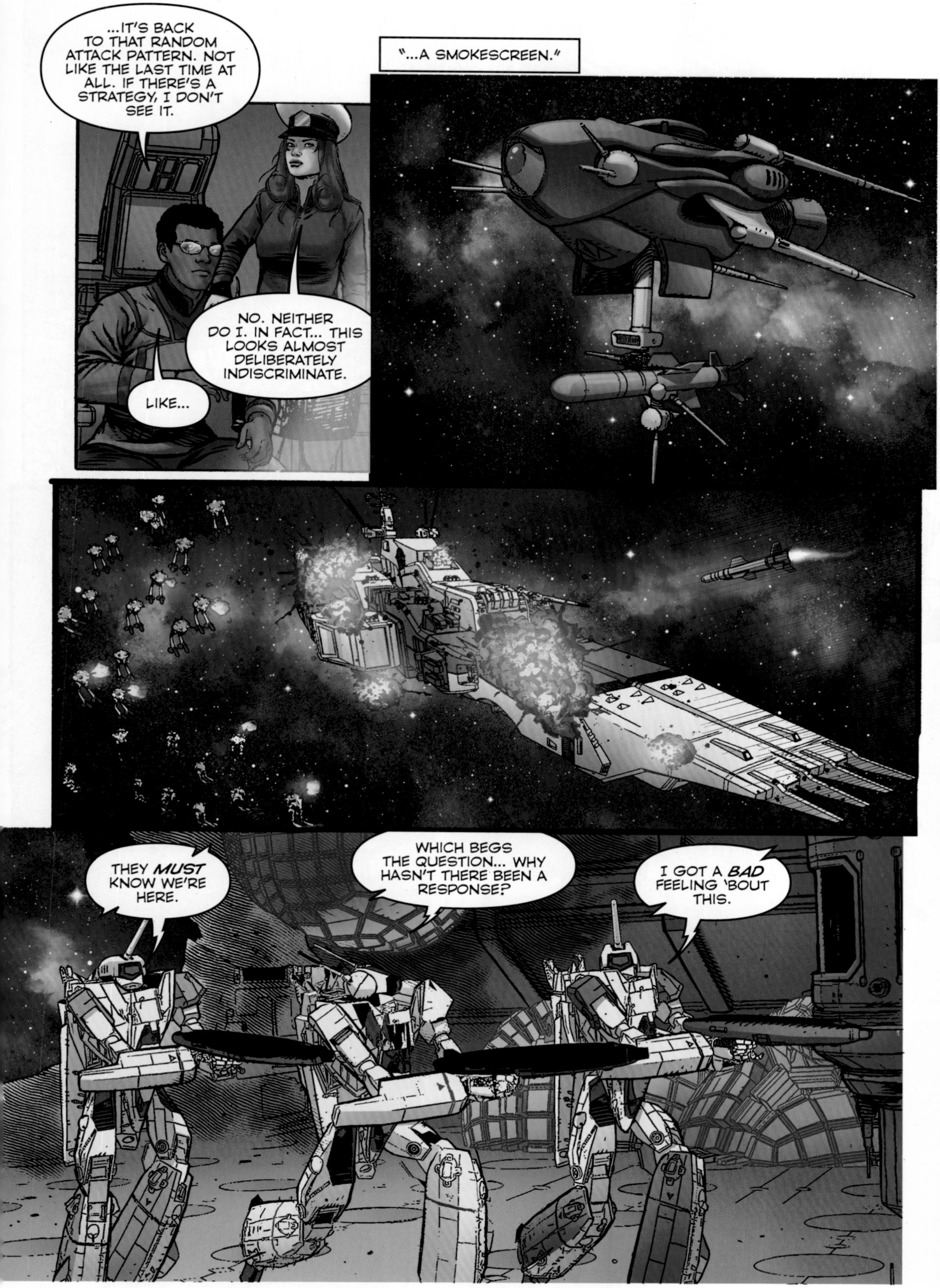
...IT'S BACK TO THAT RANDOM ATTACK PATTERN. NOT LIKE THE LAST TIME AT ALL. IF THERE'S A STRATEGY, I DON'T SEE IT.
NO. NEITHER DO I. IN FACT... THIS LOOKS ALMOST DELIBERATELY INDISCRIMINATE.
LIKE...
"...A SMOKESCREEN."
THEY MUST KNOW WE'RE HERE.
WHICH BEGS THE QUESTION... WHY HASN'T THERE BEEN A RESPONSE?
I GOT A BAD FEELING 'BOUT THIS.

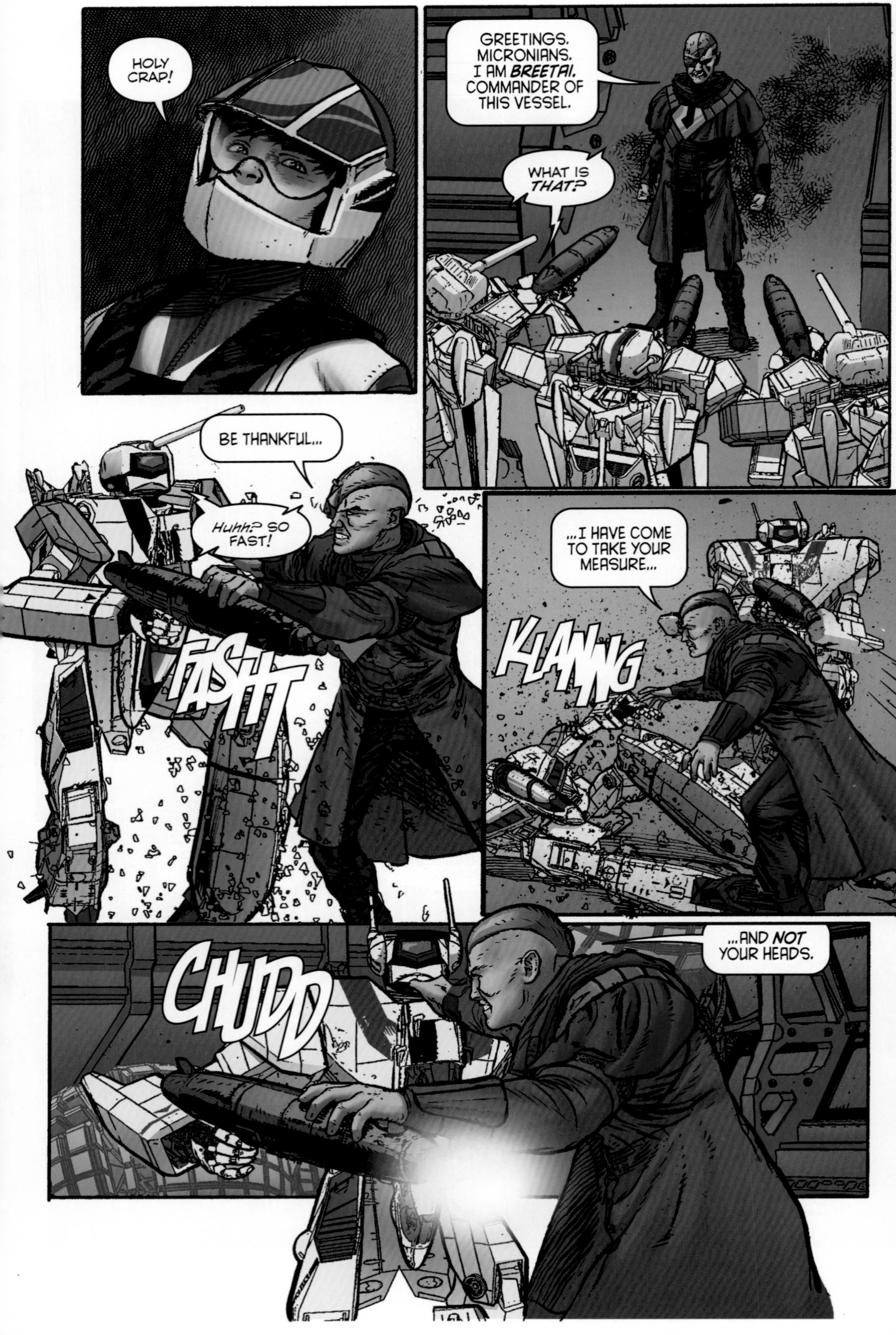
HOLY CRAP!
GREETINGS. MICRONIANS. I AM BREETAI. COMMANDER OF THIS VESSEL.
WHAT IS THAT?
BE THANKFUL...
Huhh? SO FAST!
FASHT
...I HAVE COME TO TAKE YOUR MEASURE...
KLANNG
CHUDD
...AND NOT YOUR HEADS.

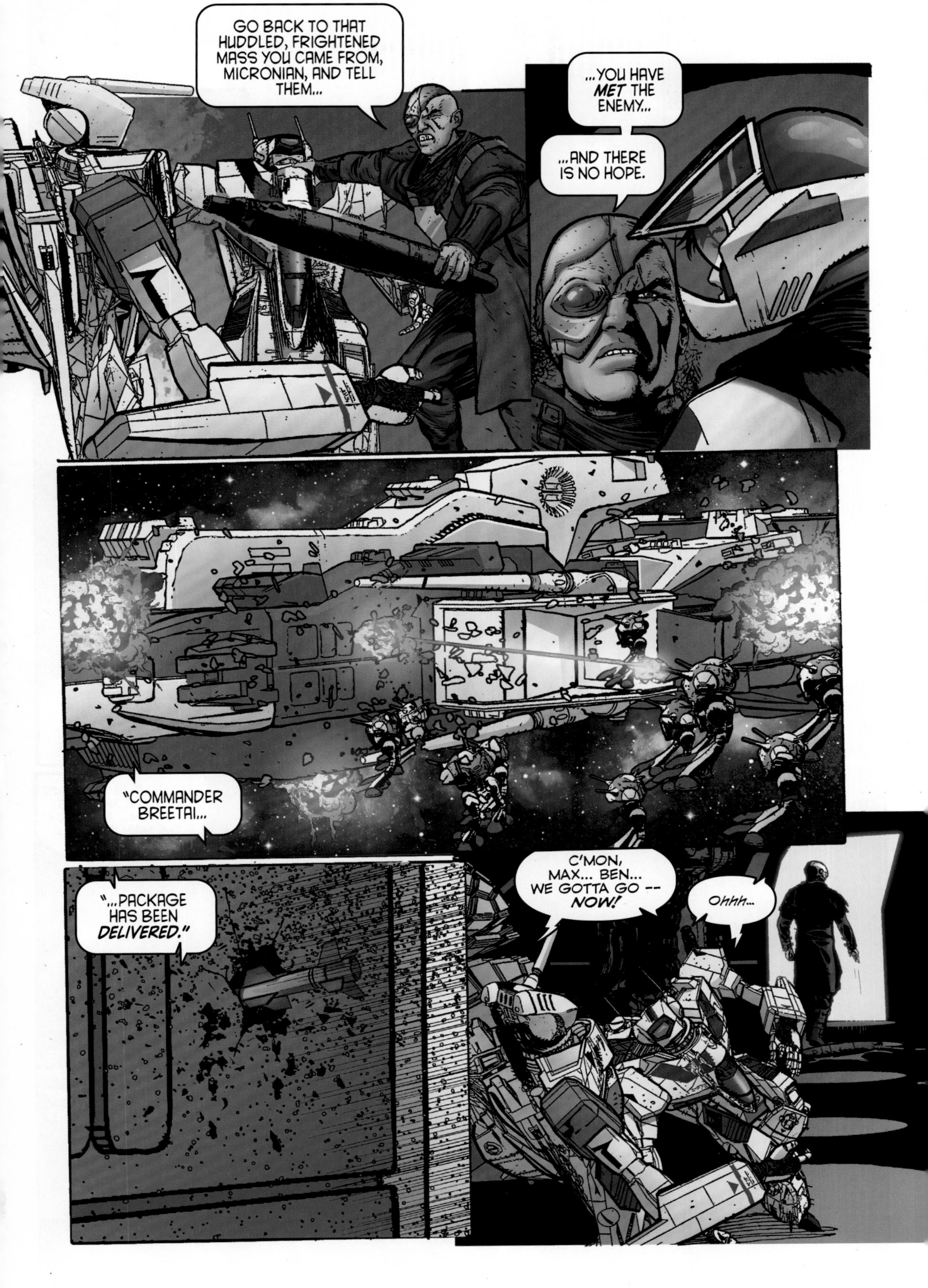
GO BACK TO THAT HUDDLED, FRIGHTENED MASS YOU CAME FROM, MICRONIAN, AND TELL THEM...
...YOU HAVE *MET* THE ENEMY...
...AND THERE IS NO HOPE.
"COMMANDER BREETAI...
"...PACKAGE HAS BEEN *DELIVERED.*"
C'MON, MAX... BEN... WE GOTTA GO -- *NOW!*
Ohhh...

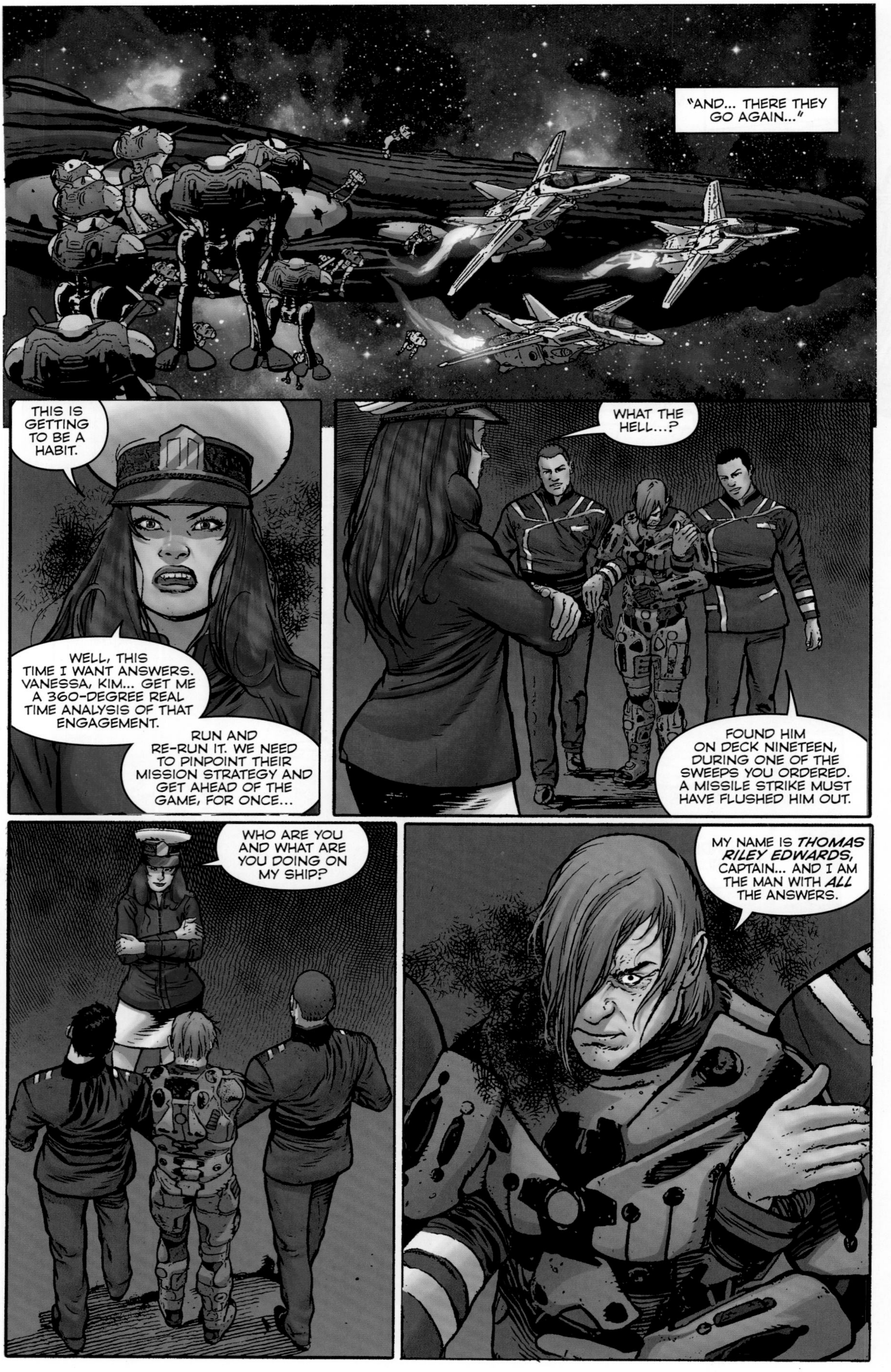
"AND... THERE THEY GO AGAIN..."
THIS IS GETTING TO BE A HABIT.
WELL, THIS TIME I WANT ANSWERS. VANESSA, KIM... GET ME A 360-DEGREE REAL TIME ANALYSIS OF THAT ENGAGEMENT.
RUN AND RE-RUN IT. WE NEED TO PINPOINT THEIR MISSION STRATEGY AND GET AHEAD OF THE GAME, FOR ONCE...
WHAT THE HELL...?
FOUND HIM ON DECK NINETEEN, DURING ONE OF THE SWEEPS YOU ORDERED. A MISSILE STRIKE MUST HAVE FLUSHED HIM OUT.
WHO ARE YOU AND WHAT ARE YOU DOING ON MY SHIP?
MY NAME IS *THOMAS RILEY EDWARDS*, CAPTAIN... AND I AM THE MAN WITH *ALL* THE ANSWERS.

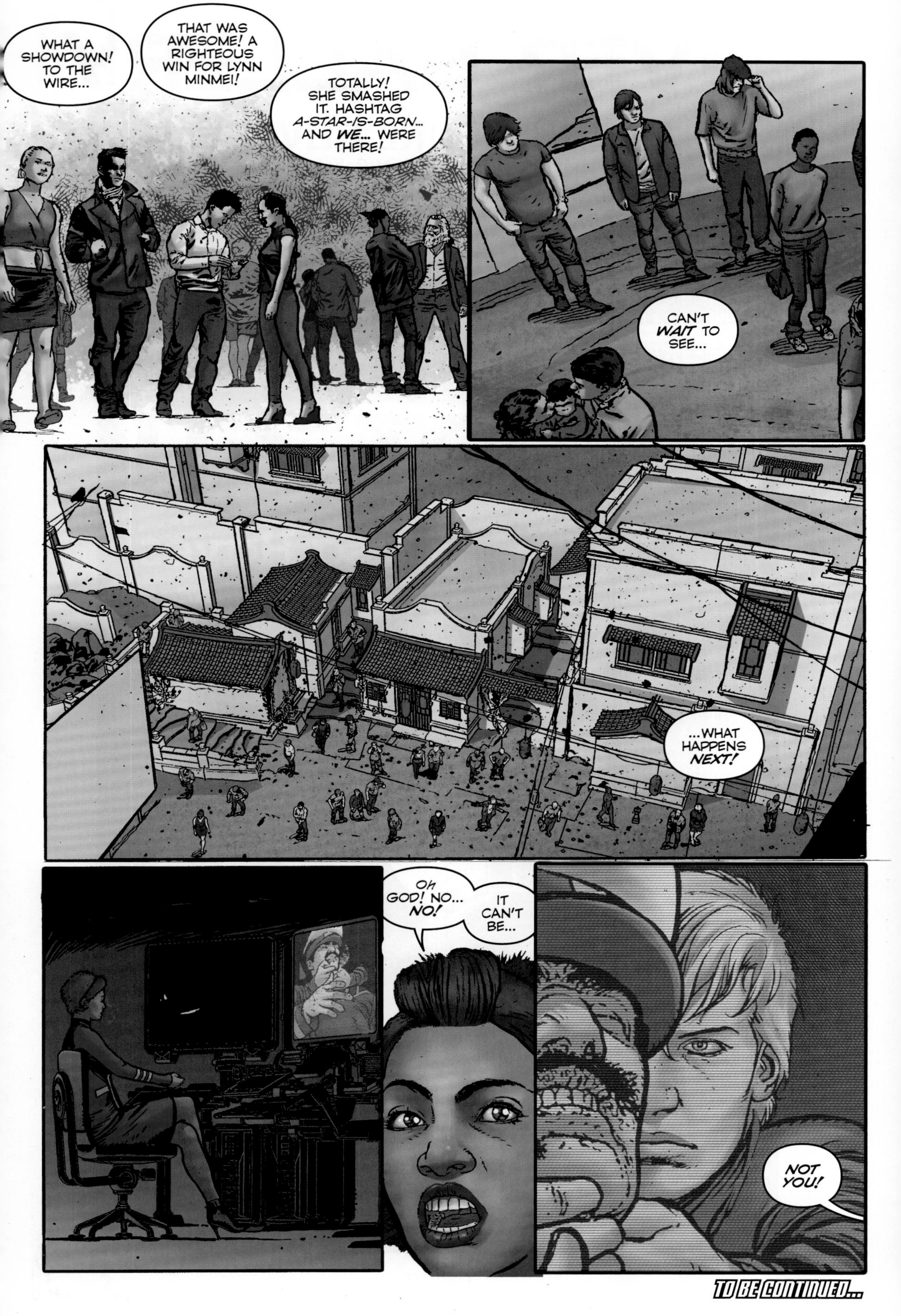
WHAT A SHOWDOWN! TO THE WIRE...
THAT WAS AWESOME! A RIGHTEOUS WIN FOR LYNN MINMEI!
TOTALLY! SHE SMASHED IT. HASHTAG A-STAR-IS-BORN... AND WE... WERE THERE!
CAN'T WAIT TO SEE...
...WHAT HAPPENS NEXT!
Oh GOD! NO... NO!
IT CAN'T BE...
NOT YOU!
TO BE CONTINUED...

COVER GALLERY

ACTION FIGURE COVERS

Blair Shedd created another excellent series of *Robotech* action figure covers, featuring never-before-seen variants based on the original action figure packaging. Claudia didn't atually have her own action figure from Matchbox in the 80s!

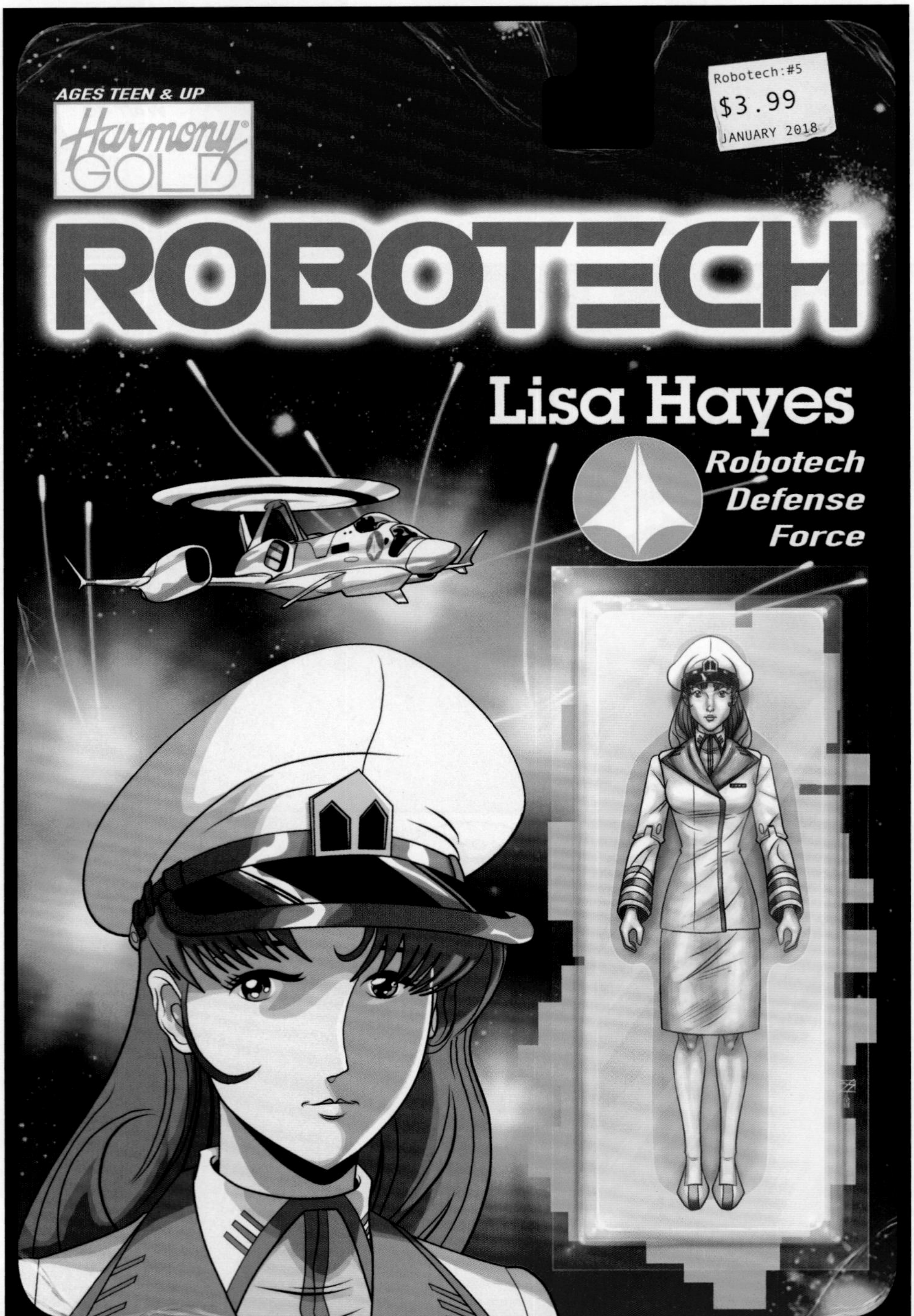
AGES TEEN & UP
Harmony GOLD
Robotech:#5
$3.99
JANUARY 2018
ROBOTECH
Lisa Hayes
Robotech Defense Force

COVER #5C

COVER #6B

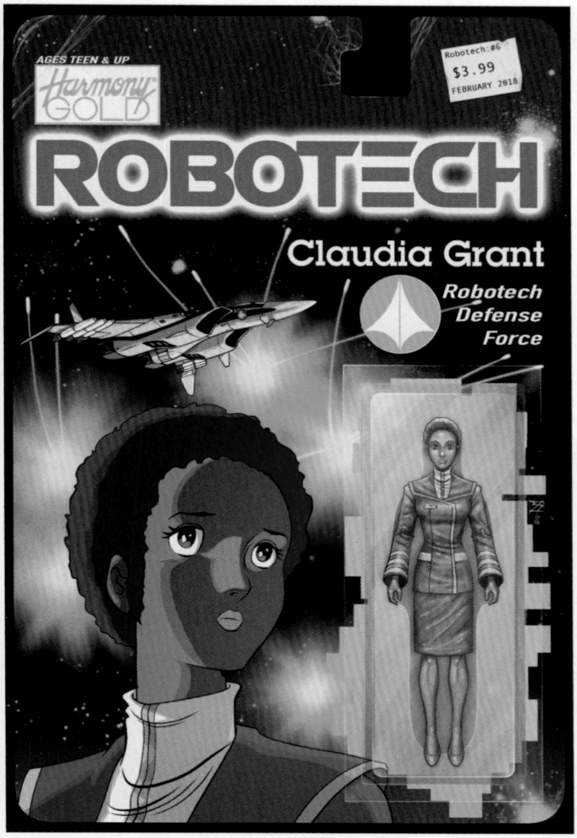
AGES TEEN & UP
Harmony GOLD
Robotech: #6
$3.99
FEBRUARY 2018
ROBOTECH
Claudia Grant
Robotech
Defense
Force

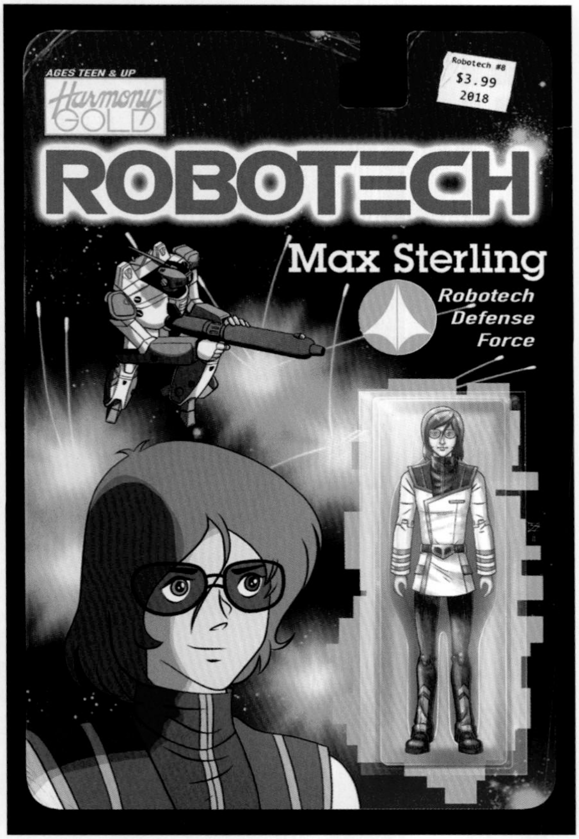
AGES TEEN & UP
Harmony GOLD
Robotech #8
$3.99
2018
ROBOTECH
Max Sterling
Robotech
Defense
Force

COVER #8B

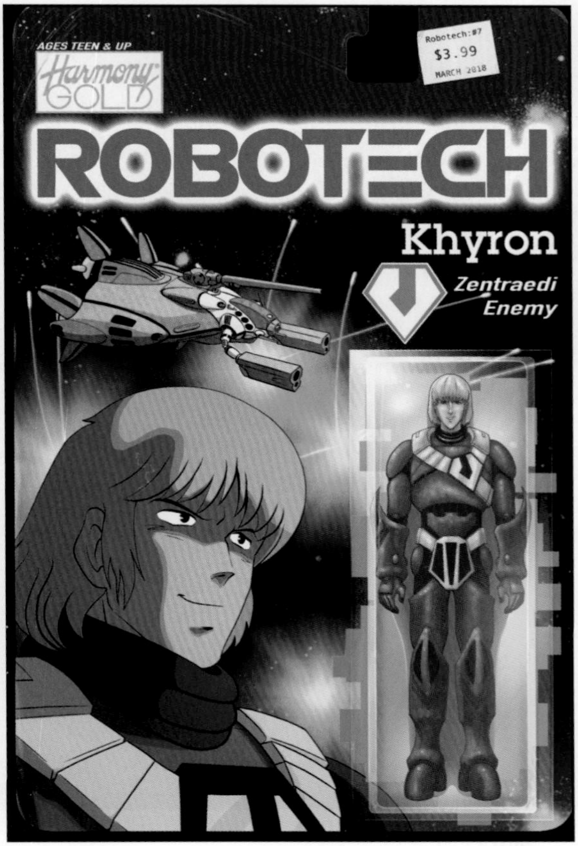
AGES TEEN & UP
Harmony GOLD
Robotech: #7
$3.99
MARCH 2018
ROBOTECH
Khyron
Zentraedi
Enemy

COVER #7B

COVER GALLERY

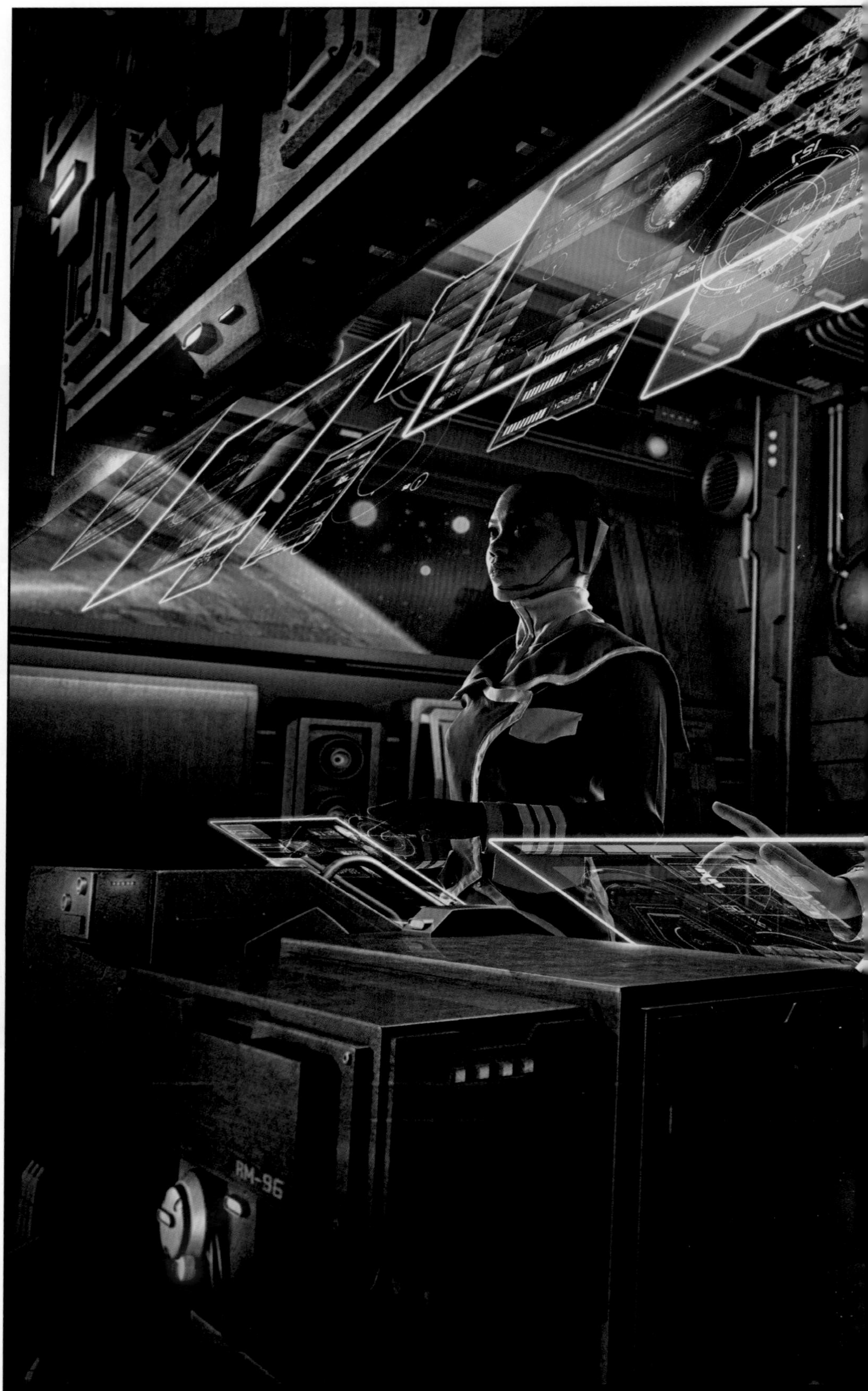
RM-96

COVER #5B
COSPLAY

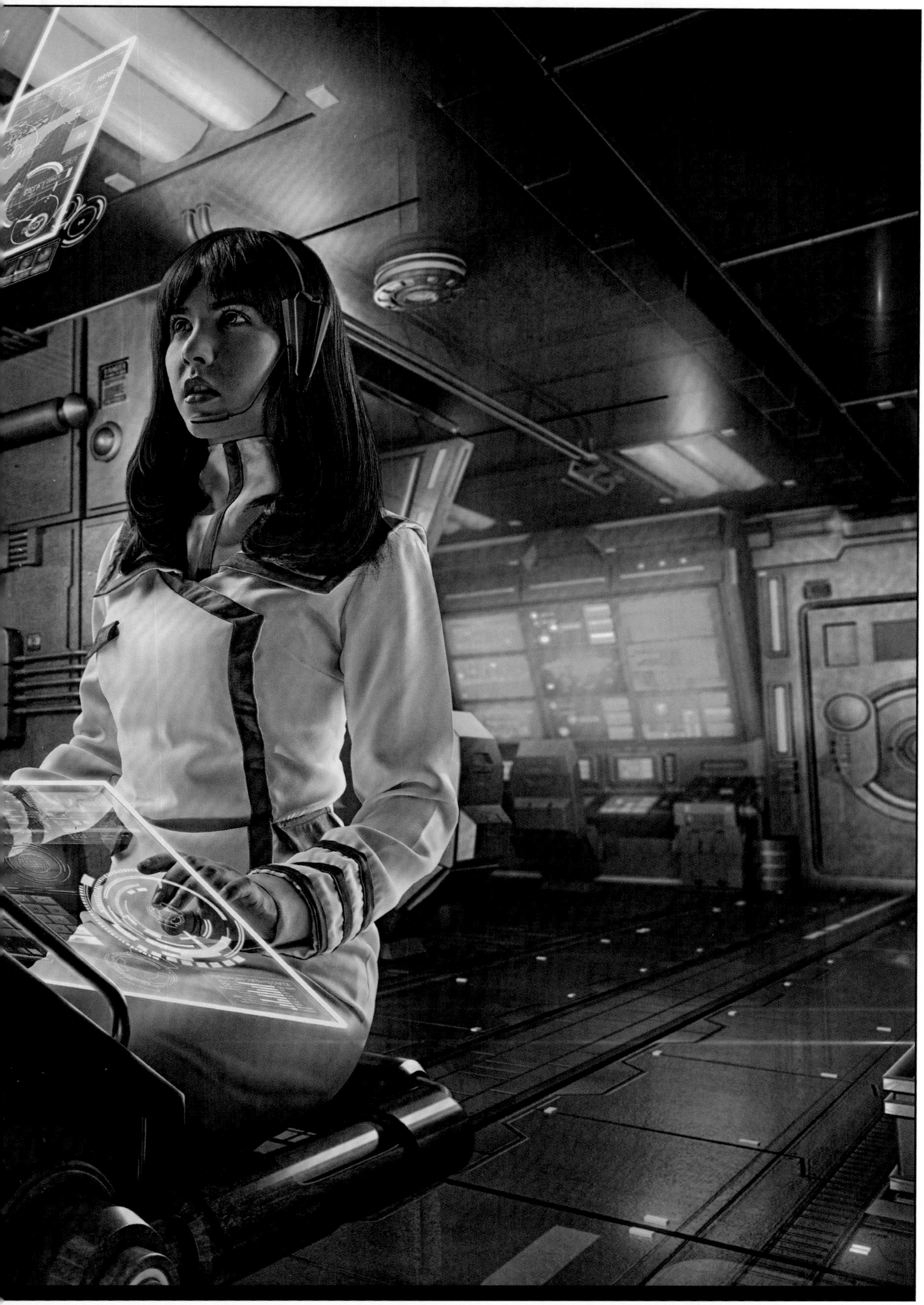

Photography/art direction: Jay Tablante; Make-up: Ara Fernando/Jopie Sanchez; Styling: Hannah Kim; Costume production: Regine Tolentino/Badj Genato; CG imaging: Riot inc. (SDF-1 interior); Digital imaging: Allan Montayre; Models: Kristine Dinglasan/Jenn Rosete

COVER GALLERY

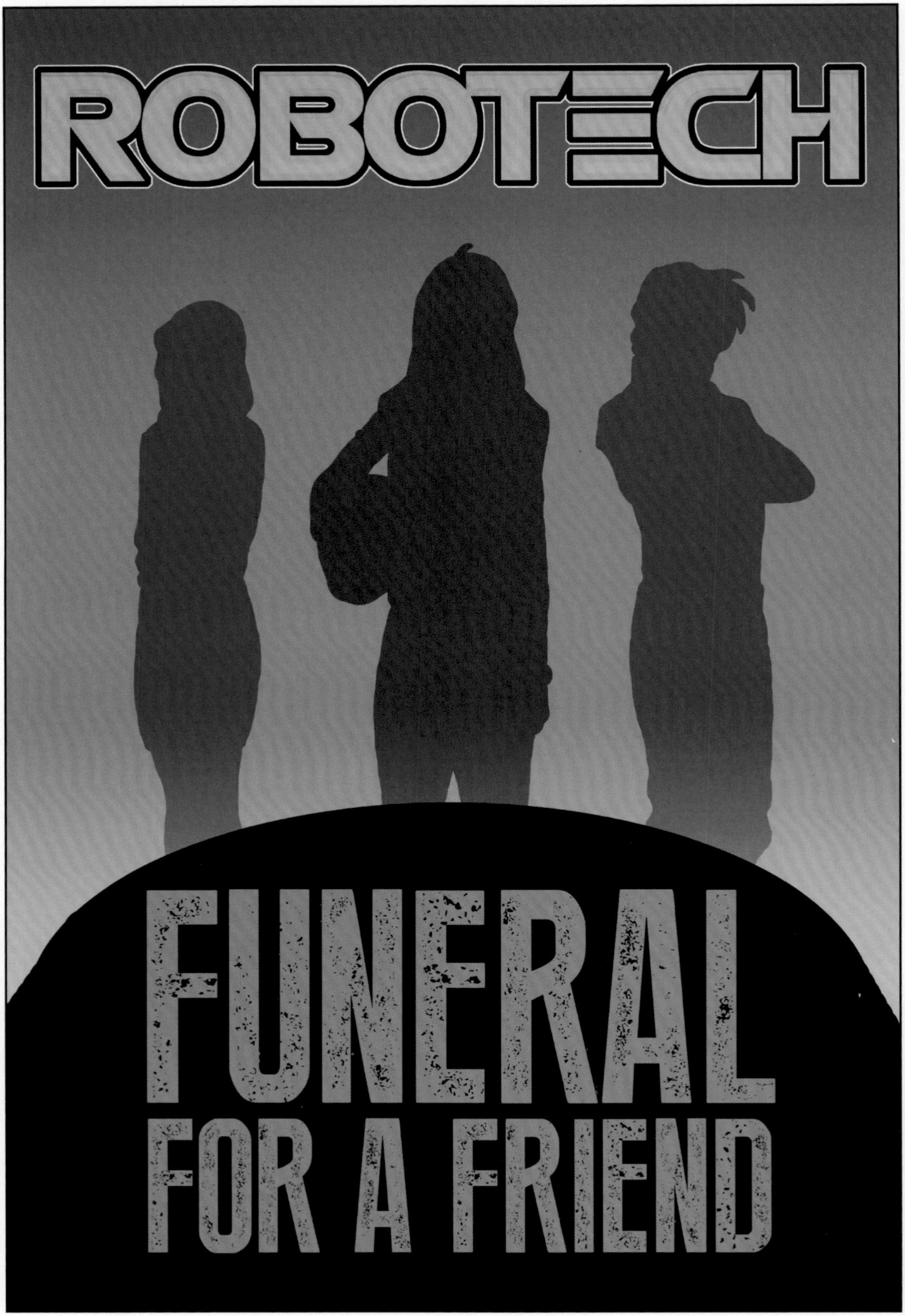
ROBOTECH
FUNERAL
FOR A FRIEND

COVER #5E
FUNERAL COVER

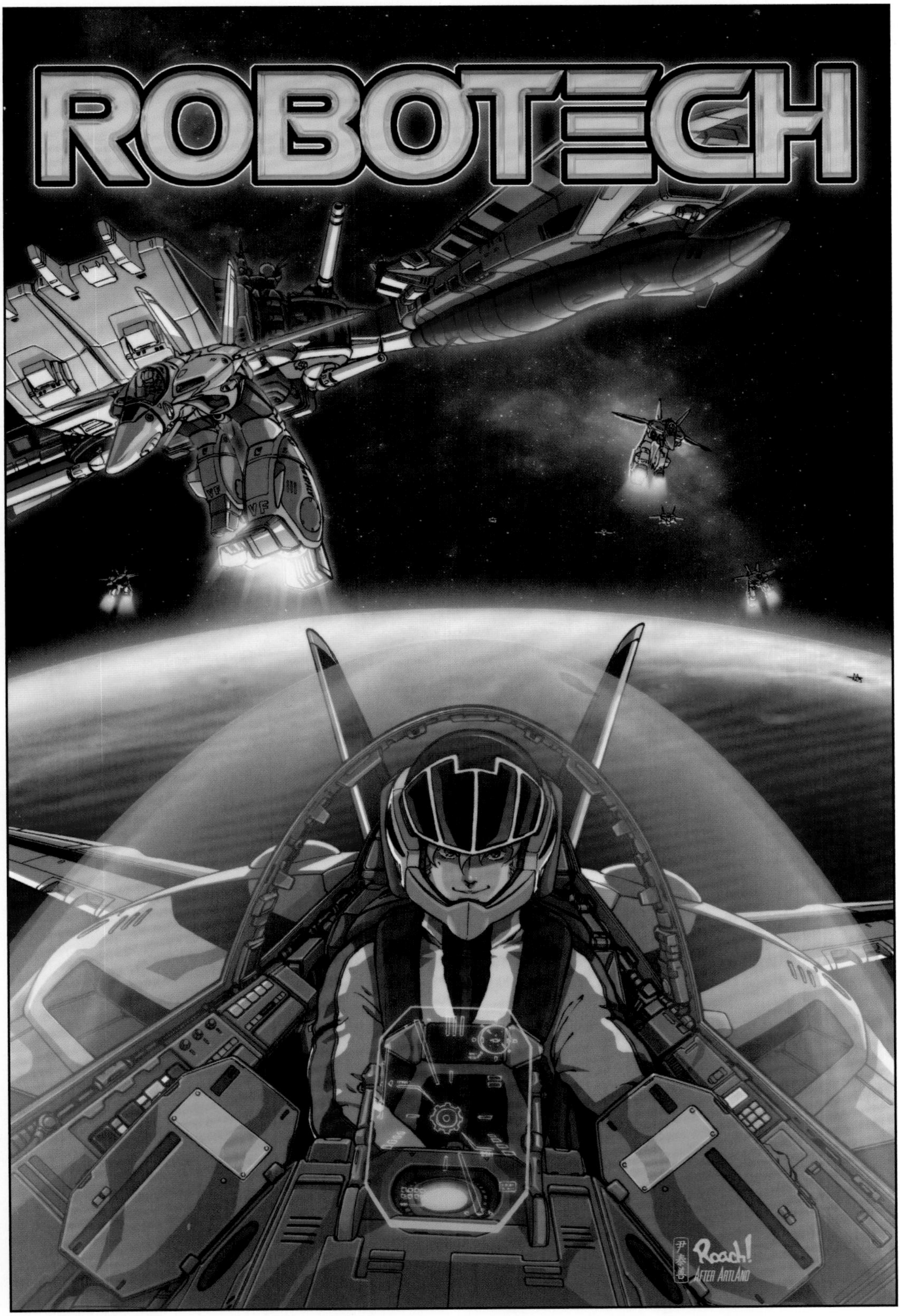
ROBOTECH
VF
VF
Roach!
After ArtLand

COVER #6C
TOMMY YUNE

COVER GALLERY

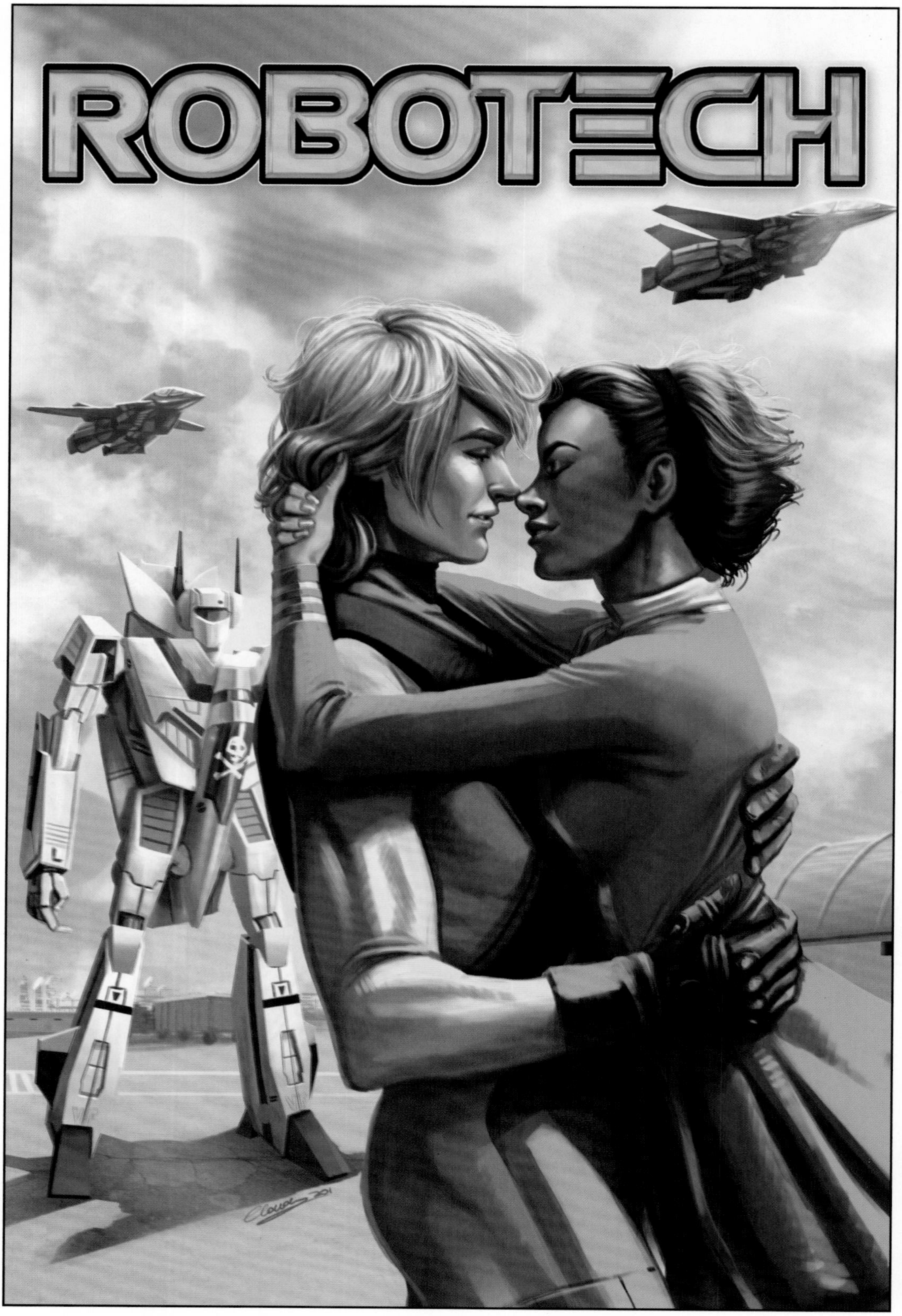
ROBOTECH

COVER #8C
CLAUDIA IANNICIELLO

EXTRAS

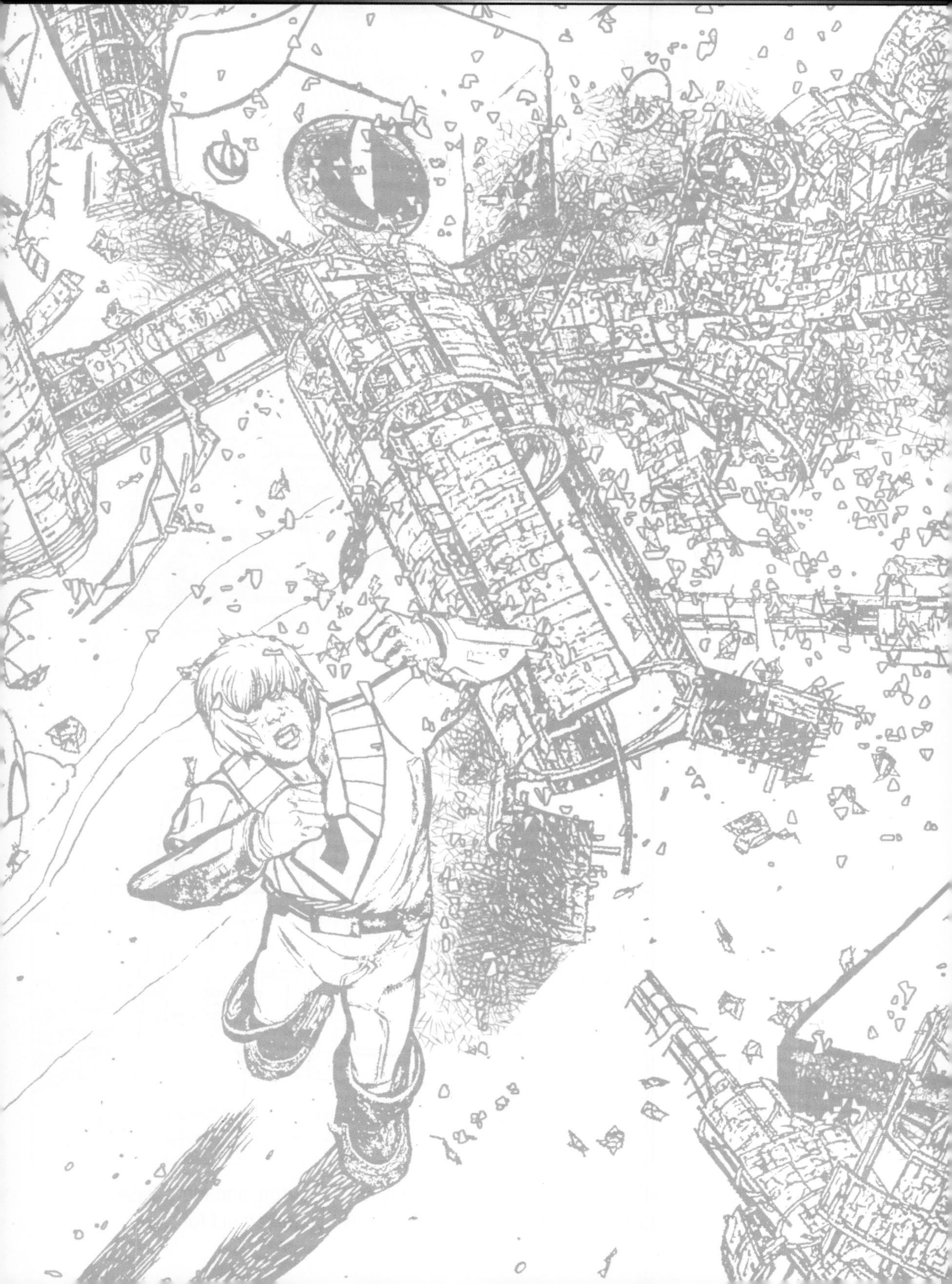

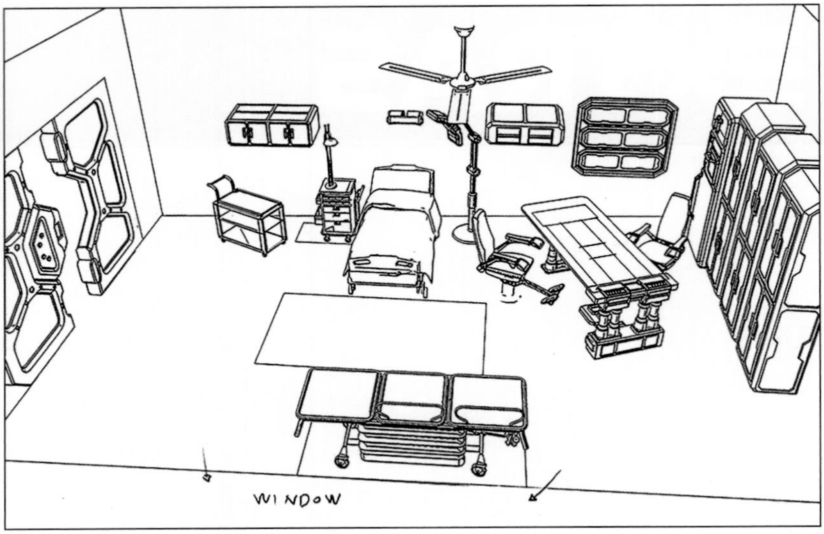
WINDOW

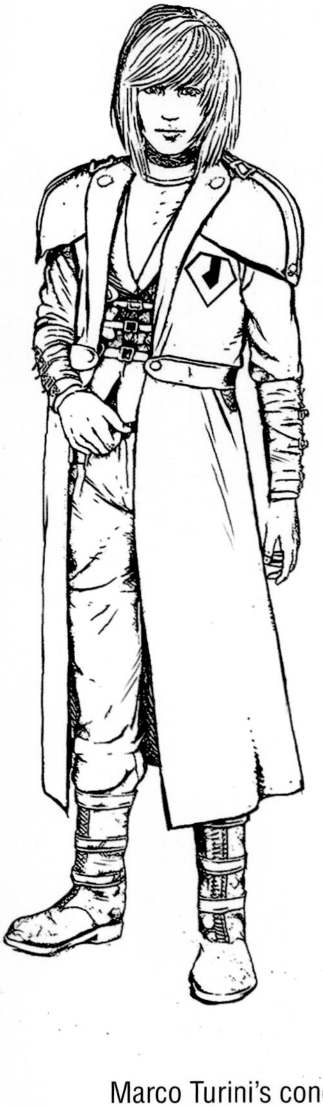

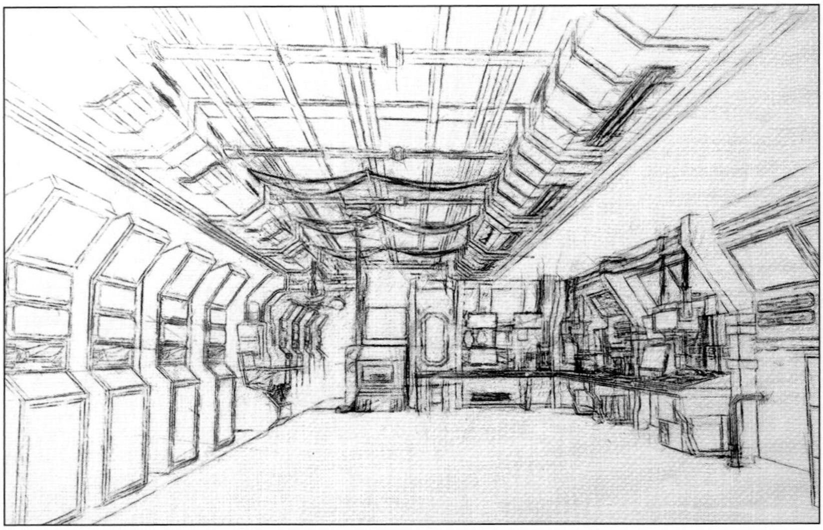

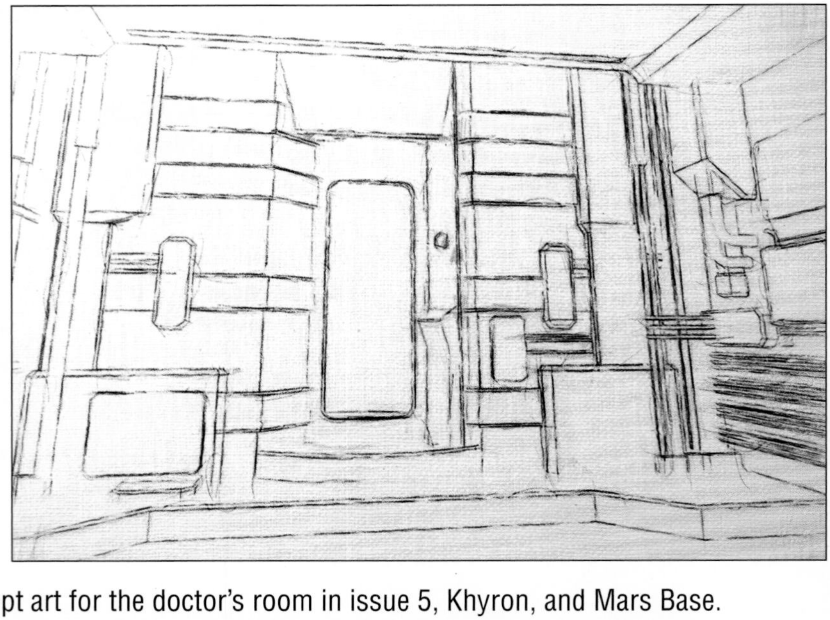

Marco Turini's concept art for the doctor's room in issue 5, Khyron, and Mars Base.
On the next two pages, you'll see Veritech paintings which Marco did for fun!

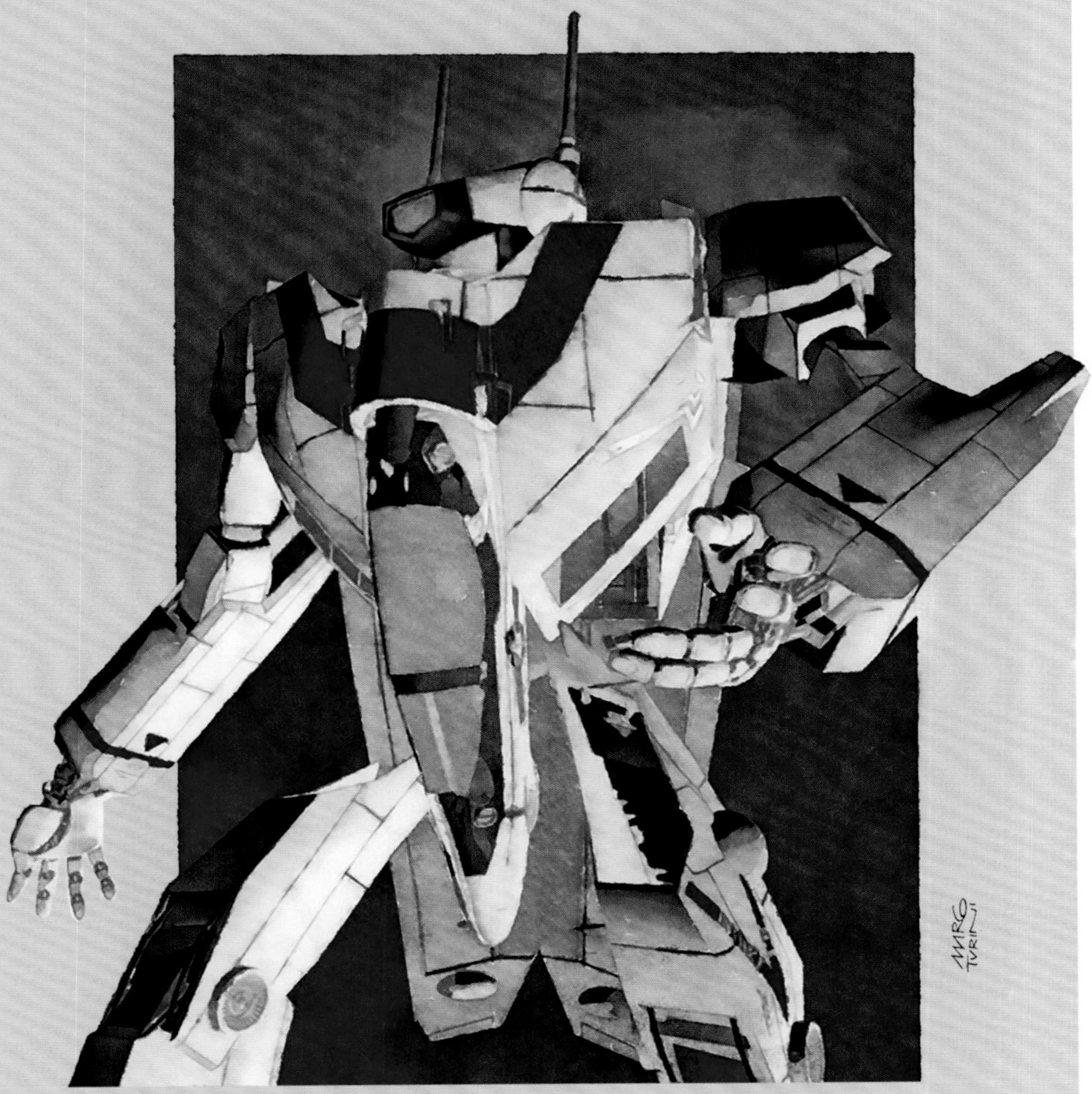

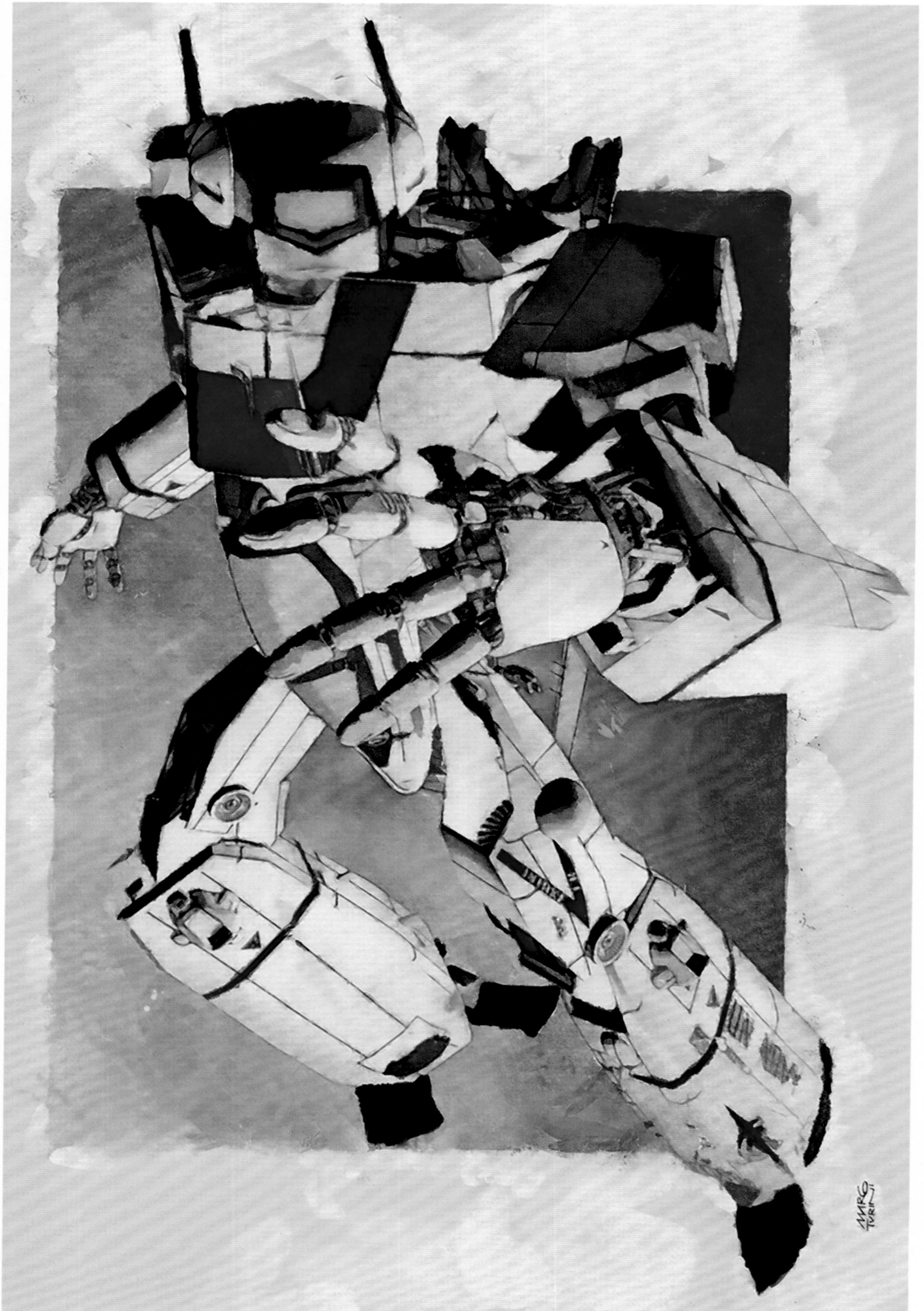

CREATOR BIOS

BRIAN WOOD

Brian Wood is a *New York Times* best-selling author, known for writing near-future world building, historical fiction, military sci-fi, and female-friendly YA, all with strong identity and socio-political themes. He launched his career 20 years ago with the groundbreaking *Channel Zero*, and has followed that with *DMZ*, *Northlanders*, *The Massive*, *Rebels*, *Starve*, *Black Road*, *The Couriers*, and *Demo*, amongst many others. He has written *The X-Men* and *Moon Knight* along with some of the biggest titles in pop culture, including *Star Wars*, *Aliens*, *Conan the Barbarian*, and *Terminator*.

Brian co-wrote the story for the award-winning video game *1979 Revolution*, and is currently adapting multiple series for television, including *Briggs Land* at AMC.

SIMON FURMAN

Simon Furman is a writer for comic books and TV animation, with a major involvement in *Transformers*, the '80s toy phenomenon. He has written literally hundreds of stories about the war-torn 'robots in disguise'. His other comic book credits include *Doctor Who*, *Dragon's Claws*, *Death's Head*, *Alpha Flight*, *Turok*, *She-Hulk*, *Robocop*, and *What If?* In the TV animation field, Simon has written for shows such as *Beast Wars*, *Roswell Conspiracies*, *Dan Dare*, *X-Men: Evolution*, *Alien Racers* and *A.T.O.M.*. Simon's recent/ current writing work includes *StarCraft*, *Transformers: Nefarious*, *Terminator – Revolution*, *Ronan* and *Death's Head 3.0*, *Transformers UK*, *Wallace & Gromit* and *Torchwood*.

He is also the author of numerous books and is currently the lead writer and script supervisor for the animated TV show *The Matt Hatter Chronicles*.

MARCO TURINI

Marco Turini was born in Italy and now lives in Prague.
He has worked on such titles as *Squadron Supreme*, *Battleworld*, *Legends of the Dark Knight*, *Cyberforce*, and *E.V.A.* Marco has also worked as a concept artist for movies and games. Find out more at www.marcoturiniart.com

MARCO LESKO

Marco Lesko is a colorist who has worked on *Doctor Who: The Ninth Doctor*, *Assassin's Creed*, *Peepland*, *The Shadow*, *Deus Ex*, *Torchwood*, *E.V.I.L. Heroes*, and more.

JIM CAMPBELL

Jim Campbell is a comic book letterer from Nottinghamshire, UK. Jim has lettered Titan Comics' DreamWorks titles, including *Kung Fu Panda* and *Dragon Riders of Berk*. He letters many American comic books, including *Diesel* and *Bill & Ted's Triumphant Return!*

TITAN COMICS' ROBOTECH SERIES

ROBOTECH GRAPHIC NOVELS

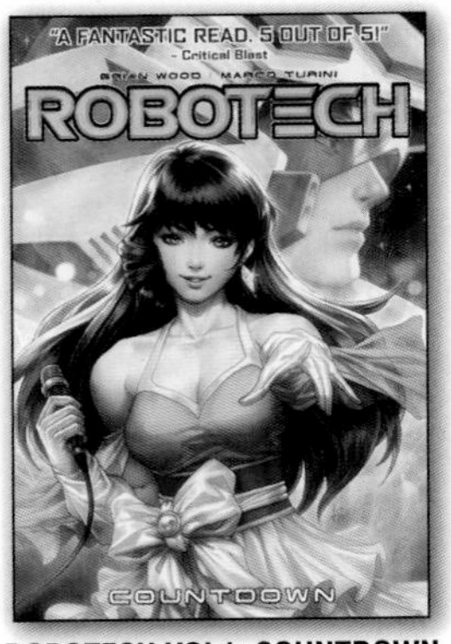
"A FANTASTIC READ. 5 OUT OF 5!"
- Critical Blast
BRIAN WOOD MARCO TURINI
ROBOTECH
COUNTDOWN

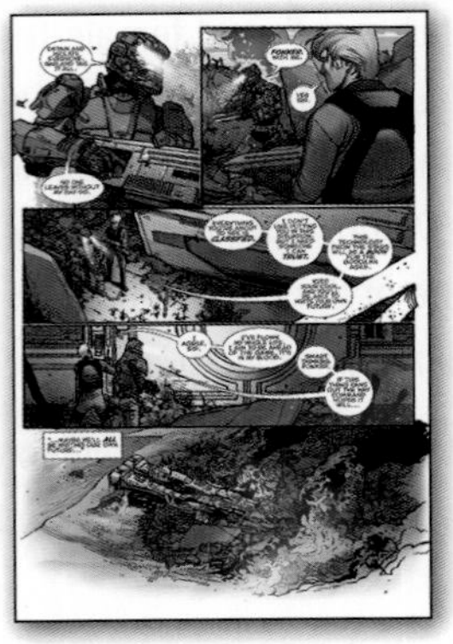

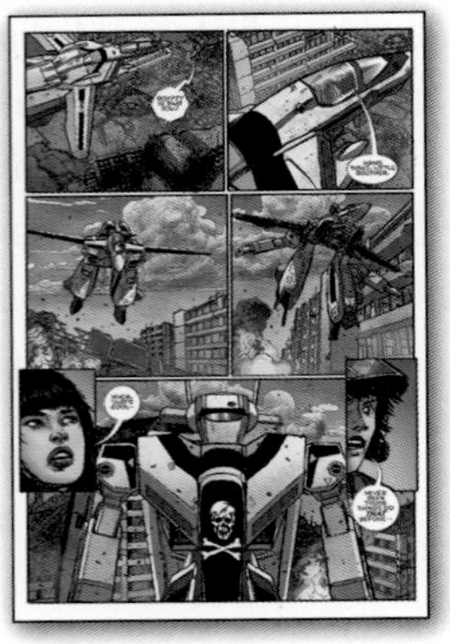

ROBOTECH VOL1: COUNTDOWN
ON SALE NOW

ROBOTECH ARCHIVES

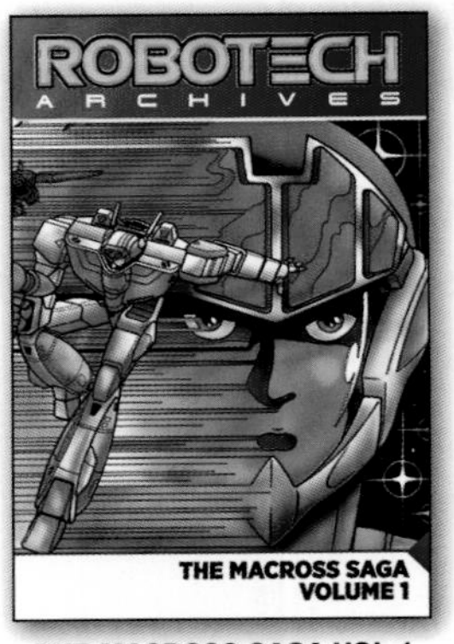
ROBOTECH
ARCHIVES
THE MACROSS SAGA
VOLUME 1

THE MACROSS SAGA VOL 1
ON SALE NOW

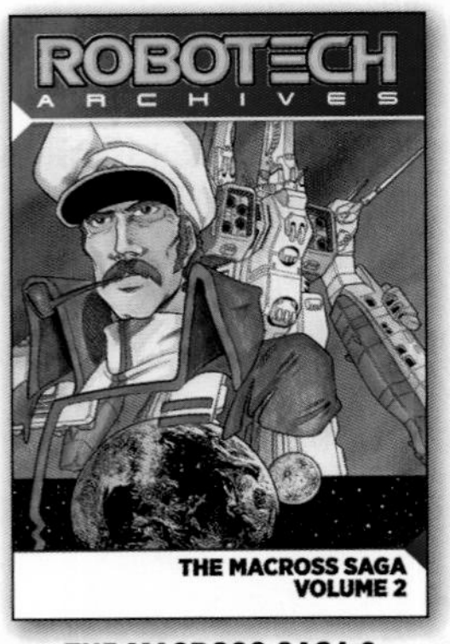
ROBOTECH
ARCHIVES
THE MACROSS SAGA
VOLUME 2

THE MACROSS SAGA 2
ON SALE AUGUST 2018

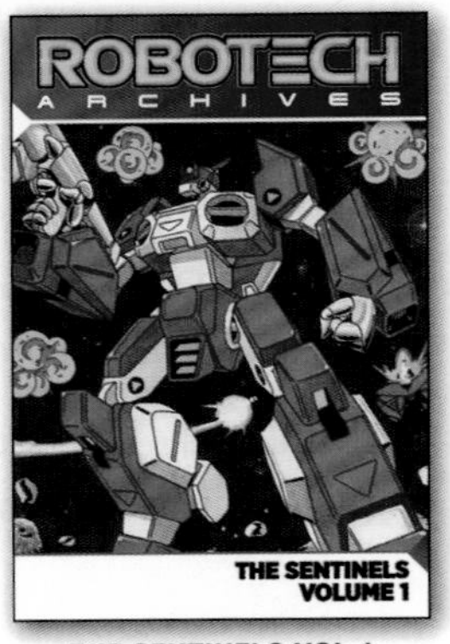
ROBOTECH
ARCHIVES
THE SENTINELS
VOLUME 1

THE SENTINELS VOL 1
ON SALE FEBRUARY 2019

ROBOTECH MONTHLY COMIC

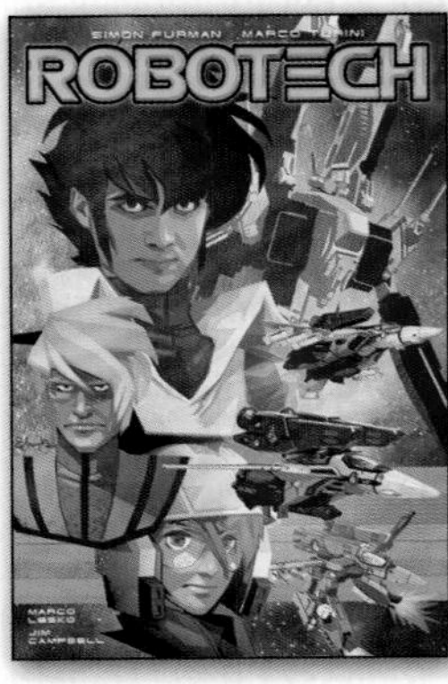
SIMON FURMAN MARCO TURINI
ROBOTECH

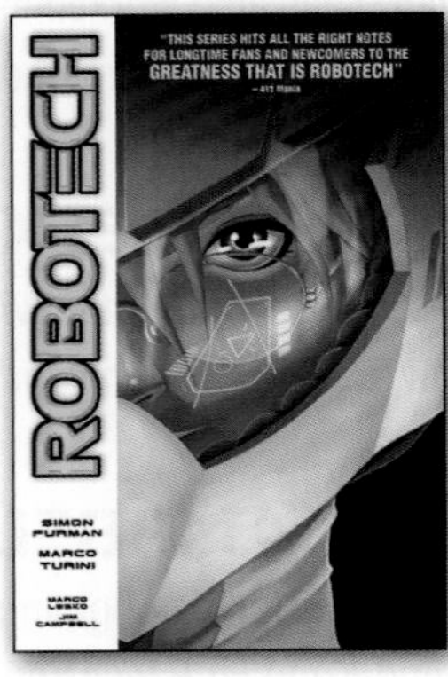
"THIS SERIES HITS ALL THE RIGHT NOTES FOR LONGTIME FANS AND NEWCOMERS TO THE GREATNESS THAT IS ROBOTECH"
ROBOTECH
SIMON FURMAN
MARCO TURINI

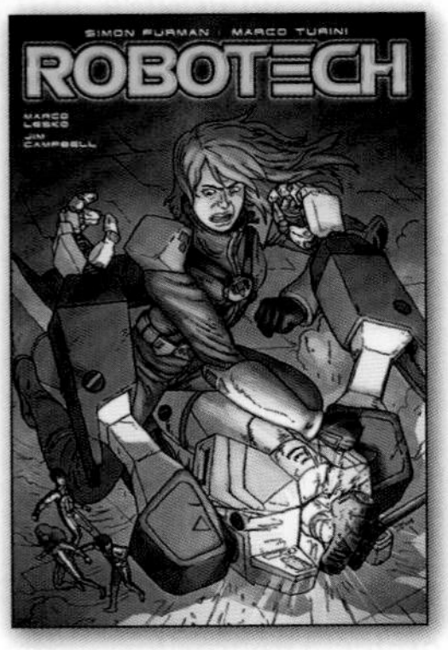
SIMON FURMAN MARCO TURINI
ROBOTECH

Harmony GOLD

ALSO AVAILABLE DIGITALLY
WWW.TITAN-COMICS.COM

TITAN COMICS

SCI-FI TITLES FROM TITAN COMICS

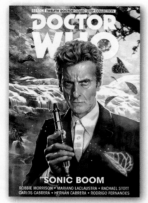

BBC TWELFTH DOCTOR COMIC STRIP COLLECTION
DOCTOR WHO
SONIC BOOM
ROBBIE MORRISON • MARIANO LACLAUSTRA • RACHAEL STOTT
CARLOS CABRERA • HERNÁN CABRERA • RODRIGO FERNANDES
DOCTOR WHO

GEORGE MANN • TAZIO BETTIN • ENRICA EREN ANGIOLINI • ROB STEEN
WARHAMMER
40,000
FALLEN
WARHAMMER 40,000

FAKHADEL • WATTERS • HOLDER • LESKO
ASSASSIN'S
CREED
UPRISING
UBISOFT
INFLECTION POINT
ASSASSIN'S CREED

WORLD
WAR
X
BOOK 1
JERRY FRISSEN / PETER SNEJBJERG
WORLD WAR X

"Huge and epic... beautiful and fresh!"
Joe Quesada, Marvel Comics
universal war one
UW1
DENIS BAJRAM
UNIVERSAL WAR ONE

INDEPENDENCE DAY
DARK FATHOM
VICTOR GISCHLER
STEVE SCOTT • RODNEY RAMOS • ALEX SHIBAO
TAZIO BETTIN • IVAN RODRIGUEZ
INDEPENDENCE DAY

Wolfenstein
THE DEEP
WOLFENSTEIN

STEFANO RAFFAELE / CHRISTOPHE BEC
UNDER
SCOURGE OF THE SEWER
UNDER

JOE HALDEMAN • MARVANO
THE FOREVER WAR
FOREVER
FREE
FOREVER WAR/FOREVER FREE

EXPLORE THE FULL RANGE AT TITAN-COMICS.COM

TITAN COMICS

facebook.com/comicstitan @ComicsTitan

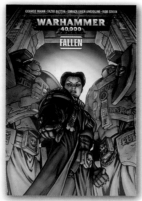

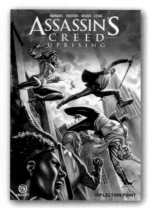

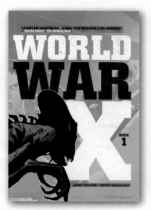

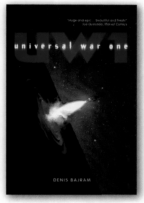

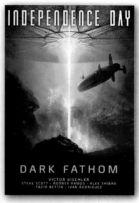

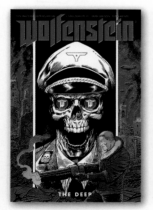

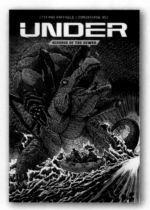

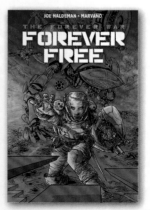

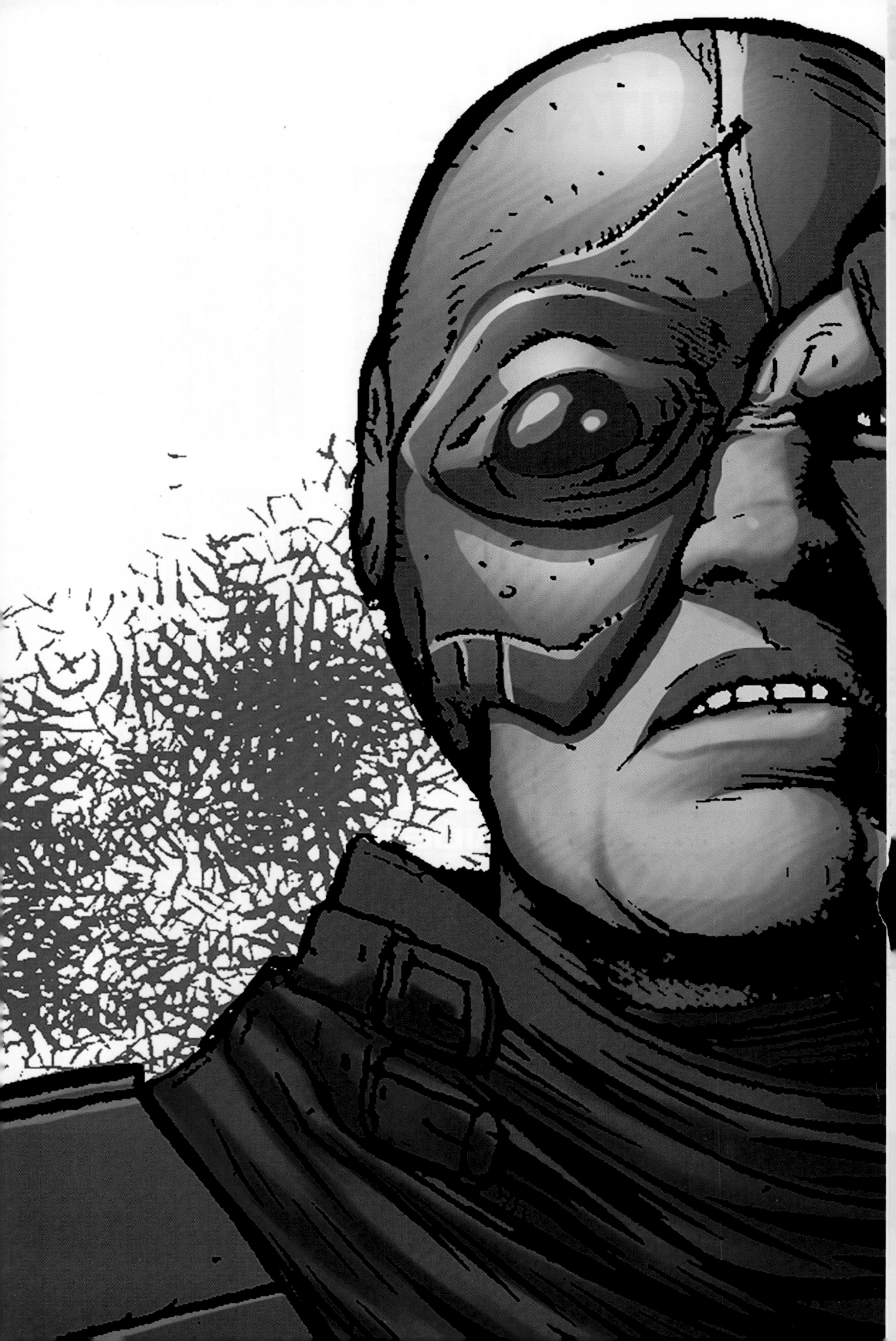